WOMEN IN INDIA
Two Perspectives

Doranne Jacobson
Susan S. Wadley

MANOHAR
1995

ISBN: 81-85425-37-X

First Published 1977
Reprinted 1986
Second Enlarged Edition 1992
Third Enlarged Edition 1995

All photographs in this volume are © Doranne Jacobson, with the exceptions of Ellora statuary and of the former Queen Mother of Jaipur, which are © Jerome Jacobson, and the photograph of Santal women, which is © Mimi Sharma.

Publishers
Manohar Publishers & Distributors
2/6, Ansari Road, Daryaganj,
New Delhi - 110002

Lasertypeset by
A J Software Publishing Co. Pvt. Ltd.
305 Durga Chambers,
Karol Bagh
New Delhi- 110005

Printed by
Rajkamal Electric Press
B-35/9, G.T. Karnal Road
Delhi - 110033

WOMEN IN INDIA

Two Perspectives

Contents

Doranne Jacobson
   Introduction   1

1. Doranne Jacobson
   The Women of North and Central India:
   Goddesses and Wives   15

2. Susan S. Wadley
   Women and the Hindu Tradition   111

3. Doranne Jacobson
   Golden Handprints and Red-Painted Feet:
   Hindu Childbirth Rituals in Central India   137

4. Susan S. Wadley
   Hindu Women's Family and Household
   Rites in a North Indian Village   157

5. Doranne Jacobson
   Women and Jewelry in Rural India   171

6. Susan S. Wadley
   The "Village Indira": A Brahman Widow and Political
   Action in Rural North India   225

Index   251

The Authors

Doranne Jacobson received her Ph.D. in Anthropology from Columbia University, where she is a University Seminar Associate at the Southern Asian Institute. Currently Director of International Images, Springfield, Illinois, she has focused on changes in women's roles in Central India, where she has conducted research for a total of more than five years. She has published more than 25 articles on women, the family, development, and change in India. She is also a widely published photographer and the author of *India*, a large-format volume illustrated with hundreds of colour photographs (W.H. Smith, London, 1992).

Susan S. Wadley is Professor of Anthropology at Syracuse University. She received her Ph.D. in Anthropology from the University of Chicago. Her research interests include women's ritual, folklore, and epic traditions, as well as socio-economic change, especially as it affects women in rural North India. She has published numerous books and articles on India, including *Struggling with Destiny in Karimpur, 1925-1984*, (University of California Press, 1994).

Introduction

Doranne Jacobson

India is currently undergoing dramatic change in nearly every sphere, and the lives of the nation's women are being altered in important respects. Many Indian women are playing major roles in effecting these changes—they are active in politics, the professions, and virtually all of the nation's occupations. Millions are seeking higher education, and millions more are employed in jobs outside their homes. Spheres of activity are widening most especially for women who live in urban areas. However, the vast majority of India's women dwell in villages, where most carry out traditional domestic and agricultural tasks and adhere to norms which have been espoused for many generations. Even in rapidly growing urban areas, traditional roles and values relating to women find wide acceptance. Although India was led for nearly sixteen years by a dynamic woman prime minister, countless numbers of the nation's women veil their faces and quietly accept the dictates of others.

Approaching their subjects from somewhat differing points of view, the papers in this volume were written with the common goal of attaining a greater understanding of women's myriad roles and statuses in modern India. My paper, "The Women of North and Central India: Goddesses and Wives," presents a general overview of some of the experiences and problems of women in the northern half of the country, placing women and their activities within social and economic contexts. Susan Wadley's essay, "Women and the Hindu Tradition," focuses in detail on traditional Hindu ideology as it pertains to women, many elements of which find expression in modern women's lives. My second paper, "Golden Hand-prints and Red Painted Feet: Hindu Childbirth Rituals in Central India," discusses women's rites performed in celebration of the centrality of pregnancy and childbearing in the lives of village women. Susan Wadley's second essay, "Hindu Women's Family and Household Rites in a North Indian Village," highlights the significance of several women's rites intended to bring happiness and prosperity to women's domestic realm. My third paper, "Women and Jewelry in Rural India," focuses on culturally valued ornaments and the multifaceted ways in which they express social and economic relationships involving women. Susan Wadley's third paper, "The 'Village Indira': A Brahman Widow and Poltical Action in Rural North India," provides a fascinating glimpse of contradictions and ambiguities in the life of a dynamic village leader.

Dr. Wadley's papers are based primarily on her extensive examination of classical and modern Hindu texts, as well as on her own anthropological research in North India and on studies conducted by others. My essays are based on data obtained during ethnographic fieldwork concentrating on rural women in Central India, and on information gained from reading the works of others who have written of Indian women. While some of the papers in this volume were written several years ago, despite changes in the nation as a whole and in the villages described, the essays focus on realities which are strikingly relevant to the lives of Indian women today.

Dr. Wadley worked in Karimpur village in the Agra region of Uttar Pradesh, which differs in some important respects from Nimkhera, the more rustic village in the Bhopal region of Madhya Pradesh where I lived. Thus, some of our perceptions of Indian women's lives may differ because of our varied experiences. It should be noted, too, that our papers barely touch on South India, where few women are veiled and where many women—even villagers—take more active parts in public life than is usually the case in North and Central India.

These papers reveal concern with women's status relative to that of men and the importance of female chastity and control of sexuality. These themes are of great importance to Indian women as they live their lives and are crucial elements of any discussion of women in India. Indian society is largely based on the family unit and wider kinship groupings, and few individuals can prosper economically without being part of a cooperating group of kinsmen. In fact, most women are significantly dependent upon their menfolk for support—especially for access to land—and consider it unwise to alienate them. Guided by traditional concepts of proper feminine behaviour and aware that their actions are inextricably linked to family honour, prestige, and ultimately, material rewards, women typically carry out their expected roles as chaste daughters and dutiful wives. These time-honoured roles require of women much self-sacrifice, yet they help uphold the family structure so vital to the well-being of all members of the group. The behaviour of men, too, reflects the limitations on indivual action that family cooperation requires. Further, hierarchically-ranked castes remain strong in India, and, as Yalman (1963, p. 43) has pointed out, control of sexuality and reproductive powers is vital to individual castes, since caste membership is ideally based upon purity of lineage.

None of the papers in this volume discusses at length the possible root causes and material bases of the cultural features we outline, but the investigation of the basic determinants of women's status in various societies has received much attention in the writings of others and is the topic of some controversy. For example, in her widely-cited work, *Woman's Role in Economic Development* (1970), Ester Boserup pointed out that male dominance and veiled women are hardly exclusive to India, but are found in many agricultural societies in which men are responsible for the ploughing and most of the labour of cultivation, while women process the food and prepare it for consumption. According to this view, it is not surprising that in South India, where certain classes of women play vital roles in rice cultivation, women tend to have more freedom of movement and a higher status relative to men than they do in North and Central India (Miller, 1981; Mencher, 1989; and Dyson and Moore, 1983). In a comprehensive overview of the position of women in widely differing societies, Martin and Voorhies (1975, p. 286) have stressed that it is unnecessary to propose a theory of male conspiracy as the cause of male dominance or of the "inside-outside" dichotomy of labour, but rather that this system exists simply because it has worked. Other writers have taken a less charitable view of women's relatively low status in South Asia--and indeed, throughout the world--as virtual slavery and socially sanctioned exploitation of one segment of society (women) by another (men) (French, 1992; Omvedt, 1986; Agarwal, 1988b).

In a cross-cultural statistical study, Peggy Sanday (1973) concluded that a major contribution to production is a necessary but not sufficient condition for the development of high female status, and that *control* over valued products and strategic resources is vital to women's status. In a later work (1981), Sanday explored several correlates of women's status. The question of the relationship of women's status to economic activities has also been discussed by Veena Das (1976), M. Sharma (1985), Jeffery *et. al.* (1989), and Agarwal (1986, 1988a) among others.

Using concepts developed by Levi-Strauss and de Beauvoir, Sherry Ortner (1974) has suggested that women have everywhere been devalued in relation to men and that such devaluation is linked to a universal association of women with inferior "nature" in contrast to the association of men with superior "culture." These notions have been strongly criticized on several grounds by Leacock and Nash (1975). They suggest that the idea of culture as separate from and superior to nature is probably of relatively recent European origin and indicate that in many pre-colonial egalitarian societies women were not derogated. They relate male assertiveness to competition over social and economic prerogatives in more technologically advanced societies. Other authors have added to these criticisms (see, for example, several articles in MacCormack and Strathern, 1980).

General features of the female condition in global perspective have been discussed in many other publications. Examples include Friedl (1975), Kessler (1976), Matthiasson (1974), Reiter (1975), Rohrlich-Leavitt (1976), Leacock and Safa (1986), Gallin and Ferguson (1991) and Agrawal (1988b). Cross–cultural studies (for example, Hammond and Jablow 1976, p. 38) document the widespread fear of the power of women's sexuality, a basic theme in the Hindu literature examined by Susan Wadley.

Seclusion and limitations on the actions of women have contributed to the practice of female infanticide, the latter practiced in some groups in India until recent times and occasionally reported even today (see Miller 1981, and Bumiller 1990). Such practices have been related to reproductive success by an anthropologist working in the highly controversial field of sociobiology (Dickemann 1979a, 1979b, and 1981). Approaching the same data with a different orientation, a demographic historian has documented the role of female infanticide in maintaining the social and economic dominance of a prosperous caste in Gujarat, North India (Clark 1989).

In India today, amniocentesis and ultrasound are becoming increasingly popular as a method of determining the sex of female fetuses so they can be aborted. In response, some Indian states have passed legislation prohibiting the use of amniocentesis for sex selection. On a wider scale, the continuing neglect of girl children throughout northern India has been demonstrated by Das Gupta (1987), Wadley (1989), and Freed and Freed (1989). Further, fertility practices are now understood to be intimately connected to female neglect as families seek to construct the most desirable family for their economic situation (Caldwell *et. al.* 1984, Wadley in 1993.)

Several other significant publications pertaining specifically to Indian women should be mentioned here. Many of these have not been referred to in the papers in this volume for reasons of space, or because they fall outside the scope of these papers, or because they became available after these essays were written. Of key importance is *Towards Equality*, the influential and eye–opening official report of the Committee on the Status of Women in India (1974, 1975). This lengthy compendium was carefully prepared for the Government of India by an august panel of Indian scholars and activists. The report, still highly regarded as relevant to current conditions, unrelentingly details the statistics of systematic discrimination against women in Indian society and proposes numerous specific measures to alleviate women's problems. Those seriously interested in the women of India should acquaint themselves with this report and its recommendations. A summary of some of the major points made in the report and numerous references to other pertinent works can be found in a subsequent article on Indian women's roles in processes of national development (Jacobson, 1976-77).

      ˙ An ever-increasing number of volumes and papers focus on Indian women as policy-makers, educators, social scientists, religious practitioners, homemakers, agricultural labourers, factory workers, and actors in a multiplicity of other roles. A few of these publications include de Souza (1975), Jacobson (1989a), Kelkar and Nathan (1991), Lebra *et. al.* (1984), Liddle and Joshi (1986), Nanda (1976), and Papanek (1975). Further discussion of purdah is provided in Papanek (1973), Papanek and Minault (1982), Mandelbaum (1988), Jacobson (1976a, 1977a, 1977b, 1978, 1982), Jeffery (1979), U. Sharma (1980b), and Wadley (1992). Information on women's pollution can be obtained from such sources as Harper (1964, 1969), Ferro-Luzzi (1974), and Thompson (1985). Other significant publications concerning Indian women's family roles include Kolenda (1968, 1990) and Vatuk (1987).

      Detailed analysis of village Hindu beliefs in Karimpur, as revealed in religious texts, myths, and songs, with further information on women, is provided in a book by Dr. Wadley (1975), while some of her papers explore various other facets of the village women's lives (1983, 1989, 1992, and in 1993). Additional articles on Karimpur deal with issues of social change (Wadley and Derr, 1988; 1989).

      Women's religious roles in other parts of India are outlined in a volume on popular Hindu thought and action in the Chhattisgarh region of Central India by Babb (1975), and in a study of women's family rituals in Karnataka by Hanchett (1988). One practice affecting women is sati, the focus of work by Harlan (1992), Gaur (1989), Hawley (1993), and Courtright (forthcoming). Issues of gender and religious pilgrimage are discussed by Sax (1991) and Gold (1988). A volume by Leslie (1989) provides extensive discussion of ideal models of feminine purity and behaviour, while a collection of essays (Leslie, 1991) yields insights into many aspects of women's religious lives.

Works on South Indian women include, among many others, Wadley (1980a), Hobson (1982), and Ullrich (1987a, 1987b). Women of the Himalayan region are the focus of works by U. Sharma (1980a) and Bennett (1983), while Bengali women are discussed by Roy (1975), Mazumdar and Forbes (1989), and Fruzetti (1982).

An extensive annotated bibliography on South Asian women compiled by Carol Sakala (1980) presents a wealth of references to relatively recent as well as long-respected publications. Another bibliography on women in India is Dasgupta (1976), and annotated references to works on South Asian women appear in Tinker *et al.* (1976). A bibliography of sources pertaining to Hinduism, including important references to women's .roles in religious practice and ideology, has been published by Hopkins *et al.* (1980).

Susan Wadley's article, "Women and the Hindu Tradition," in the present volume, was written in 1976 and revised in 1978. An abridged version of the paper was published in *Signs* in 1977 (Wadley, 1977).

"The Women of North and Central India" was originally published in Matthiasson (1974) and is here reprinted as it initially appeared, with minor typographic corrections and the addition of some new photographs and footnotes. Since the paper was written, many changes have, of course, occurred in India, and two of these relevant to the article should be noted. Mrs. Indira Gandhi is no longer prime minister. After nearly sixteen years in office, including an electoral defeat in 1977 followed by a return to India's most powerful political position, Mrs. Gandhi was tragically assassinated in 1984. Some have likened Mrs. Gandhi to the Goddess Durga, and memories of her prominence remain strong in India. Another powerful feminine force, Sitala Mata, the Goddess of Smallpox, has also been vanquished--at least in her original form--through conquest of the disease by workers of the World Health Organization. Worshippers of the goddess are now free to reinterpret her powers and link her to other, less deadly, illnesses involving skin rashes, such as measles and chicken pox (see, for example, Wadley, 1980b). Some other changes are mentioned in footnotes in the article.

Both of the papers on women's rituals included here were originally published in 1980 and were based on fieldwork completed prior to that time. Slightly revised versions of the articles appeared in *Unspoken Worlds: Women's Religious Lives*, edited by Falk and Gross (1989). The rituals described remain a vital part of women's experiences today. Photographs have been added to the present printing. The final two papers in the volume were originally published in volumes focusing on social change. "Women and Jewelry in Rural India" appeared in *Family and Social Change in Modern India; Main Currents in Indian Sociology,* Vol. II, edited by Giri Raj Gupta (Jacobson 1976b). "The 'Village Indira': A Brahman Widow and Political Action in Rural North India" was published in *Balancing Acts: Women and the Process of Social Change,* edited by Patricia Lyons Johnson (Wadley 1992).

Several research trips and visits to the village of Nimkhera in Madhya Pradesh between 1973 and 1994 have revealed changes in women's lifestyles there. Almost all of the village Hindus continue to follow traditional patterns of veiling and seclusion, yet women of all status groups are now travelling more frequently to seek medical attention in the district town. Even within Nimkhera's lanes, the village women are exposed to urban styles, since some women wedding guests, visiting from distant villages and towns, now wear their saris draped over their shoulders, leaving their heads uncovered. Several high-status Muslim women of the village have given up the wearing of the veil (*burka*) and occasionally move about unveiled in city markets. However, even as high-status Muslims begin to regard traditional purdah as old fashioned and disadvantageous to women, upwardly mobile Muslim women of lower status are enthusiastically adopting the *burka* and seclusion as marks of increased prestige.

As anticipated in the paper on jewelry, women in rural Madhya Pradesh are currently wearing much less silver jewelry than in past decades, preferring smaller gold pieces similar to those worn by urban women. Among those who can afford such expenditures, family funds are increasingly being invested in a wider variety of assests than before, including tractors, tube wells, and improved houses.

Family planning measures, especially female sterilization, are presently meeting with more favour than in the past (particularly as infant mortality rates decline), and various innovations in agriculture are affecting women's work outside the home (for some details, see Jacobson 1975, 1977b, 1982, and 1989b). Two young women of the village are working as part-time primary school teachers, and one village matron runs a government-sponsored preschool program in her home. Four daughters of the village are being educated in nearby towns. More than twenty-five television sets now play within the mud-plastered wall of Nimkhera homes, and veiled village women, along with their male kinsmen, can regularly watch the activities of sophisticated urban Indian women as well as CNN broadcasts of foreign women. Education, along with television images of the outside, beamed into what was once a relatively isolated rural area, will doubtless help shape changing roles for village women.

In Karimpur, too, continuing research over the past few decades has revealed important changes in village life. Today, in this village of classic "mud walls" fame, television is leaving its mark, as villagers crowd around sets to watch highly popular enactments of the *Ramayan* and other epics. Yet even now, most Karimpur women have never seen a movie or television broadcast. Education for men and women is increasing, but women are divided on the issue of modernization, many lamenting changes that can leave educated sons without jobs and educated daughters-in-law without basic domestic skills. Still agricultural innovations have brought increased leisure and prosperity to many, providing opportunities to pursue religious activities more vigorously now than in the past. Karimpur women's rituals are often more elaborate and frequent that they were even twenty-five years ago.

Throughout much of India, awareness of the disadvantages women suffer is growing dramatically, and strong efforts are being made on many fronts to increase women's economic and decision-making powers and to improve their general well-being. The Indian women's movement is expanding rapidly, and activists are busy in many venues (see Bumiller, 1990; Calman, 1992; and Jacobson, 1992). The journal *Manushi*, published since the late 1970s, regularly informs its readers of issues and action pertaining to key feminist concerns. In cities, towns, and villages across the land, large numbers of women are working to mitigate the enormous problems of poverty, illiteracy, and inequity that challenge India's women and the nation as a whole, even as valued Indian traditions are maintained.

The authors wish to thank The Free Press, the editors of *Signs*, and the Wadsworth Publishing Company, Westview Press, and Giri Raj Gupta for granting permission to reprint the articles in this volume.

REFERENCES

Agarwal, Bina. "Women, Poverty, and Agricultural Growth in India," *Journal of Peasant Studies*, vol. 13, pp. 165-220, 1986.

——. "Who Sows? Who Reaps? Women and Land Rights in India," *Journal of Peasant Studies*, vol. 15, pp. 531-581, 1988a.

Agarwal, Bina (ed.). *Structures of Patriarchy: the State, the Community, and the Household.* Zed Press, London, 1988b.

Babb, Lawrence A. *The Divine Hierarchy: Popular Hinduism in Central India.*

Columbia University Press, New York, 1975.

Bennett, Lynn. *Dangerous Wives and Sacred Sisters: Social and Symbolic Roles of High-Caste Women in Nepal.* Columbia University Press, New York, 1983.

Boserup, Ester. *Women's Role in Economic Development.* G. Allen and Unwin, London, 1970.

Bumiller, Elisabeth. *May You Be The Mother of a Hundred Sons: A Journey Among the Women of India.* Fawcett Columbine, New York, 1990.

Caldwell, J., P.H. Reddy, and P. Caldwell. "The Determinants of Fertility Decline in Rural South India," in Tim Dyson and Nigel Crook (eds.), *India's Demography: Essays on the Contemporary Population.* South Asian Publishers, New Delhi, pp. 187-207, 1984.

Calman, Leslie. *Toward Empowerment: Women in Movement Politics in India.* Westview Press, Boulder, 1992.

Clark, Alice. "Limitations on Female Life Chances in Rural Central Gujarat," in J. Krishnamurty (ed.), *Women in Colonial India: Essays on Survival, Work, and the State.* Oxford University Press, New York and Delhi, pp. 27-51, 1989.

Committee on the Status of Women in India. *Towards Equality: Report of the Committee on the Status of Women in India.* Government of India, Ministry of Education and Social Welfare, New Delhi, 1974.

———. *Status of Women in India.* (abridged edition of *Towards Equality*), Allied Publishers, New Delhi, 1975.

Courtright, Paul. *The Goddess and the Dreadful Practice.* Oxford University Press, London, forthcoming.

Das, Veena. "Indian Women: Work, Power, and Status," in B.R. Nanda (ed.), *Indian Women: From Purdah to Modernity.* Vikas Publishing House, New Delhi, 1976.

Das Gupta, Monica. "Selective Discrimination against Female Children in Rural Punjab, India," *Population and Development Review*, vol. 13, pp. 77-100, 1987.

Dasgupta, Kalpana. *Women on the Indian Scene: An Annotated Bibliography.* Abhinav Publications, New Delhi, 1976.

de Souza, Alfred (ed.). *Women in Contemporary India: Traditional Images and Changing Roles.* Manohar Book Service, New Delhi, 1975.

Dickemann, Mildred. "Female Infanticide, Reproductive Strategies, and Social Stratification: A Preliminary Model," in Napoleon A. Chagnon and William Irons (eds.), *Evolutionary Biology and Human Social Behavior: An Anthropological Perspective.* Ducksbury Press, N. Scituate, Mass., pp. 321-367, 1979a.

———. "The Ecology of Mating Systems in Hypergynous Dowry Societies," *Social Science Information*, vol. 18, no. 2, pp. 163-195, 1979b.

———. "Paternal Confidence and Dowry Competition: A Biocultural Analysis of Purdah," in Richard A. Alexander and Donald W. Tinkle (eds.), *Natural Selection and Social Behavior: Recent Research and New Theory*. Chiron Press, New York, pp. 417-438, 1981.

Dyson, Tim, and M. Moore. "On Kinship Structure, Female Autonomy, and Demographic Behavior in India," *Population and Development Review*, vol. 9, pp. 35-59, 1983.

Falk, Nancy Auer, and Rita M. Gross (eds.). *Unspoken Worlds: Women's Religious Lives*. Wadsworth Publishing Company, Belmont, Calif., 1989.

Ferro-Luzzi, G. Eichinger. "Women's Pollution Periods in Tamilnad," *Anthropos*, vol. 69, pp. 113-161, 1974.

Freed, Ruth S., and Stanley A. Freed. "Beliefs and Practices Resulting in Female Deaths and Fewer Females than Males in India," *Population and Environment: A Journal of Interdisciplinary Studies*, vol. 10, no. 3, pp. 144-161, 1989.

French, Marilyn. *The War Against Women*. Summit Books, New York, 1992.

Friedl, Ernestine. *Women and Men: An Anthropologist's View*. Holt, Rinehart and Winston, New York, 1975.

Fruzetti, Lina M. *The Gift of a Virgin: Women, Marriage, and Ritual in a Bengali Society*. Rutgers University Press, New Brunswick, N.J., 1982.

Gallin, Rita S., and Anne Ferguson (eds.). *The Women and Development Annual Review*, vol. 2. Westview Press, Boulder, 1991.

Gaur, Meena. *Sati and Social Reforms in India*. Publication Scheme, Jaipur, 1989.

Gold, Ann Grodzins. *Fruitful Journeys: The Ways of Rajasthan Pilgrims*. University of California Press, Berkeley, 1988.

Hammond, Dorothy, and Alta Jablow. *Women in Cultures of the World*. Cummings Publishing Co., Menlo Park, Calif., 1976.

Hanchett, Suzanne. *Coloured Rice: Symbolic Structure in Hindu Family Festivals*. Hindustan Publishing Corporation, Delhi, 1988.

Harlan, Lindsey. *Religion and Rajput Women: The Ethic of Protection in Contemporary Narratives*. University of California Press, Berkeley, 1992.

Harper, Edward B. "Ritual Pollution as an Integrator of Caste and Religion," *The Journal of Asian Studies*, vol. 23, pp. 151-197, June 1964.

——————. "Fear and the Status of Women," *Southwestern Journal of Anthropology*, vol. 25, no. 1, pp. 81-95, 1969.

Hawley, John S. *Sati, the Blessing and the Curse*. Oxford University Press, New York, 1993.

Hobson, Sarah. *The Family Web*. Academy Chicago, Chicago, 1982. [*Family Web: A Story of India*. John Murray, London, 1978].

Hopkins, Thomas, *et. al. Guide to Indian Religion*, The Asian Religions and Philosophies Resource Guides. G. K. Hall, Boston, 1980.

Jacobson, Doranne. "Separate Spheres: Differential Modernization in Rural Central India," in Helen E. Ullrich (ed.), *Competition and Modernization in South Asia*. Abhinav Publications, New Delhi, 1975.

—————. "The Veil of Virtue: Purdah and the Muslim Family in the Bhopal Region of Central India," in Imtiaz Ahmad (ed.), *Family, Kinship, and Marriage among Muslims in India.* Manohar Book Service, New Delhi, pp. 169–215, 1976a.

—————. "Women and Jewelry in Rural India," in Giri Raj Gupta (ed.), *Family and Social Change in Modern India; Main Currents in Indian Sociology,* Vol. II. Carolina Academic Press, Durham, N.C., and Vikas, New Delhi, pp. 135-183, 1976b.

—————. "Indian Women in Processes of Development," *Journal of International Affairs,* vol. 30, no. 2, pp. 211-242, 1976-77.

—————. "Purdah in India: Life Behind the Veil," *National Geographic Magazine,* vol. 152, no. 2, pp. 270-286, 1977a.

—————. "Flexibility in Central Indian Kinship and Residence," in Kenneth David (ed.), *The New Wind: Changing Identities in South Asia.* World Anthropology, Sol Tax (General Editor). Mouton, The Hague, pp. 263-283, 1977b.

—————. "The Chaste Wife: Cultural Norm and Individual Experience," in Sylvia Vatuk (ed.), *American Studies in the Anthropology of India.* American Institute of Indian Studies and Manohar Publications, New Delhi, pp. 95-138, 1978.

—————. "Purdah and the Hindu Family in Central India," in H. Papanek and G. Minault (eds.), *Separate Worlds: Studies of Purdah in South Asia.* South Asia Books, Columbia, Mo., and Chanakya Publications, New Delhi, pp. 81-109, 1982.

—————. *Women and Work in South Asia: An Audiovisual Presentation.* Women and Development Issues in Three World Areas. The Upper Midwest Women's History Center Collection, St. Louis Park, Minn., 1989a.

—————. "Nimkhera Today," in S.H. Gross and M.H. Rojas, *Contemporary Issues for Women in South Asia: India, Pakistan, Bangladesh, Sri Lanka, Nepal, and Bhutan.* The Upper Midwest Women's History Center Collection, St. Louis Park, Minn., p. 56, 1989b.

—————. "Gender Relations: Changing Patterns in India," in Myron L. Cohen (ed.), *Asia: Case Studies in the Social Sciences: A Guide for Teaching.* M.E. Sharpe, Armonk, N.Y., pp. 119-139, 1992.

Jeffery, Patricia. *Frogs in a Well: Indian Women in Purdah.* Zed Press, London, 1979.

Jeffery, Patricia, Roger Jeffery, and Andrew Lyon. *Labour Pains and Labour Power: Women and Childbearing in India.* Zed Books, London, 1989.

Kelkar, Govind, and Dev Nathan. *Gender and Tribe: Women, Land, and Forests in Jharkand.* Kali for Women, New Delhi, and Zed Books, London, 1991.

Kessler, Evelyn S. *Women: An Anthropological View.* Holt, Rinehart and Winston, New York, 1976.

Kolenda, Pauline M. "Region, Caste, and Family Structure: A Comparative Study of the Indian 'Joint' Family," in M. Singer and B. Cohn (eds.) *Structure and Change in Indian Society*. Aldine Publishing Co., Chicago, pp. 339-396, l968.

—————. "Untouchable Chuhras Through Their Humor: 'Equalizing' Marital Kin Through Teasing, Pretence, and Farce," in Owen M. Lynch (ed.), *Divine Passions: The Social Construction of Emotion in India*. University of California Press, Berkeley, pp. ll6-153, 1990.

Leacock, Eleanor, and June Nash. "Ideologies of Sex: Archetypes and Stereotypes," unpublished paper, 1975.

Leacock, Eleanor, and Helen I. Safa, *et. al. Women's Work: Development and the Division of Labor by Gender*. Bergin and Garvey Publishers, South Hadley, Mass., 1986.

Lebra, Joyce, J. Paulson, and J. Everett (eds.). *Women and Work in India: Continuity and Change*. Promilla and Co., New Delhi, 1984.

Leslie, I. Julia. *The Perfect Wife: The Orthodox Hindu Woman According to the Stridharmapaddhati of Tryambakayajvan*. Oxford University Press, Delhi, 1989.

Leslie, Julia (ed.). *Roles and Rituals for Hindu Women*. Fairleigh Dickinson University Press, Rutherford, N.J., 1991.

Liddle, Joanna, and Rama Joshi. *Daughters of Independence: Gender, Caste, and Class in India*. Zed Books, London, 1986.

MacCormack, Carol, and M. Strathern. *Nature, Culture, and Gender*. Cambridge University Press, Cambridge, 1980.

Mandelbaum, David G. *Women's Seclusion and Men's Honor: Sex Roles in North India, Bangladesh, and Pakistan*. University of Arizona Press, Tucson, 1988.

Manushi: A Journal about Women and Society. C/202 Lajpat Nagar l, New Delhi-ll0024.

Martin, Kay M., and Barbara Voorhies. *Female of the Species*, Columbia University Press, New York, 1975.

Matthiasson, Carolyn J. (ed.). *Many Sisters: Women in Cross-Cultural Perspective*. The Free Press, New York, 1974.

Mazumdar, Shudha (edited by Geraldine H. Forbes). *The Memoirs of an Indian Woman*. M.E. Sharpe, Armonk, N.Y., 1989.

Mencher, Joan P. "Female Cultivators and Agricultural Laborers: Who are they and What do they do?" *Michigan State University Working Papers on Women in International Development,* No. 192, November, 1989.

Miller, Barbara D. *The Endangered Sex: Neglect of Female Children in Rural North India*. Cornell University Press, Ithaca, 1981.

Nanda, B.R. (ed.). *Indian Women: From Purdah to Modernity*. Vikas Publishing House, New Delhi, 1976.

Omvedt, Gail. "'Patriarchy': The Analysis of Women's Oppression," *Insurgent Sociologist*, vol. 13, pp. 30-50, 1986.

Ortner, Sherry B. "Is Female to Male as Nature is to Culture?" in M.Z. Rosaldo and L. Lamphere (eds.), *Woman, Culture, and Society*, Stanford

University Press, Stanford, 1974.

Papanek, Hanna. "Purdah: Separate Worlds and Symbolic Shelter," *Comparative Studies in Society and History*, vol. 15, no. 3, pp. 289-325, 1973.

—————. "Women in South and Southeast Asia: Issues and Research," *Signs: Journal of Women in Culture and Society*, vol. 1, no. 1, pp. 193-214, 1975.

Papanek, Hanna, and Gail Minault (eds.). *Separate Worlds: Studies of Purdah in South Asia*. South Asia Books, Columbia, Mo., and Chanakya Publications, New Delhi, 1982.

Reiter, Rayna R. (ed.) *Toward an Anthropology of Women*. Monthly Review Press, New York, 1975.

Rohrlich-Leavitt, Ruby (ed.). *Women Cross-Culturally: Change and Challenge*. Mouton, The Hague, 1976.

Roy, Manisha. *Bengali Women*. University of Chicago Press, Chicago, 1975.

Sakala, Carol. *Women of South Asia: A Guide to Resources*. Kraus International Publications, Millwood, N.Y., 1980.

Sanday, Peggy R. "Toward a Theory of the Status of Women," *American Anthropologist*, vol. 75, no. 5, pp. 1682-1700, 1973.

—————. *Female Power and Male Dominance: On the Origins of Sexual Inequality*. Cambridge University Press, Cambridge, 1981.

Sax, William S. *Mountain Goddess: Gender and Politics in a Himalayan Pilgrimage*. Oxford University Press, New York, 1991.

Sharma, Miriam. "Caste, Class, and Gender: Production and Reproduction in North India," *Journal of Peasant Studies*, vol. 12, pp. 57-88, 1985.

Sharma, Ursula. *Women, Work, and Property in Northwest India*. Tavistock, London, 1980a.

—————. "Purdah and Public Space," in A. de Souza (ed.), *Women in Contemporary India and South Asia*. Manohar Books, New Delhi, pp. 213-239, 1980b.

Thompson, Catherine. "The Power to Pollute and The Power to Preserve: Perceptions of Female Power in a Hindu Village," *Social Science and Medicine*, vol. 21, pp. 701-711, 1985.

Tinker, Irene, Michele Bo Bramsen, and Mayra Buvinic (eds.). *Women and World Development; With an Annotated Bibliography*. Praeger Publishers, New York, 1976.

Ullrich, Helen. "Marriage Patterns among Havik Brahmins: A 20-Year Study of Change," *Sex Roles*, vol. 16, pp. 615-635, 1987a.

—————. "A Study of Change and Depression Among Havik Brahmin Women in a South Indian Village," *Culture, Medicine, and Psychiatry*, vol. 11, pp. 261–287, 1987b.

Vatuk, Sylvia. "Authority, Power and Autonomy in the Life Cycle of North Indian Women," in Paul Hockings (ed.), *Dimensions of Social Life: Essays in Honor of David G. Mandelbaum*. Mouton de Gruyter, Berlin, pp. 23-44, 1987.

Wadley, Susan S. *Shakti: Power in the Conceptual Structure of Karimpur Religion*. The University of Chicago Studies in Anthropology, Series in

Social, Cultural, and Linguistic Anthropology 2, Chicago, 1975.

——————. "Women in the Hindu Tradition," *Signs: Journal of Women in Culture and Society*, vol. 3, no. 1, pp.113-125 , 1977.

——————. *Powers of Tamil Women*, South Asia Series, No. 6. Syracuse University, Syracuse, 1980a [reprint, Manohar Books, New Delhi, 1991].

——————. "Sitala: The Cool One," *Asian Folklore Studies*, vol. 39, pp. 33-62, 1980b.

——————. "Vrats: Transformers of Destiny," in V. Daniel and C. Keyes (eds.), *Karma: An Anthropological Inquiry.* University of California Press, Berkeley, pp. 147-162, 1983.

——————. "Female Life Changes in Rural India," *Cultural Survival Quarterly*, vol. 13, pp. 35-39, 1989.

——————. "The 'Village Indira': A Brahman Widow and Political Action in Rural North India," in P. Johnson (ed.), *Balancing Acts: Women and the Process of Social Change.* Westview Press, Boulder, 1992.

——————. "Family Composition Strategies in Rural North India," *Social Science and Medicine*, in press.

——————. *Struggling with Destiny in Karimpur, 1925-1984,* University of California Press, Berkeley, 1994.

Wadley, Susan S., and B.W. Derr. "Karimpur Families Over 60 Years," *South Asian Anthropologist*, vol. 9, pp. 119-132, 1988.

——————. "Karimpur 1925-1984: Understanding Rural India Through Restudies," in P. Bardhan (ed.), *Conversations Between Anthropologists and Economists: Issues in the Measurement of Economic Change in Rural India.* Oxford University Press, Delhi, pp. 76-126, 1989.

Yalman, Nur. "On the Purity of Women in the Castes of Ceylon and Malabar," *Journal of the Royal Anthropological Institute*, vol. 93, pp. 25-58, 1963.

The Women of North and Central India: Goddesses and Wives

Doranne Jacobson

Her red sari bespangled with tiny mirrors, a statuesque village woman balances gleaming brass pots brimming with water atop her head as she returns to her whitewashed home from the well. In a suburb of New Delhi, a well-to-do housewife draws water for her bath in a pink bathtub. With only her hands and feet protruding from an all-enveloping black cloak, a Muslim woman rides in a curtained, horse-drawn carriage to a city bus station. A bareheaded young lecturer in English drives her family's car to a college in a large town. Outside a village, a woman carries a head load of gravel in an iron pan for a road construction project as her tiny child sleeps in a cloth hammock hung from a nearby tree. A slight, gray-haired woman brings to order the Parliament of the world's largest democracy. With an emaciated child astride her hip, a gaunt woman in a tattered sari stretches out her hand to beg for coins from a plump civil servant's wife in a busy railway station. Completely covered by a white cloth over her silken sari, a young village bride huddles apprehensively in a corner, awaiting her first encounter with the youthful husband she has never seen. A bare-breasted girl of the Muria tribe walks arm-in-arm with her lover in the moonlight at a country fair. A Christian woman of old Delhi sweeps her small apartment in a crowded tenement. High atop a heavily loaded bullock cart, a nomadic blacksmith woman rides to a new roadside camp. In a small village, a woman prostrates herself before a mud shrine and beseeches Goddess Durga to save the life of her sick child. A Calcutta woman physician hurries to the home of a patient stricken with typhoid. Social workers, road sweepers, college students, field labourers, matriarchs, and quiet brides; these are all women of India.

From *Many Sisters : Women in Cross-Cultural Perspective,* edited by Carolyn J. Matthiasson. Reprinted by permission of the publisher. © 1974 by The Free Press, a Division of Macmillan Publishing Co., Inc.

At the rock temples of Ellora, sculptures 1500 years old depict idealized feminine beauty. (c) Jerome Jacobson

Ornamented with finery, revered as mother and goddess, concealed behind a veil, or despised as a widow, the Indian woman has long been an object of interest and fascination to Westerners and to her own countrymen. The subject of countless works of art and literature through the ages, from the ancient epics and the cave paintings and voluptuous statuary of Ajanta and Ellora to the cinema, novels, and greeting cards of today, the Indian woman has been depicted as graceful and loving, a gentle creature in need of protection and guidance, yet hard-working and strong enough to withstand with dignity cruel blows dealt her by fate.

Those who have attempted to know the women of India have never been successful in finding a stereotype, because there is no single Indian woman. In fact, the diversity of women in India defies imagination. Geographic, occupational, economic, religious, and caste differences are vast.

Each region is unique in many respects — verdant Bengal, the hot Gangetic plain, the mountainous Kashmiri and Himalayan areas, the productive Punjab, desert Rajasthan, fertile and forested Central India, and the humid rice lands and airy uplands of South India. Within each region the crowded urban centres and busy market towns contrast with the rural villages, where four-fifths of India's population lives. The cities are peopled with clerks, merchants, labourers, officials, factory workers, teachers, and other workers engaged in thousands of different tasks. The villages are inhabited mostly by farmers and craftsmen and people who perform services for them. In the cities, elegance and wealth, squalor and poverty are found in close proximity. Even in the villages, a few landlords drive cars while many villagers are too poor to own bullock carts. Hindus, Muslims, Sikhs, Parsis, Christians, Jains and Jews all bargain in the bazaars and markets, but in most parts of the country the majority of the people are Hindus.

Almost all of India's nearly 575 million[*] people are born into and marry within one of thousands of caste and castelike groups. Each such group is ritually ranked in relation to other groups, and most castes are traditionally associated with an occupation, from high-ranking Brahmans (priestly castes) and middle-ranking farmer and artisan groups, such as potters, barbers, and carpenters, to "untouchable" latrine cleaners, washermen, and butchers. The greatest number of castes are found among the Hindus, but even Muslims and Christians recognize

---

[*] In 1991, India's population was estimated at 860 million (Population Reference Bureau, Inc., Washington, D.C.).

caste differences among themselves. Additionally, there are many groups, usually referred to as tribes, whose members often live in forest areas and are considered to be somewhat outside the caste system. Even a small village of a few hundred people may count among its citizens representatives of a score of different castes, several economic groups, and two or three religious groups.

An essay such as this can barely touch upon the great variety of life-styles to be found among the women of even half of India — those of the regions lyings north of the Narbada River, which almost bisects the country. Broadly, these areas are known as North and Central India and are characterized by a general similarity of environment and culture, the basic patterns of which are overlaid with diversities large and small. This paper does not discuss the women of the South India, who have much in common with women of North but whose lifeways differ significantly in some respects. The women of India's many and diverse tribes are only mentioned.

Although urban women are also discussed, this chapter focuses on the rural women of North and Central India, women who are often depicted in idyllic scenes by India's modern artists wearing colourful traditional clothing, peacefully grinding wheat in hand mills or carrying pots of water. Mostly illiterate and unable to write about themselves, village women, who constitute 80 per cent of India's female population, are often slighted in treatises and official writings that purport to analyze "the status of women" in India. Three important threads wind through the lives of these women: separation of the sexes, concern with hierarchy, and restraint.

As an anthropologist, I lived and did research in a small village in the Central Indian state of Madhya Pradesh, and many of the women I discuss are those I met in Nīmkherā village and adjacent areas near the city of Bhopal. I also draw upon other studies of rural and urban Indian women carried out in recent years by other researchers.[1]

North and Central India

North and Central India include many different kinds of terrain, from mountains in the north to desert in the far west and lush greenery in the east. But most of North India is occupied by the great plain of India's most sacred river, the Ganges. Upon this densely populated, open, flat land lie wheat fields thickly dotted by clusters of windowless, mud-walled houses. Much of Central India consists of the black-soiled Malwa Plateau, a rich wheatland bordered by forested hills sheltering deer, antelope, tigers leopards, and wild boar. Here mud-plastered stone houses roofed with handmade tiles are grouped a few miles apart, separated by fields and forest. Throughout most of India north of the Narbada, wheat is the staple crop, and herds of humped cattle are omnipresent. Rice, lentils, and millet are other important food crops. Water buffaloes, valued almost everywhere as milk producers, are used in some areas as draft animals.

Most of these parts of India have a monsoon climate, with three distinct seasons. From late March through June the land is parched by hot winds and soaring temperatures. Fields lie dry and empty of all but stubble, while the people busy themselves with weddings and visits to kinsmen. In cities, offices are often empty as their occupants take long tea breaks and vacations. In late June the skies darken and the desiccated land is rejuvenated by torrents of rain pouring down unceasingly for days at a time. Greenery appears everywhere, and children wear fragrant blossoms in their hair. Bullocks pull ploughs through the sodden wheat fields, and rice plots are sown by hand. At night, villages reverberate with sounds of exuberant singing.

Days gradually become drier and cooler throughout the green season until November, when the rain stops and the nights are clear and cold. The wheat has been sown and grows tall, even as rice is harvested. Many religious festivals and holidays are observed during the cool months, and villages and city dwellers alike make pilgrimages to the holy sites of Hinduism. Suddenly it is March again, and the wheat is harvested just as the days become unbearably hot.

Even city dwellers are attuned to the agricultural cycle, the timeliness and sufficiency of the rains, and the abundance of the harvest, for any aberration in the cycle means food shortages for all but the most prosperous. The phases of the moon are closely watched by both urban and country dwellers, since calendrical religious activities are timed in accordance with the lunar phases. Thus virtually all Indians are constantly aware of the physical world and cosmos around them.

In North and Central India, ancient civilizations were born. Kingdoms rose and fell, and invaders from the northwest — Aryans, Greeks, Persians, and Afghans — added their biological and cultural heritages to the Indian melange. Hindu emperors were superseded by Muslim sultans, and graceful Muslim monuments like the Taj Mahal challenged the architectural pre-eminence of the intricately wrought, carved Hindu caves and temples like Ellora and Khajuraho.

Today, although most of the inhabitants of the northern half of India speak varieties of Hindi, more than a dozen other languages and dialects — almost all classed within the far-reaching Indo-European language family — are also spoken.

A group of Lambadi women wear mirror-studded clothing.
Originally from Rajasthan, these former gypsies now
live in Pune where they work as day labourers.

Appearance and Dress

Physically, most North and Central Indians are taller and fairer than most South Indians, but the range of physical types is great, even within a single village or a single caste. Skin tones range from light olive to dark brown, and hair varies from dark brown to jet black. Most women are slender and small-boned.

Generally, fairness of skin and a slight plumpness are considered essential to beauty. A girl who has been ill may be told, "Oh, you poor thing. You've become very black and skinny". Movie stars are typically rather fleshy, with skin the colour of wheat paste.

Most Indian women wear saris, garments consisting of several yards of cloth that may be draped about the body in different ways. Urban women usually wear the sari draped into an ankle-length skirt and then pulled across the bosom and over the left shoulder. Under the sari are worn a tight-fitting open-midriff blouse and a long petticoat. City saris are made of colourful printed cottons and silks, almost always immaculately clean and neatly ironed (village women tend to be less fastidious). Muslim women wear a head scarf, long gathered pants, and a tunic. This costume, freshly starched, is also a favourite of high school and college students. In cheaper cottons and synthetics, it is worn by many Muslim village women as well.

In the cities, much of the jewellery women wear is of gold, including dangly earrings, bangles, necklaces, and tiny nose ornaments worn through a small hole in the nostril. Essential to the costume of the nubile girl and married woman are colourful glass bangles that cover the wrists and a cosmetic mark on the forehead — for Hindus a dot of vermilion or a gilt spangle and for Muslims a small black line. Married Hindu women also put vermilion in the part of the hair. Virtually all city women have long dark hair, oiled and braided into one or two long plaits or wound into a bun. Unlike villagers, most urban women keep their hair uncovered.

Throughout North and Central India, city women dress very much alike, with only a few regional differences in the manner of draping the sari. It is among the Hindu villagers that regional variations in styles of dress are pronounced. In the Delhi area, village women wear a head scarf and a long-tailed shirt over a full skirt. Punjabi Hindus and Muslims don tunics and pantaloons, and in Rajasthan, tie-dyed saris are worn over colourful cutwork blouses and full, hand-printed skirts. There, clothes and lacquer jewellery may be studded with tiny mirrors, and some women bind their hair into a conelike shape atop the head. Arms, ankles and heads are bedecked with heavy silver and ivory jewellery.

In Madhya Pradesh, villagers wear long, full skirts, puffed-sleeved blouses, and colourful cotton saris. Their jingling silver and gold jewellery includes a head peak, earrings in upper ear and lobe, nose plug, necklaces, three or four heavy bracelets and half a dozen glass bangles on each wrist, rings, thick chain belt, and clunky ankle and toe ornaments. Here, an undecorated wrist or ankle is considered naked. Hair is arranged in several small braids and pulled back into a large one, tightly bound with string.

Eastward and closer to the Ganges, in eastern Uttar Pradesh and Bihar, village women wear drabber costumes — little jewellery, often no blouse or petticoat, and a thin-bordered white or maroon sari pulled around the body and over the head to cover a single plait of hair. Bengali villagers wear blue-bordered white and coloured saris without much jewellery, although festival days are enlivened by the appearance of young women in brilliant colours. The tribal women of Bengal, Bihar, and Madhya Pradesh seldom wear blouses with their mostly white, knee-length mini-saris and heavy jewellery. Nomadic blacksmith and gypsy women are conspicuous in multi-coloured mirror-work clothing and ivory bangles from wrist to shoulder. Village women usually go barefoot, but in public almost all city women wear sandals.

For all Indian women, clothing and decoration of the body are very important. The soft draping of fabrics — sari or long head scarf — about the face and shoulders and the frequent manipulation of the cloth are the essence of femininity. To feel pretty, the woman must also have long, braided hair, musical and glittering jewellery, and eyes outlined with lampblack. Hands and feet are objects of great aesthetic concern and are often decorated with intricate designs in scarlet paint or russet-coloured henna. Tattoos ornament the limbs of many village women. Much of the artistry of India is devoted to personal adornment of the feminine figure. Hindu goddesses are depicted wearing not the drab drapery of the Virgin Mary but gold-bordered red saris, dazzling jewellery, and luscious garlands of flowers.

For the Indian woman, sumptuous personal decoration symbolizes material and social well-being. Jewellery is an important form of wealth and is usually a woman's most important material asset. In most parts of India, it is only the destitute woman who displays no jewellery and the unfortunate widow who breaks her bangles, shaves her head, and wears only white.

In contrast to their womenfolk, Indian men often look quite drab. City streets teem with men in pure white shirts and pants, their oiled black hair glistening in the sun. Villagers and a few city men wear white caps or turbans, but only in the desert areas of western India is it usual to see yellow and red turbans and intricately embroidered flared shirts. Most village men wear a long piece of white cloth wound around and between the legs and heavy leather shoes or sandals. The contrast between the men and women's dress is sometimes striking. Among well-to-do Sikhs, it is customary for a bride to wear fine silks and jewellery for thirty days after her wedding. One evening on the streets of Bhopal, I met a recently married Sikh friend, Harlal Singh, who introduced me to his new bride. Mrs. Singh wore an elegant purple brocaded sari and heavy earrings and necklace studded with small pearls and rubies. Her arms were encased in dozens of pure gold bangles. Harlal wore a pair of grey cotton trousers and a brown plaid sport shirt.

In the seclusion of her courtyard, a young Brahman wife of Madhya Pradesh uses a winnowing fan to separate edible grains from chaff.

Growing up in North and Central India

Rambai, a middle-aged Hindu woman of the high-ranking Bagheli Thakur caste, first came as a girl of fifteen to live with her young husband and his family in Nimkhera, a village of about 550 people in Central India. The joint family household of which she became a part consisted of her husband's parents, his two older brothers, their wives and children, and her husband's younger sister and brother, all sharing a home and the produce of the family fields. Their house, of whitewashed mud-plastered stone, was roofed with country tiles and decorated with well-worn wooden carvings of horses' heads set into the door frame. Like the house in which she had grown up in a not too distant village, her new home was furnished with large, built-in grain bins, rope-strung cots, metal trunks, quilts, and a variety of shining brass water pots, cooking utensils, and earthenware storage jugs.

In most of North and Central India, a bride usually leaves the village of her birth to reside with her husband and his family in another village. After her marriage, she is considered a member of her husband's kin group, a lineage including patrilineally related males, their wives, and their unmarried daughters.

When Rambai first realize she was pregnant, she was about eighteen, and she was delighted at the prospect of having a baby. Some of the neighbour women had begun to whisper that it was taking Rambai a long time to conceive, but at last her own baby was to be born! Rambai hoped it would be a boy; after all, it was best to have a boy first. She wanted to have several children, including girls, but it was important to have a boy. Rambai's mother-in-law, Hirabai, suspected the girl might be pregnant when she continued to cook every night for three months straight. When a woman menstruates, she does not cook or enter the kitchen or touch others, since she is considered ritually unclean for five days. But Rambai had failed to ask anyone to take over her cooking tasks for three months, and finally the older woman asked her, "Is something there"?

Shyly dropping her eyes, Rambai mumbled, "Who knows?" Suddenly engulfed in a warm glow, Hirabai admonished, "Then don't go anywhere, and don't drink too much tea." Rambai knew that her mother-in-law was advising her to keep away from places where evil spirits might lurk to harm her or her baby and to refrain from eating foods said to be inherently "hot" — such as tea, meat, eggs, and onions — because they would cause too much heat to build up in the womb.

Rambai knew that during her pregnancy she would be regarded as a very special and auspicious person.

Rambai's husband Tej Singh also began to suspect something when his wife did not sleep apart from him for three months. And one day his older sister-in-law laughed and said, "You should keep away from your precious one, you know! But I suppose you won't be able to do that!" Rambai had been too shy to tell him and he too shy to ask.

It was not too long before her mother-in-law had hinted to the neighbours of Rambai's condition, and Rambai noticed that visitors to the house smiled at her and sat at a little distance from her. She knew they did not want to be accused of unwittingly carrying a spirit or ghost into contact with her, since, after all, no one knew if the baby would be born properly and live. One visitor, old Mograwali, told Rambai and her mother-in-law about her own unfortunate experience with a woman possessed by a ghost.

> Once, not long after I had a baby, I went to the well to get water. A strange woman was there at the well. She came rushing up to me and put her wet hands flat against my chest. I was young then and didn't know what she was doing, and I didn't think anything of it. But when I got home, I began to have a burning sensation in my chest, and my milk dried up. My baby got very weak and died. I found out later that woman was possessed by a ghost, and the ghost made her do that to me so it could attack me and my baby.

"Yes, bride, you see me now with only three daughters, but sitting before you is the mother of twelve children". Mograwali's eyes filled with tears as she remembered her nine dead babies. She held up her hand, fingers outstretched, "Five, five were boys".

Rambai knew it was a special tragedy of Mograwali's life that she had been deprived of sons. Fortunately, her husband was still alive, but if he died, who would support the old woman? Her daughters were married and living in other villages with their husbands and their families, and Mograwali was too old to work. Perhaps she would be able to visit her daughters for long visits, but after all, she would not want to be considered a beggar, dependent upon her daughters. Maybe that was why Mograwali was such a miser; perhaps she was saving money for her possible widowhood. How much luckier her own mother-in-law was. With sons and daughters-in-law in her house, her mother-in-law would never be without someone to look after her.

For the next several months, Rambai refrained from strenuous work. There were others in her large household who fetched water and cleaned the cow dung out of the cow sheds. But as the youngest daughter-in-law, Rambai continued doing most of the cooking, squatting beside the small earthen oven to prepare *rotīs* - flat, tortillalike wheat cakes — and to stir pots of vegetables and lentil sauce in the dark kitchen, over a fire of cow dung and wood. She was glad she did not have to work in the fields, the way poor pregnant women do, or to continue with all the household work, as do women who have no sisters-in-law to help them.

Rambai went for a visit to her parents' village, where she rested and enjoyed herself for about a month. She would have loved to stay there with her mother and her dear family members to have her baby, but it was forbidden. A girl's first baby had to be born in its father's house, or something terrible would happen. So, as the imminence of her motherhood became obvious, Rambai returned to her husband's home. (In some other parts of India, a baby is born in its mother's parents' home.)[2]

One evening a few weeks later Rambai felt labour pains. She did not know what to do, how to tell her mother-in-law; it was so embarrassing. Sitting quietly next to her husband's little sister, she felt afraid. "Lalta, go ask you mother if I could have a little *nīm* tea, I have a stomach-ache". The leaves of the *nim*[3] tree are good for soothing many pains. Soon her mother-in-law was beside Rambai, feeling her stomach and then whispering to Rambai's brother-in-law to go and call the midwife. The time had come.

Rambai lay on an old sari on the earthen floor of a tiny room used by five or six generations of parturient women before her. With her were her mother-in-law and the midwife, a member of an untouchable caste who was allowed in the house only to assist in childbirth. As the pains grew worse, Rambai felt like screaming, and she moaned loudly. "Sssh, bride. What will the men think? They can all hear you", her mother-in-law admonished. Rambai thought of her father-in-law and his overnight guests sleeping just a few feet away on the other side of the wall and grit her teeth silently. The midwife urged her to squat. "If you lie down, the baby will never come out." With every contraction, the woman pressed hard on Rambai's belly, trying to force the baby down and out.

Finally, at dawn, when Rambai thought she could stand it no longer, it was all over. "Eh. It's little girl," the midwife announced. Rambai's heart sank. A girl. Was it worth all the pain? Her mother-in-law was consoling. "Never mind, all babies are made by God. You'll have a boy next time". After the afterbirth had been delivered and the cord cut with a sickle, the midwife wrapped the baby in a bit of old cloth. Rambai took her squalling infant in her arms. She was beautiful.

There were a number of rituals to be taken care of. Lalta was asked to fetch a flat basket of wheat, a bit of salt, a few red chillis, and a betel-nut cutter. The baby was laid in the basket alongside these items. "This will make sure she's clever," Hirabai murmured. The baby was given a sponge bath and rubbed with a ball of dough, "to make sure she isn't hairy." The placenta and umbilical cord were buried in a small hole under the cot that was now brought in for Rambai to lie on, and a smouldering chunk of cow dung was placed atop the filled-in hole. No one said so, but Rambai knew this was done to prevent spirits or evil persons from harming the baby through magic performed on the discarded matter so intimately associated with her. Rambai's husband's young brother was called and informed of the birth. Through him the menfolk would learn the news and note the time, necessary for drawing up a horoscope. The Potter woman was sent for and soon appeared with a special earthenware water pot dabbed with cow dung. In this pot Hirabai prepared a special brew of medicinal herbs, a strength-giving tea for the new mother to drink during the coming days of recovery. The midwife was paid a rupee and a few pounds of wheat; she would have received more if the baby had been a boy.

That evening, as Rambai and her baby lay on the cot in the birth room with the door shut, a score of women and girls gathered in the courtyard to celebrate the birth. The pleasant strains of childbirth songs lulled the new mother to sleep.

> The new mother has appeared with a tiny baby in her arms.
> She is standing in the courtyard.
> Her mother-in-law has come, prepared the herb tea,
> And is asking for a gift.
> Instead of giving, the new mother says,
> "My husband has gone with the key..."
> Sister-in-law has come, bringing a sweet,
> And is asking for a gift . . .

> Listen, oh my Raja, your mother is sleeping upstairs, go call her
>   to help me.
> Listen, oh mother, your daughter-in-law's waist is tiny, come
>   share her pain.

Listen, son, hearing the words of that woman pierces my heart.
Listen, mother, she's an outsider, do this not for her but for me...

For three days Rambai and her baby were in a state of ritual pollution and no one came too close to them. Her mother-in-law asked the Brahman next door to determine the most auspicious moment for the new mother to begin suckling her child and came to the door of the room to let her know. No one except the closest family members were allowed to see the baby, whose forehead and the bottom of one foot were dabbed with spots of lampblack to protect her from the evil eye. When the Barber woman came to give Rambai her cleansing bath and massage after three days, Rambai casually draped a bit of cloth over the baby so she could not be seen. After the bath, mother and baby moved into the main room of the house.

For the next week Rambai did nothing but rest and tend to her baby daughter, whom she called simply Munni ("little girl"), a common nick-name. The baby was later named Radhabai, but everyone continued to call her Munni.

Then a special blessing ceremony, the *Chauk*, was held. At dusk, dressed in her finest clothing and jewellery and draped with a white coverall sari, Rambai was made to sit with her baby in her lap on a tiny wooden platform over a pile of grain and a design drawn in flour, inside the house. Munni's father's sister blessed the mother and child by waving a small lighted oil lamp around them seven times and dabbing them with a bit of turmeric paste. With wet, bejewelled hands, Rambai touched the water pots as if to imbue the sources of the household's food and water with her own fertility. The Barber woman, who directed Rambai in the ceremony, told her to throw some small bits of fried pastry toward the sun. "If you want another baby soon, don't throw them very far." Rambai barely moved the pastry bits; maybe she would soon have a son. Next, she worshipped a design her sister-in-law had made of cow dung on the wall near the front door and went into the house. Her mother-in-law paid the Barber woman some coins and grain. Later, after supper, a large group of women assembled to sing more childbirth songs. Again, Rambai and her baby remained unseen throughout the evening, although they could hear the songs. Hirabai distributed large chunks of brown sugar to the women to celebrate the successful completion of ten days of life by her son's first child.

Forty days after Munni's birth, the last vestiges of ritual birth pollution were removed in a special bath, and Rambai again began

A young Thakur woman takes pride in her daughter.

cooking and sitting with other members of the family, her tiny baby on her lap.

About a month later, Rambai's father and brother came to visit her and her baby. They brought with them a special collection of gifts traditionally given to a daughter's first baby — a colourful painted cot, a pair of silver ankle ornaments, a patchwork cap, and a bright little dress. They also brought new clothing for Rambai and all the adult members of her husband's family. When they went home, they took Rambai and Munni with them for a long visit.

Four months later, when Rambai and the baby returned, Munni's head was ceremonially shaved and her birth hair offered to the gods to ask them to protect her.

Little Munni was a treasured child, beloved of her parents and her grandparents on both sides. She spent her childhood amid the large jointly family all living under one roof, and she and her mother visited for long weeks with her mother's family. Her mother's brother and his wife were as dear to her as those in whose house she was born. Like other children, she was reared to perceive herself as a member of a circle of kinsmen rather than as a unique individual.

Munni helped her mother with household tasks and caring for her little brothers and sister, who were born before she was ten. As a child she was never particularly aware of any special treatment being given to her brothers; in fact, it was she who often felt superior. Whenever Munni visited her maternal grandparents, her grandmother always touched her feet and gave her a few pennies for her very own. "Little girls are like goddesses; it's good to touch their feet," she heard people say. Boys never had their feet touched. And when she was six, she was one of nine little girls selected to take part in the annual village worship of Matabai, the Mother Goddess who protects the village. She felt very honoured as she and the other girls sat on the festival platform where all the important men of the village were helping the Brahmans in the worship service. In front of several hundred people, the village headman and two Brahman men touched the girls' feet, draped their shoulders with new saris, and served them a fine dinner, which they ate on the spot. She was a *kanyā*, a pure little girl.

Had Munni been born in another time or place, she might not have been so fortunate. Among the warrior-caste Rajput and Thakurs of Rajasthan and parts of the Ganges area, female infanticide was often practiced until about fifty years ago, and even today girls are not treated as well as boys in many places. In Senapur, a village near Varanasi (formerly called Banaras), on the Gangetic plain, women do not sing to welcome a baby girl, although the arrival of a boy is celebrated with drumming and singing. In fact, the birth of a girl may be cause for dejection and recrimination. Upon the arrival of her son's first child, a village Brahman woman of Kashmir exclaimed, "Natha my firstborn, did not deserve a daughter. My daughter-in-law is unlucky and has brought bad luck into the family" (Madan, 1965, p. 78).

In northern India, male offspring are valued not only because of the economic security they represent to their parents but also because they assure the continuation of the family line. Further, in much of North India, a girl is a considerable liability, since her parents must sponsor a costly wedding for her, provide her with a large dowry, and, after every visit to them, send her to her husband's home with a trunkload of gifts for her in-laws. In the Gangetic area, a Thakur girl must be wed to a boy of a family of higher status than her own, and this often presents problems to the girl's parents. Mildred Luschinsky, who lived in Senapur village and has written about its women, overheard a high-caste woman say to her baby granddaughter as she held her up in the air, "Now she should die. I tell her she should die. She is growing bigger and soon there will be the problem of finding a husband for her. . . It's a great worry." Still, she treated the baby with love and affection (Luschinsky, 1962, p. 82). In Khalapur, a large village north of Delhi, girls are similarly considered a financial liability to their parents. Although they are loved, girls do not receive the medical care boys do, and twice as many girls as boys die before reaching maturity (Minturn and Hitchcock, 1966, p. 97). In Central India, where Munni was born, a girl is much less of an expense to her parents, and her husband is usually from a family whose status is similar to that of her own family.

In most parts of North and Central India, there are fewer females than males. In Uttar Pradesh, the state in which Khalapur is located, there are 909 females per 1,000 males. In Madhya Pradesh State, where Nimkhera is situated, there are 953, in Rajasthan 908, and in West Bengal 878 females to 1,000 males. These figures probably reflect the fact that in some rural areas, better medical care is made available to males not only in infancy but also in adulthood. Women are prey to all the contagious diseases that afflict men and suffer the additional hazards of pregnancy and childbirth (usually at home, at the hands of midwives who are uneducated and unfamiliar with the germ theory of disease). They are also in frequent proximity to dangerous cooking fires which all too often set clothing ablaze. Most villages have no medical facilities, and travel to towns and cities — even to see a doctor — is generally disapproved for women. In any case, villagers often distrust urban medical facilities and prefer to try their own remedies. Rambai's mother-in-law is proud of the fact that not once in her life has she ever seen a doctor.

In cities, although boys are still highly desired, the birth of a girl is not considered a disgrace or a calamity; a few modern, Westernized families seem not to prefer boys over girls.

Yet even in Khalapur, where baby girls were sometimes killed in the last century, some mothers admit to actually liking their daughters better than their sons. Throughout much of North and Central India, girls are viewed sentimentally, treasured as creatures who stay with their parents but a short time and then are sent away to live with their husband's families. Mother and daughter are often very close, since they spend most of their waking hours together, and the mother sees in her child a diminutive of herself, a girl now happy in the security of her home but destined to be exiled among strangers after her marriage.

Cooking is considered one of women's main tasks. Here, a Brahman wife prepares flat wheat breads (rotis) *over her kitchen fire.*

As soon as she is able, perhaps at the age of six, a girl is encouraged to help care for her younger siblings. Little girls playing together often carry babies with them on their hips. In a village, dolls are scarce, but there are babies in abundance. Whenever a baby cries, its big sister carries it to its mother to be nursed. Thus, from a very young age, a girl is trained to care for babies, and she considers child care an essential and important part of her life. Adolescent girls seem to love being with babies and seek opportunities to carry them about.

Small girls enjoy imitating their mothers in daily work. They practice balancing water pots on their heads, try to push the heavy grinding stone in its circular path, and crouch beside the stove while dinner is being prepared. Seldom overtly praised, children learn primarily through observation and participation rather than direct instruction. Although some North Indian mothers consider their daughters to be guests in their homes and expect little work of them, in Senapur a mother may admonish her daughter to learn household tasks well, lest she embarrass her family when she goes to live with her husband.

In most parts of India, free schooling is available to all. Many village boys attend classes, but relatively few village girls do so. "What's the sense of teaching a girl to read and write? A woman's work is cooking and grinding" is a commonly expressed sentiment, reflected in the all-India rural literacy rate of 29 per cent for males and 8.5 per cent for females. Further, some villagers believe that an educated woman will be cursed by bad fortune — barrenness, widowhood, or, at the very least, dissatisfaction with traditional family life. Many villagers feel that if education is to prepare a child for its role as an adult, it is logical to keep a girl at home beside the hearth where she can learn the skills she will use throughout her married life as a farmer's or artisan's wife, while men must be literate to deal sensibly with district officials, tax collectors, accountants, and moneylenders. Nevertheless, in some areas, an increasing number of village girls are being educated.

A higher percentage of city girls are in school. In India, literacy rates are 57 per cent for males and 34 per cent for females.[*] Wearing shiny braids and neat white frocks, bright-eyed girls pore over their books at public and private schools. Like their country cousins, these girls too are preparing themselves for marriage, not to farmers but to clerks, bank tellers, merchants, government officials, and industrialists. A very few, perhaps unknowingly, are laying the groundwork for future careers as teachers, social workers, or doctors. After school, a girl is

---

[*] Literacy rates are rising slowly. According to provisional 1991 Census of India figures (which are more optimistic than United Nations estimates), 52% of India's population over the age of seven is literate— 39% of females and 64% of males. Despite these gains, since 1981, the absolute number of illiterate women in India has increased by 16 million to a total of nearly 200 million. In contrast, an estimated 127 million Indian males are illiterate — up by 6 million since 1981.

expected to go straight home, where she helps her mother in the kitchen or with younger siblings. Although she may have servants, the educated city girl is also expected to know the domestic arts when she marries.

These daughters of prosperous Thakur and Brahman families
study in the Nimkhera village primary school. They are
soon to be married and taken out of school.

Like her friends, Munni gradually learned the complex rules of purity and pollution pertaining to castes and foods. Before she was five, she was taught to avoid playing with or touching children of the "unclean" castes — Tanners, Washermen, Sweepers, and even Weavers. She learned that water and cooked foods become polluted by the touch of a lower-caste person, although sugar and raw foods do not. At women's gatherings, which she attended with her grandmother, she saw women of different castes sit in separate groups to receive helpings of boiled wheat from a high-ranking hostess, then hurry home before the food could be polluted. Whenever Munni came in from the village lanes where she might have come in contact with something impure, her mother sprinkled her with water before allowing her into the kitchen, which always had to be kept ritually pure. She learned that a person of her caste was allowed to eat small portions of mutton on occasion but would be terribly defiled by consuming beef, pork, fish, or even chicken. Sweepers, she learned, sometimes ate pork, which she considered most disgusting.[4]

As a little girl in Nimkhera, Munni spent most of her time with her mother, but her uncle sometimes carried her about on his shoulders. When he sat in groups with other men of the village, Munni — still a mere toddler — sat in his lap and listened to the conversation. She jumped around and was treated nicely by all the men as long as she did not urinate on their sitting platform. But by the time she was five, she began to feel funny sitting with the men. She had already realized that girls and boys should not play together very much and that older girls and women never sat with men. In fact, some men and women never talked to each other at all, and many women veiled their faces whenever men came near. When her cousin's new bride came to live in the joint family, Munni observed that she hardly ever unveiled her face. Gradually, Munni learned the rules governing interaction between men and women in her village.

Hindu girls and women who have been born in the village — that is, daughters of the village — never veil their faces in the village. They talk to all residents of the village, whom they consider their uncles, aunts, cousins, brothers, and sisters in accordance with the ties of fictive kinship that bind those who dwell in the same village. They are free to attend all women's social gatherings and festival observances in the village, fetch water from the well, and work in the fields if called upon to do so.

In contrast, a girl or woman married into the village is considered a daughter-in-law (*bahū*)of the village, and she cannot move about and interact with the same freedom. As a young bride, she must veil her face and refrain from talking to almost everyone in her husband's home, most especially her father-in-law, her husband's older brothers, and all older men of the village. Whenever an older family member or villager enters the courtyard, he gives a warning cough and the *bahu* immediately pulls her sari down over her face. Only by accident or under rare circumstances does a man see the face of his son's or younger brother's bride. Motibai, an elderly high-caste woman, remembers such an event which occurred when she was very young. She tells the story proudly and with humour:

> Once on Jhanda Torna [a raucous holiday] I drank a lot of hemp drink. I wasn't in my senses; neither was my father-in-law; he

was in the same condition. I went into the kitchen to cook, and I
sat there with my head uncovered. I was plopping the *rotis* here
and there, not even getting them on the fire. My father-in-law
came in and saw me sitting like that. He said, "How are you
cooking"? and then I realized and I covered up. He went and told
my mother-in-law and said, "What a fine *bahu* we have; she's so
fair!"

*Young Hindu wives keep their faces veiled when they go
out to visit the fields at dusk.*

A young *bahu* should be circumspect in talking to her mother-in-
law and not address older women of the village unless spoken to. In the
presence of others, she should veil her face from husband and refrain
from talking or handing anything to him. (Munni rarely heard her
parents exchange even a few words.) Further, she should not leave the
house or go out in the village without the permission of her husband's
mother. She should not expect to attend village social functions unless
there is a specific need for her presence, such as at a ritual honouring
the Mother Goddess (who blesses and helps brides bear children) or a
family wedding or other ceremony in which she plays a role. However,
a young woman who lives alone with her husband and children or a
woman of a poor family often finds it necessary to go out to fetch water
and do farm work. On the occasions when she does leave the house, a

young wife should keep her face covered and peer out through the cloth. As she grows older, restrictions on her activities diminish. Not until a woman is very mature and becomes the senior woman in her household, however, is she free to visit neighbours, attend social functions, and work outside according to her own wishes.

This veiling and seclusion of wives is called purdah. Muslims also observe purdah, but in a different way. Adolescent Muslim girl begin to veil themselves and stay at home even before marriage. Once a girl reaches puberty, she should wear a cover-all garment called a *burkā* whenever she leaves her house. No matter how hot it is outside, a

A Muslim woman wearing a burka *in public prepares to travel outside her village home.*

woman in a *burka* keeps her face covered and looks out only through tiny eyeholes in the veil. Unlike Hindus, Muslim women do not veil specifically from their husband's elder relatives and residents of their conjugal villages but from all strange men, men who are not their close blood relatives or close in-laws. Muslim girls are often too shy to have long conversations with their elder male in-laws, but they tend not to veil from them, as Hindus do. In villages, poor Muslims work in the fields without *burkas*, but in towns and cities, even the poor often wear the ghostlike garments. In general, it is considered unseemly for a Muslim woman to go out unless she has specific work to do or is going to visit a relative. Both Hindus and Muslims consider shopping in the bazaar man's work.

In conservative circles adhering to the rules of purdah is a mark of high status and prestige. In conservative Bhopal, most Muslim students at a girls' college go unveiled inside the college compound but don *burkas* at the gate. One Pathan Muslim girl, studying to be a doctor, gave up the *burka* but was protectively escorted to and from college each day by a servant boy. In other cities, however, few highly educated Hindus or Muslims veil themselves today, and even in some villages, purdah has been relaxed over the past few decades. In Senapur, Mildred Luschinsky knew a young Thakur woman who refused to observe purdah at all, and her conduct was tolerated by the villagers, many of whom were lax in their own veiling behaviour (Luschinsky, 1962, pp. 343-344).

Men and women are segregated under most conditions throughout much of North and Central India, but the segregation is especially pronounced in the Gangetic plain area. In many North Indian villages, there are separate houses for men and women, with husbands quietly visiting their wives at night in the women's quarters. In Khalapur, the narrow village lanes are used by men and village daughters, while wives travel from house to house via the flat rooftops of the women's houses (Minturn and Hitchcock, 1966, p. 23). In Central India there are no separate houses, but men gather on open-air porches and platforms while women remain inside courtyards. North and Central Indian village men often visit nearby towns and cities, but women rarely do so. When women travel on trains, they frequently ride in the separate women's compartments.

Rambai emphasized to her daughter that it was becoming more important for her to be modest in her demeanor and her dress. Her sari should be carefully wrapped and her skirt held in such a way that no one could see up her dress. This was important now that she was growing up, although when she was a child no one took notice of her bare bottom. She was told to keep away from boys and stay close to home unless she was sent on a specific errand, or her reputation would be in jeopardy. "Just look at that Sweeper girl, she roams here and there all day. Who knows what she does!" Rambai admonished.

During early adolescence, village and city girls alike learn that they must now segregate themselves from boys except those who are close relatives and that they must act like young ladies. Any village girls who are in school are usually taken out before puberty. One city girl from a well-educated, prominent family told me that when she reached the age of twelve her father informed her she could no longer swim in their club pool, even if she wore long slacks and a tunic for swimming as some girls did. "You're too big for that sort of thing now," her father said, and his decision was final.

In her autobiography, Ishvani, a member of wealthy Bombay Khoja Muslim family, resentfully described the restrictions placed upon her behaviour:

> Then we passed the Chappatti seashore....[T]he promenade was thick with people taking the evening air....The public consisted chiefly of men; however there was a good sprinkling of Parsi and Hindu women in carriages; they did not adhere to the purdah system so strictly as the Muslims....When I was a little girl my father used to bring me here on Sundays and allow me to fly the biggest kite I could find. The sands were full of small girls and boys, screaming with laughter...and the sky was dotted with kites that looked like some gigantic birds of paradise. My greatest joy was to get into a fight and bring down the biggest and highest kite belonging to the other fellow, according to the rules of the game. It was a lot of fun. Now at the age of fourteen such things were not to be thought of — I was much too old. Even stopping the car for a few minutes on the promenade, or taking a walk, was absolutely forbidden. There were thousands of girls like me. Our faces were not covered with veils, but we were denied the most innocent liberties. Visiting a relative in one's own car was permitted but a hired taxi or vehicle would have given our parents heart failure. We were escorted to weddings or religious ceremonies under a gimlet-like surveillance (Ishvani, 1947, pp. 90-91).

As part of their training in feminine modesty, city girls learn to walk gracefully, keeping their arms close to the body, not swinging like a boy's (Cormack, 1953, p. 37).

Munni had heard older girls whispering about "*mahinā*", something that happened to a woman every month. She had an idea what it was, but still she was not prepared for its happening to her. One day she found a spot on her clothes. She knew it was something embarrassing and tried to hide it, but her cousin's wife noticed it and took her aside. *Bhābhī* explained to Munni what *mahina* was and told her how to deal with it. She told her to use cotton batting or even fine ash wrapped in bits of old saris and other rags for padding and to dispose of the pads very carefully. "Put them under a stone or a thick bush when you go out to eliminate. That way no one can get hold of them and do magic on them, and they won't cause trouble to anyone else". *Bhabhi* told Munni a trick to ensure that her period every month would be a short one. "Secretly put three dots of blood on the cowshed wall, then draw a line through one of the dots. That way your period will only be $2\frac{1}{2}$ days long". *Bhabhi* also told Munni never to touch a man or even a woman during her period. She should sit apart from others and not go to religious or social events, because a menstruating woman is considered "dirty" until she takes a full bath five days after the start of her period. After her bath, she can again enter the kitchen, draw water, and resume normal interaction with others. Muslim women do not follow all these restrictions, but they refrain from praying or touching the holy Koran.

Munni never discussed menstruation with her mother, and no men of the family learned of the event. But Munni's *bhabhi* quietly told Rambai, "Your little girl has begun to bathe".

Marriage

When she was young, Munni and her friends sometimes played "wedding". A small child posed as the bride and was draped in a white sari. Laughing children carried the "bride" to meet her "groom", a baby brother being cared for by one of the girls. But as Munni and her friends approached puberty, playing wedding was no longer fun. Their own weddings were not too far off, and the game became embarrassing.

It was very embarrassing to be married. First of all, even if a girl should want to be married, it would be shameless for her to admit it; her parents must arrange her marriage. Only a very brazen girl would ever ask questions about what it was like to have a husband. And a wife must never say her husband's name. Even to mention the name of his village is embarrassing. Sometimes girlhood friends whispered to each other about their husbands, but to discuss marriage with an older person would be shameless. Munni had heard older girls talking about sex, but she could never ask anyone about it. It is most embarrassing when a girl's husband comes to visit in her parents' village, where she does not veil her face. She must veil in front of her husband, but she should never cover her face in front of her parents. The only thing to do is run and hide. Munni knew a girl should never talk to her husband in front of anyone; it would be mortifying. Still, marriage would be very exciting, and Munni anticipated it with a mixture of eagerness and dread.

Unknown to Munni, her parents had already begun making inquires about her marriage several years before she reached puberty, and they had hoped to have the wedding before the girl "began bathing." A generation ago, parents who had an unmarried pubescent girl in the house would have been severely criticized, but today villagers are more tolerant of marriages after puberty. Still, the average age of marriage for village girls in the Bhopal area is about eleven, and brides of seven or eight are not unknown in Central India. In 1955 the Government of India enacted a law providing legal penalties for those responsible for the marriage of a girl younger than fifteen or a boy younger than eighteen, but this law is widely ignored.* Most villagers are ignorant of its existence, and since village marriages are not registered with any government authority, "child marriage" occurs with great regularity throughout the northern half of India. In Senapur village, near Varanasi, high-caste weddings usually unite couples older than the legal age, but low-caste children often marry before twelve. Despite early marriage, most village marriages are not consummated until after a second ceremony, the *gaunā*, which usually occurs after the bride has reached puberty or is fifteen or sixteen. City brides are usually older than seventeen, and college girls typically marry after graduation. In general, the age of marriage is rising throughout India.

Munni, like most Indian girls, considered marriage to be something that would happen to her without her having to do anything to make it happen. She never for a moment worried about the

---

* Recently enacted legislation has set the minimum legal marriage age for grils at 18 and for boys at 21. The average age of marriage for village girls in the Bhopal area is gradually rising and many brides are now in their late teens.

*Latif Khan and Birjis Jahan sit on their veranda, openly
showing affection for each other.*

possibility of becoming an old maid — even the ugliest and most
deformed girls were always married, even if not to the most desirable
husbands. One old woman in Nimkhera, Langribai, had been stricken
with a crippling paralysis when she was about nine. Though she could
only creep about in a crouching position, she was wed to an older man

blind in one eye. Now widowed, she is the mother of four grown children and still runs her own household. Only once did Munni hear of an unmarried girl past fifteen — an idiot girl in a distant village. Somehow, every girl's parents found her a husband.

Munni would have been startled to learn that, in cities not too far from her village, there are scores of spinsters. Among educated urban classes, there are nurses, teachers, social workers, and other women who for a variety of reasons have never wed. These women must walk a difficult path, for unmarried women attract attention even in cities. Forbidden by ultra-Victorian mores still in vogue in urban Indian to date men or to receive gentlemen callers who are not close relatives, the career woman must constantly guard her reputation and check her desires for pleasure. The network of communication in India is so efficient that a minor transgression would bring immediate disgrace to a woman and her family. In some coed colleges, teachers are quick to note a budding romance and report it to the girl's parents.

In rural India, too, chastity for the single girl and fidelity for the wife are considered ideal, but quietly committed sins are far from uncommon. In fact, old Mograwali sometimes whispered to Rambai's mother-in-law that they were about the only women in the village who were unsullied. This was an exaggeration, but it was true that barely a dozen of Nimkhera's 160 postpubescent females had never been the subject of innuendo or gossip. In fact, any grown girl or woman seen alone with an unrelated male is like to be quietly criticized, but a public scandal rarely results unless a woman is extremely promiscuous or an illicit pregnancy occurs. In some areas, a woman is likened to an earthen pot which, once polluted, can never be cleansed, and a man is compared to a metal pot which is easily purified with water. Thus a promiscuous girl may find her reputation irreparably damaged, while an errant boy is forgiven. In North India, if a girl who goes to her husband pregnant is rejected by his family, she may even be killed by her own shamed father (Freed, 1971). High-ranking Muslims insist that a bride be a virgin, and the marital bed sheet may be inspected by the husband's female kin. Birjis Jahan, a Pathan Muslim, told me that a sullied bride would be returned to her family in disgrace, but she had never heard of such an incident. Hindus need pass no such test, and a village bride suspected of being non-virgin is almost always accepted by her husband.

An unarranged "love marriage" is considered by most Indians to be a daring and perhaps ill-fated alternative to an ordinary arranged marriage. Many urban youths who have studied and dated abroad return home to wed mates selected for them by their parents. Even a tribal girl who has lovers before marriage usually expects to marry a boy chosen by her parents (Elwin, 1968, p. 200). Intercaste marriages (seldom arranged) occur now with increasing frequency, particularly in cities, but they are still disapproved by the vast majority of Indians. Only in the most Westernized circles, among less than 1 per cent of the population, do young couples date and freely choose their own mates.

In Nimkhera, one Pathan Muslim couple told me proudly of their arranged "love marriage". Muslims are often encouraged to marry cousins (although North and Central Indian Hindus forbid it), and young cousins who are potential mates normally know each other well. Seventeen-year-old Latif Khan and his sixteen-year-old cousin Birjis Jahan had a crush on each other and were secretly heartbroken when Birjis Jahan's parents engaged her to an older man. "Birjis Jahan's mother offered me some of the sweets Birjis's fiance had sent to her", Latif Khan remembered, "but I couldn't take any. I said I was sick and left quickly. I felt terrible." Each hesitantly confessed their true feelings to a relative, and their parents had a conference. Soon Latif and Birjis Jahan were happily wed, and even now, as the parents of twelve children, they say their love for each other is the most important thing in their lives.

By contrast, virtually all village Hindus are married to someone they have never met before or have perhaps only glimpsed. Although a Hindu girl should marry within her own caste, her groom cannot be someone to whom she is known to be related by blood. Most Hindus belong to a named patrilineal clan (*gotra*); a girl cannot be matched with a youth of her own or her mother's clan.[5] In some areas, members of other clans are also ineligible, as are members of lineages from which men of her own kin group have taken brides. From Rajasthan to Bihar, over much of northern India, a girl should not marry a boy of her own village. In the Delhi area, a boy of a neighbouring village or even one in which the girl's own clan or another clan of her village is well represented must be avoided (Lewis, 1965, pp. 160-161). In Central India, although village exogamy is preferred, some marriages unite unrelated village "brothers" and "sisters".

Hindu men ask about available mates for their children among their in-laws and relatives in other villages, and they discuss the virtues of each candidate with their womenfolk. Munni's father and uncles spoke with many relatives and caste fellows and heard of several prospects. One youth seemed acceptable on all counts, but then Ramabai learned from a cousin that his mother had been widowed before she married the boy's father. Although widow remarriage is acceptable among members of Munni's caste, children of remarried widows are considered to have a very slightly tainted ancestry. Munni's parents looked further and finally decided that the best candidate was a seventeen-year-old youth named Amar Singh, from Khetpur, a village 20 miles away. He was the eldest son of a well-to-do farmer hitherto unrelated to their family. Munni's father's brother was able to visit Khetpur on the pretext of talking to someone there about buying a bullock, and he made inquiries and even saw the youth. Amar Singh had no obvious disabilities, had attended school through the fifth grade, and his family had a good reputation. Thus, after all in the family agreed, they asked the Nimkhera barber to visit Khetpur and gently hint at a proposal to Amar Singh's family. His relatives sent their barber to similarly glimpse Munni as she carried water from the well and to learn what he could about her and her family. Before too long, the fathers of the two youngsters met and agreed that their children would be married. A Brahman examined the horoscopes and saw no obstacle to the match. Each man gave the other five rupees as a gift for his child. Later, larger gifts were exchanged in a formal engagement ceremony.

In Bengal, a prospective bride may have to pass a rigorous inspection by her prospective father-in-law. At one such public examination, a village girl was tested in knowledge of reading, writing, sewing and knitting, manner of laughing, and appearance of her teeth, hair, and legs from ankle to knee.

> Rishikumar...asked the girl to drop the skirt and walk a bit.
> The bride began to walk slowly.
> "Quick! More quick!" and silently the girl obeyed the order.
> "Now you see there is a brass jar underneath that pumpkin creeper in the yard. Go and fetch that pot on your waist, and then came here and sit down on your seat."
> The girl did as she was directed. As she was coming with the pot on her waist, Rishikumar watched her gait with a fixed gaze to find out whether the (toes) and soles of the feet were having their full press on the earth. Because, if it is not so, the girl does not possess good signs and therefore would be rejected.

The man read her palm, quizzed her on her knowledge of worship, demanded her horoscope, and asked that she prepare and serve tea. Even after he had found her acceptable and a dowry had been agreed upon, her bridegroom, eager to be modern, insisted upon seeing her— and could thus himself be seen by the girl and her people (Basu, 1962, pp. 97-102).

In cities, prospective marriage partners may exchange photographs, and the youth and his parents may be invited to tea, which the girl quietly serves to the guests. Each group assesses the other's candidate quickly under these awkward circumstances. Frequently, a girl is rejected for having too dark a complexion, since fair skin is a highly prized virtue in both village and town.

For city dwellers, matrimonial advertisements in newspapers often provide leads to eligible spouses. These advertisements typically stress beauty and education in a prospective bride and education and earning capacity in a groom. Regional and caste affiliations are usually mentioned.

> **REQUIRED FOR OUR DAUGHTER** suitable match. She is highly educated, fair, lovely, intelligent, conversant with social graces, home management, belongs to respected Punjabi family of established social standing. Boy should be tall, well educated, definitely above average, around thirty years of age or below, established in own business or managerial cadre. Contact Box 44946, The Times of India.

> **MATRIMONIAL   CORRESPONDENCE   INVITED** from young, beautiful, educated, cultured, smart Gujarati girls for good looking, fair complexioned, graduate bachelor, well settled, Gujarati Vaishnav Vanik youth of 27 years, earning monthly Rs. 3000/-. Girl main consideration [i.e., large dowry not important]. Advertisement for wider choice only. Please apply Box 45380, The Times of India.

Discussions of dowry are important in marriage negotiations in conservative Hindu circles in many parts of North India. The parents of a highly educated boy may demand a large dowry, while a well-educated girl's parents may not have to offer as large a dowry as the parents of a relatively unschooled girl. In Central India, dowries are not important, although expensive gifts are presented to a groom.[*] In a few groups, the groom's family pays a bride price to the girl's kinsmen. Almost all weddings involve expensive feasts, and the number of guests to be fed is sometimes negotiated.

---

[*] Among some high-status groups of Central India, dowries are currently increasing in size and importance. Such a trend has been noted in many parts of the country.

Sikh and Hindu college girls in Bhopal sing in celebration of a classmate's wedding to a man she met through a matrimonial advertisement.

As her wedding approached, Munni heard her relatives discussing the preparations. She pretended not to hear but was secretly excited and frightened. No one spoke directly to her of the wedding, but nothing was deliberately kept from her.

For Munni as for other villagers, her wedding was the most important event in her life. For days she was the centre of attention, although her own role was merely to accept passively what happened to her. She was rubbed with purifying turmeric, dressed in fine clothes, and taken in procession to worship the Mother Goddess. Her relatives came from far and near, and the house was full of laughter and good food. Then excited messengers brought news of the arrival of her groom's all-male entourage from Khetpur, and fireworks heralding their advent lit the night sky. Munni was covered with a white sari, so that only her hands and feet protruded, and amid a wild din of drumming, singing, and the blaring of a brass band, she was taken out to throw a handful of dust at her groom.

The next day was a rush of events, the most exciting of which was the ceremony in which she was presented with an array of silver jewellery and silken clothing by her father-in-law and his kinsmen.

A Brahman bride is closely veiled as she receives gifts
from her groom's kinsmen.

Under her layers of drapery, the bride could neither see nor be seen, but could hear the music and talking all around her. Many of the songs, sung by the Nimkhera women and female guests, hilariously insulted the groom and his relatives. Later, at night, in the darkest recesses of the house, her mother and *bhabhi* dressed Munni in her new finery. These valuable and glistening ornaments were hers, a wonderful treasure. Bright rings were put on her toes, a mark of her impending married state. Munni's little sister watched every ritual with wide eyes, realizing that one day she too would be a bride.

The wedding ceremony itself was conducted quietly at the astrological auspicious hour of 4 A.M by a Brahman priest, before whom the couple sat. Amar Singh looked handsome in his turban and red wedding smock, but Munni was only a huddled white lump beside him. The priest chanted and offered sacrifices to the divine, and then, in a moving ritual, Rambai and Tej Singh symbolically gave Munni away to Amar Singh. As women sang softly, the garments of the couple were tied together, and the bridal pair were guided around a small sacrificial fire seven times. With these acts, Munni and Amar singh were wed and Munni officially became a *bahu*, a daughter-in-law and member of her husband's lineage.

As a *bahu*, she became a symbol of fertility, of promise for the continuation of her husband's family line. She also became an auspicious *suhāgan*, a woman with a living husband. In the word *suhagan* is emphasized the concept that neither man nor woman is complete as an individual but only in their union. Traditionally, no woman except a prostitute remained unmarried and villagers believe that men who die single become ghosts who haunt the descendants of their more fortunate brothers. For some devout individuals, asceticism may be a stage of life, but except for a few holy men, all people are expected to marry.

The next day was another round of feasting, fun fests, ceremonies, and gift giving. As a send-off for the groom's party, Munni's kinswomen playfully dashed red dye into their faces. The relatives departed, the house was quiet. Only tattered coloured paper decorations and her new jewellery served to remind Munni of her change in status. Life continued as before.

But Munni and Amar Singh, though strangers to each other, were now links between two kin groups, and their male relatives began to meet each other and become friendly. Munni's relatives were always properly deferential to Amar Singh's, as befitted the kinsmen of a bride in relationship to those of her groom. It would have been improper, too, for Munni's mother to meet Amar Singh or his mother or to speak to any of his male relatives. Having given a bride to Amar Singh's family, it now would be shameful for Munni's family ever to accept their gifts or hospitality.

At a Thakur wedding, the bride's veiled kinswomen mock the groom's relations with insulting songs and dash red dye into their faces.

Among Thakurs in North India, a girl is given in marriage to a boy who belongs to a group of higher rank than her own. Thus the bride's kinsmen are not merely deferential but are considered actually inferior to the groom's kin. This lower status of the bride's family adds to the relatively low status all North Indian brides have in their new homes. Among most Muslims, however, the kin of both bride and groom consider themselves equals, particularly since they often are close blood relatives (for example, the children of two siblings may marry).

The Muslim wedding consists of a series of rituals, gift exchanges, and feasts. The couple are legally united in a simple ceremony during which both bride and groom indicate their assent to the marriage by signing a formal wedding contract in the presence of witnesses. The groom and his family pledge to the bride a sum of money, known as *mehr*, to be paid to her upon her demand. (Most wives do not claim their *mehr* unless their husbands divorce them.) During the wedding the bride and groom sit in separate rooms and do not see each other. Latif Khan's mother was married by mail to her first cousin, living hundreds of miles away, and did not see her husband for over a year.

Munni expected to spend the rest of her married life as Amar Singh's wife, but she could remarry if he died. In her caste, as among most high-ranking groups, divorce is always a possibility, but it involves shame. For a Brahman girl, her first marriage would definitely have been her last until recently. Although most Brahman widows are expected to remain celibate for life, some Brahman groups now allow young widows to remarry without suffering ostracism. Among high-ranking Muslims, divorce is relatively rare but it does occur, and remarriage is usually easy. In educated urban Hindu circles, divorce is almost unthinkable; but among tribals and low-status Hindus and Muslims, it is not uncommon, and scandalous elopements occasionally take place. In any case, a second marriage for a woman never involves the elaborate ceremonies of the first wedding but may simply entail setting up house with a new man.

During past centuries, very high castes prohibited widow remarriage, and a widow was sometimes expected to immolate herself on her husband's funeral pyre. This practice, known as *satī*, occurred in only a very small percentage of families and was legally abolished over a century ago. Rajputs remember with pride the *johār*, the rite in which the widows of warriors slain in battle died in a communal funeral pyre (Carstairs, 1967, p. 111). Today, reports of *satis* appear in North Indian newspapers once or twice a year.

In the past, a widow was sometimes treated harshly, since the death of her husband was thought to be punishment for her misdeeds in a previous life. However, widows of lower-ranking castes have always been allowed to remarry.

Under Indian law today, any woman may divorce her husband for certain causes and any widow can remarry, but considerations of property and social acceptability rather than legality usually determine whether or not a woman seeks a divorce or remarriage. Among Hindu villagers, a widow who remarries customarily loses her rights in her husband's land. If she has young sons, a widow usually remains unmarried in order to protect her children's right to their patrimony.[6]

In North and Central India, monogamy is generally practiced. Hindus may legally have only one wife, but Muslims are allowed four wives under both Indian and Muslim law. Village Hindus, whose marriages are seldom registered with legal authorities, occasionally take two or three wives, and the women of some Himalayan groups have several husbands.[7] Wealthy Muslim men occasionally avail themselves of their legal limit, but most cannot afford to do so. When Yusuf Miya, a Bhopal man, wanted to marry a second time, his wife spoke of suicide and the matter was dropped. Some women, particularly those who have borne no children, do not openly object to having a co-wife. In Nimkhera, one untouchable Sweeper man has four wives, all of whom contribute to his support.

Munni spent three more years in the bosom of her family, happily taking part in household and agricultural work and enjoying the frequent festivals observed in the village. Not long after her wedding, she went with her brothers and father to a fair in the district market centre, where they watched the Ram Lila, a religious drama, and bought trinkets in the bazaar.

The next winter, her grandfather was stricken by pneumonia and died. This tragic event deprived the family of its patriarch and Hirabai of her husband. As she wept beside her husband's bier, her glass bangles were broken, never to be replaced. After the cremation, relatives arrived to pay their condolences and to take part in ritual gift exchanges and a large death feast. Munni joined the visiting women in weeping and singing sad songs.

The following year she went with her parents, uncle, and a large group of villagers by train on a pilgrimage to Varanasi and Allahabad, where they bathed in the sacred river Ganges. Her father's older brother carried with him a small packet of his father's charred bones, which he threw into the river. The trip was exciting and eye-opening. Although it was expensive, the journey allowed the pilgrims to carry out important religious and family obligations and was therefore considered more a necessity than a luxury.

Munni knew that her idyll among her natal kin would not last much longer. Many of her friends had already been sent to their husband's homes, and Munni too would soon go. Her *gauna* (consummation ceremony) was set for March.

The night before her *gauna*, Munni's *bhabhi* (her cousin's wife) took her aside and told her about sex and what to expect from her husband. Munni had heard some stories from her friends but was shocked to hear the details. (Parents and children never discuss sex.) Her mother reminded her that she was going among critical strangers and that she should do whatever work was asked of her without complaint.

Beating drums and blaring trumpets soon announced the arrival of Amar Singh and a group of his male kinsmen. Munni sat passively as her mother and the Barber woman dressed her in finery and ornamented her with silver. She was truly agitated: now she would meet her husband and her in-laws and see Khetpur, the village in which she would spend her adulthood. Her life would be forever changed.

Her departure from her parents, grandmother, brothers, sisters, uncles, aunts and cousins was heartrending. Clinging to each in turn, she sobbed piteously and pleaded not to be sent away. They too cried as they put her into a small covered palanquin and saw her borne away by her in-laws. With her went baskets of food and clothes and a little cousin to act as intermediary.

Heavily veiled, she was transferred to a bus and sat miserable and silent for the entire journey. At Khetpur she was put into a palanquin again and carried to her new home. Women's voices all around were talking about her, referring to her as *dulhan* (bride), *bahu* (daughter-in-law) and *Nīmkherāwālī* (the woman from Nimkhera). Here in her husband's home she would never be known as Munni.

There were some "games" she had to play with her husband before a group of village women who had gathered to sing and welcome her. Almost overcome with shyness and apprehension, she was made to sit near her husband and compete with him in finding some silver rings in a platter of turmeric water. Whichever partner won this game was said to be likely to dominate in the marriage. It is rare for a veiled and shy bride to win, and Munni, too, lost the competition. Then the couple were taken inside the house and told to feed each other some rice pudding. Embarrassed and awkward attempts ended when Amar Singh ran out of the house. Finally, Munni's mother-in-law escorted her to a decorated cot, left, and locked her in the room. Clutching her veil, Munni apprehensively awaited her husband. He came in quietly, after the house was silent, and put out the lamp.

Modesty required that she try to fend him off and succumb only after great protestation (even an experienced girl must feign modesty), but Munni was sixteen at her *gauna* ceremony and her introduction to her husband was not traumatic. Some younger girls have been genuinely terrified of their husbands, and their *gauna* nights have involved virtual rape. One Brahman girl, Kamladevi, who met her husband when she was just thirteen, described her *gauna* as follows:

> I had my *gauna* when I was still little; I hadn't started bathing yet. My *bhabhi* told me about sex and what to expect; I was really frightened. I came to Nimkhera and stayed for three days. The first night I slept with Amma (her husband's grandmother). The second night Jiji (her husband's cousin's wife) took me into the house and told me to sleep there. She said she'd be coming in shortly. She spread the blankets on the bed, and then she went out and locked the door from outside. I was really scared; I cowered

near the door. I didn't know it, but he (her husband) had gone in before and hidden in the dark near the hearth. He came out then and grabbed hold of me. I let him do whatever he wanted to do; I just clenched my sari between my teeth so I wouldn't cry out. But I cried a lot anyway, and there was lots of blood. In the morning I changed my sari before I came out of the room, and bundled the dirty sari up and hid it from everyone. I had a fever; and I was so sick that some people criticized him for sleeping with such a young and weak girl. My brother came to get me on the third day and took me home.

Munni stayed in her husband's home for a week before her father and a group of male relatives came to fetch her. During the week she became acquainted with her husband and was viewed by all his female relatives and friends. Each woman paid her a small sum for the privilege of looking under her veil at her shy face with downcast eyes. All commented on her complexion (they said she was fair) and on the clothing she had brought. She spoke almost nothing to anyone but her own little cousin and Amar Singh's little sister, to whom she was *bhabhi*. Several songfests were held by the women, most of whom had themselves been brought to Khetpur as brides.

At home again, Munni unveiled, relaxed, and enjoyed her normal life for several months until her husband's father came to escort her to Khetpur again. On her second visit, she was no longer a guest but was treated more like a member of the household. She began cooking, sweeping, and grinding. Her mother-in-law was polite, and Munni docilely performed the tasks expected of her. After three weeks she again went home for several months.

Munni is now a young woman of about twenty-one, the mother of a baby daughter. She continues to spend a few months of each year in her parents' home.

Not all girls have a *gauna* ceremony. Most Muslim girls and educated urban girls marry after puberty and go immediately to their husbands' homes. Nor do all girls have such an easy transition between their natal and conjugal homes as did Munni.

In much of North India, a girl is sent on her *gauna* and remains in her husband's home for a year or more, sometimes until she has produced a child, before she is allowed to visit her parents. Such an abrupt transition is a difficult one for a young girl. In Senapur, among a sample of sixteen Thakur women, five had remained with their in-laws between seven and eleven years on the first or second visits there.

Four had never returned to their parents' villages because their parents had died (Luschinsky, 1962, pp. 350-351).

In Central India, older wives go home at least once or twice a year for visits and festival observances, but in parts of North India several years may elapse between visits. This is partly because of the expectation that the parents of a visiting daughter will send expensive gifts to her in-laws when she returns to them—so that few parents can afford frequent visits from their daughters. In Central India, however, a visiting daughter receives relatively modest gifts and may provide vital services in her natal home (for example, helping with the harvest or doing housework for a sick mother). Consequently, whereas a North Indian bride is clearly shifted from one household to another at her *gauna*, the Central Indian bride may become an important participant in the activities of two households. However, as expressed in the childbirth song (p. 28), the young mother may feel herself to be and may be considered to be an outsider in her marital home for some time.

Given the fact that a wife is expected to live with her husband's family, usually in a village other than that of her birth, teenage marriage makes sense. A young girl easily falls under the tutelage of her mother-in-law and can be socialized to life in her husband's family. The new bride, although the centre of attention for a while, has the lowest status of any adult in her new residence. Young and alone among strangers, effaced by her veil, the bride can be happy in her new surroundings only by adjusting her behaviour to satisfy her in-laws. If she quarrels with her mother-in-law, her husband cannot take her side without shaming himself before his elders. Thus she quickly learns the behaviour appropriate to her role as a young *bahu* in a strange household.

Virtually every new bride longs to return to the security of her natal home. Even though she may be secretly thrilled by her relationship with her husband, a bride rarely enjoys being sequestered and ruled by her mother-in-law. Songs stress the unhappiness of the the young wife in her new residence, and young girls eagerly seize any opportunity to return home. Sometimes a young wife is so unhappy she commits suicide, typically by jumping in a well. Few girls can go home when they wish; a young wife must be formally called for, with the permission of her in-laws, and escorted by a responsible male from her natal household.

For the village bride, marriage does not mark attainment of independent adulthood but signals the acquisition of a new set of relatives to whom she is subordinate. Her actions had previously been guided by sometimes indulgent parents; with marriage and *gauna*, they fall under the control of adults who are far less likely to consider her wishes. She herself can attain a position of authority only by growing older, becoming the mother of children, and outliving her mother-in-law. Until she is at least middle-aged, a woman is usually subordinate to and protected by others.

Women's Status

According to ancient Hindu texts and tradition, until about 500 B.C. women in India enjoyed considerable freedom in choosing their mates and taking part in public functions. Equal to men in religious matters, upper-class women were well-educated and married late. Divorce and widow remarriage were acceptable. But during the next thousand years, women's position gradually deteriorated: educational and religious parity was denied them and widow remarriage was forbidden to those of high-status families.[8] Still quoted on the proper role of a woman are the laws of Manu, written during this period:

> She should do nothing independently, even in her own house.
> In childhood subjected to her father, in youth to her husband,
> And when her husband is dead, to her sons, she should never
>   enjoy independence....
> Though he be uncouth and prone to pleasure,
> though he have no good points at all,
> the virtuous wife should ever
> worship her lord as a god. (Basham, 1959, pp. 180-181).

In this treatise and in more recent Indian writings is embedded the notion that a woman must always be subordinate to men. In fact, virtually everywhere in India today, women's status relative to that of men appears to be low. As one Nimkhera woman said, "Men are high and women low; this is the rule of the world. Men are the breadwinners. In the wedding ceremony, the woman is given to the man, and she belongs to him." In villages, a woman walks behind her husband, and a *bahu* sits on the ground in the presence of her father-in-law. A woman asks permission from her father or husband before travelling far from home.[9] A woman is considered polluted monthly and is segregated from others. She should eat after her husband does and may consume his leavings; her leavings would defile him. Even if she is a Brahman, she cannot become a priest and conduct ceremonies as men do. If she is of high status, she marries only once, but any widowed or divorced man may marry again if he can find a bride.

Very importantly, by traditional Hindu custom, a woman does not inherit land or house from either parents or husband; such property is inherited patrilineally only by sons and can only be used by a widow during her lifetime. A widow cannot sell her husband's land or give it to her natal relatives, and if she has no sons, the land is claimed by her husband's closest male patrilineal relatives upon her death or remarriage. In fact, the only property over which a village Hindu woman has full rights of ownership is her jewellery, particularly that given to her by own relatives (jewellery received from her in-laws may be borrowed or pawned by them and would not be hers to keep in case of divorce). Only occasionally does a Hindu man with no sons formally will his property to his daughter. Modern Indian law assures widows, daughters, and mothers the right to inherit and absolutely own property, but few village women would risk alienating their kinsmen by challenging tradition.

Some observers feel that the veiling and seclusion of women indicates low female status and that men prevent women from taking part in community politics and commerce and restrict them to home activities.

Although it is true that, in general, women's status is lower than men's, it is not as low as these outward signs might indicate. In any case, men did not consciously organize a system to dominate women. Both men and women are actors in a complex social and ecological system which functions reasonably smoothly and provides benefits to both sexes. Men do dominate activities outside the home — they take positions of leadership in their communities, make important decisions pertaining to agriculture, and make most purchases. Nevertheless, women affect men's actions and have important spheres of influence of their own. It is really a mistake to see women as competing with and being restricted by men; rather, male and female roles are clearly distinguished, and the sexes are seen as complementary to each other. As one educated Muslim girl explained, "We don't feel inferior or superior to boys. We each have our separate roles" (Cormack, 1953, p. 36).

A number of cultural symbols stress the value of women. Another ancient text, the *Mahabharata*, says:

> Even a man in the grip of rage will not be harsh to a woman, remembering that on her depend the joys of love, happiness, and

A woman of Rajasthan works at the family threshing floor, tossing grain high so it can be winnowed by the wind.

virtue. For woman is the everlasting field, in which the Self is born. (Basham, 1959, p. 182).

Goddesses are worshipped throughout India, and in the village Hindu wedding ceremony, the bride is likened to Lakshmi, the goddess of wealth. And in a Central Indian ceremony (p. 30), nine young girls are worshipped and offered gifts by priests and important men.

Nevertheless, men's view of women — and women's view of themselves — is ambivalent. Throughout India, the concept of motherhood is revered. The words *Mātā* and *Mā* ("mother") connote warmth, protection, and life-giving power. Ideally, a child should always honour his mother. The cow, sacred to Hindus because of her usefulness as a producer of milk, dung, and bullocks, is called *Gao-Mātā* ("mother cow"). The most powerful local goddesses, responsible for the care and protection of whole villages and regions, are known as *Mata*. Yet it is *Sītalā Mātā* who brings smallpox and may injure those who displease her.

Normally, sexuality must be assumed as a prelude to motherhood, yet it is as a sexual being that woman is feared and despised. Brahmanical tradition views women as shameless temptresses lacking in self-control and likely to go astray unless controlled by their menfolk. A woman can bring devastating shame to her family by engaging in sexual activity with a man of lower caste. Further, a menstruating woman may use her pollution to harm others — for instance, if she goes near a smallpox patient, the patient will die, because the smallpox goddess is thus offended.

A goddess gains power by controlling her sexuality; a mother goddess is not a mother in the normal sense. Shiv Prasad, a learned Nimkhera Brahman, explained the position of Matabai, the goddess most worshipped by the villagers: "Matabai is not married. She is the mother of us all, the mother of the world. She creates everyone and also destroys them. She is a form of the goddess Durga". The ceremony at which the young girls (*kanyas*) are worshipped takes place at the Matabai shrine. "The *kanyas* are like the goddess Durga, like nine Durgas", he explained. Thus chaste womanhood is powerful and worthy of adulation.[10]

Most Hindus, however, are not consciously aware of this association. On a day-to-day basis, women are neither idealized nor despised but treated as ordinary mortals with normal human strengths and weaknesses.

Some men believe that women have a stronger sex drive than men do, but others realize that it is men who usually initiate lovemaking and who secretly visit prostitutes. Some men regard women as weak and flighty and in need of male guidance, while others recognize feminine expertise and strength in particular areas of life. Nearly every man feels that having a wife is essential to his happiness and to the smooth running of the home. A few men perhaps suspect that it is difficult for a woman to always behave properly. A Weaver man of Nimkhera who is very devoted to his wife contrasted masculine and feminine behaviour:

> For instance, at a religious drama, a man can laugh loudly, but a woman has to laugh quietly. She shouldn't raise her voice, and she should obey her husband. She can't roam around at night. But a man can do all he likes, except drink, or go to prostitutes.

Women are usually dominant in home activities — in matters relating to birth, child care, housework, and food preparation. Further, even though men are usually in charge of work outside the house and bringing home food and money, women are responsible for storing and allocating these resources. When a farmer wants to buy a bullock, he usually discusses it with his wife, and it is from her that he gets the money. She usually tells him when to buy new clothing for the family and which foodstuffs are needed from the bazaar. However, many urban wives do their own shopping, and a high percentage of merchants and customers in tribal bazaars are women. In any case, both men and women must make their purchasing decisions within the limits imposed by each family's financial situation.

In ritual matters, too, women perform essential roles. They vigilantly ensure ritual purity of household food and water, although their husbands may transgress caste food rules at urban restaurants. Through prayers, fasting, and ceremonial observances, women enlist divine succour for their families. In the Varanasi area particularly, women are almost wholly responsible for seeking divine aid to ensure the health and well-being of their menfolk and children.

Women also help make important decisions in other family matters, especially in the selection of mates for their children. Men do some of the scouting, but, through their networks of ties with women in other towns and villages, women frequently have access to information vital for evaluating prospects. Muslim women particularly play essential roles in the selection of wives for sons and nephews, since most marriageable Muslim girls are in purdah and can be seen only by other women and a few male relatives. And women control other women — mothers and mother-in-law control their daughters and *bahus*. In Khalapur, reflecting the social and residential cleavage between men and women, the Rajput woman who heads a woman's house has considerable authority over others (Minturn and Hitchcock, 1966, p. 46).

The fact that women are secluded and veiled does in some ways contribute to male domination, but in other respects purdah is a mark of high status. In ancient times noble women veiled their faces and travelled in curtained litters to protect themselves from the profane gaze of commoners. Today, the association of seclusion and prestige remains. Poor Muslim women strive to remain housebound as much as possible, in emulation of the strict seclusion only wealthier Muslims can afford. One upward-mobile Muslim woman in Nimkhera told me, "I never go out in the village without my *burka*. One of those farmers or even a Sweeper might see me." Her tone implied that such an occurrence would degrade her. Well-to-do village Hindu men take pride in their ability to afford farm hands and water bearers, thus freeing their wives from the need to leave the courtyard to visit the fields or wells. The women value their status as well-cared-for ladies of relative leisure.

In addition to its association with economic well-being and high rank, purdah has other meanings. Traditional town women appreciate the protection the veil affords them from the stares of lecherous men. For Hindus, veiling is an expression of distance between a woman and her husband's relatives. Noting that a young high-caste woman of Khalapur village covers her face even in front of older low-caste serving men, Hitchcock states that this is a sign of respect for the man's status as a man (Minturn and Hitchcock, 1966, p. 34). But this is not really so: the woman veils from the servant because of his position as village "older brother" of her husband, a relative in whose presence she feels shy and to whom she should show respect. She also veils from older women in her husband's village, but in her parental village she never covers her face, whether in the presence of men or not. For Hindus, veiling also contributes to harmonious family living.

Nevertheless, purdah restrictions on the mobility of traditional women do contribute to their subservience to males. A village woman of good reputation should not travel to another village or town except for an approved purpose. It is significant that in a country where travel has traditionally been by bullock cart, women never drive bullock carts. Even among the wealthy urban classes one seldom sees a woman driving a car. Thus, unless she has access to a bus line, a woman cannot journey far without a male accompanying her. Attendance at a school or non-religious public meeting would usually be disapproved by family elders. As a result, sequestered women are often poorly educated and ignorant of events outside their own villages. Even within her conjugal village, the young wife is isolated by restrictions on her movement. She is unable to visit freely with neighbours and consequently forms few bonds of friendship within her husband's village.

The former Queen Mother of Jaipur, Rajasthan leaves the Jaipur polo grounds after viewing a match. © Jerome Jacobson.

It is not surprising, then, that the vast majority of women do not obviously play any part in extrafamilial politics. In villages it is rare to find a leader among women. Every village now elects representatives to a government-sponsored village council, and traditional caste and village councils also meet to consider disputes. Almost never is a woman a member of a traditional council, but in some villages a seat on the government-sponsored council is reserved for a woman (Mayer, 1960 p. 114). Indian women have had full suffrage since 1949, yet many either fail to vote or cast their ballots for the candidates of their husbands' choice. The Prime Minister of India is a woman,[*] and women have been chosen to serve as cabinet ministers, governors or

---

[*] Mrs. Indira Gandhi was the Prime Minister of India for sixteen years. She was assasinated in 1984.

states, ambassadors, United Nations officials, and members of state legislatures and the national parliament. But India's politically eminent women are hardly representative of the populace; they are mostly of the highest urban educated classes and include former Prime Minister Nehru's daughter and sister as well as the Queen Mothers of Gwalior and Jaipur. These are women who were part of a select elite before they entered politics.

The relationship of a woman to her husband is not simple to characterize despite the formal trappings of female subservience. At first, husband and wife are usually strangers shyly meeting each other at night. Their first encounters may be cold enactments of the sex act, but later meetings may become romantic. Embarrassment gives way to warmth and pleasure. The traditional bride shyly veils her face from her husband, but he gradually encourages her to talk. Publicly, the young Hindu couple pretend indifference to each other, and the wife veils her face from her husband. Neither utters the other's personal name. They cannot be daytime companions, and not until middle age do they exchange words in the presence of other adults. Among the Brahmans of Kashmir, a wife is called "the parrot of the pillow", in reference to the fact that she is free to talk with her husband only when they are in bed (Madan, 1965, p. 136). Even very Westernized couples usually refrain from public displays of affection. A well-educated young woman from a large city told me that in her entire life she had never seen a couple embrace or kiss.

In cramped quarters, lack of privacy in the joint family may stifle development of understanding between husband and wife. A Bania (merchant caste) youth of Jaipur City wrote in his autobiography:

> Wife wants to learn alphabet — but because there is no separate room I cannot coach her. She may like to go with me to the garden or cinema or exhibition, but the fear of family members, which is quite genuine, closes her mouth. All her intentions have been killed — she has never asked me for anything. It proves sufficiently that it is my family circumstances which have killed all her enthusiasm. . . . If I can have one year living (alone) with my wife, I can get to know her and teach her things (Carstairs, 1957, pp. 296, 306).

A husband may attempt to exert dominance over his wife. One young Brahman groom in Nimkhera threatened his bride that he would beat her if she fought with his mother and grandmother, although he will probably never carry out his threat. Women also speak of male dominance as is given: asked what would happen to her if her husband caught her in an affair with another man, a young woman replied, "He would beat me till I had no skin left." If he were caught cheating, she said, she would merely stop talking to him for a while or go home for a long time.

*Motibai, a self-assured village woman of high caste, treasures
traditional values.*

In fact, some spouses are indifferent to each other and some husbands do beat their wives, but many couples become quite devoted and, particularly in nuclear families, enjoy equal partnerships, making decisions jointly and showing consideration for one another. Most older couples treat each other as equals.

Yusuf Miya and his wife are an example of a couple who really care for each other. Yet Yusuf has made his wife unhappy by becoming involved with other women, and her only defense is to withdraw affection and weep. Still, after they make up, they make love and are friends again.

Among the Bhils of Rajasthan and other tribal peoples, genuinely affectionate marriages are common, since either partner can abscond with a lover if he or she is dissatisfied with his or her current spouse (Carstairs, 1957, p. 132).

Old Motibai and her husband, the Nimkhera temple priest, have an easygoing relationship in which she takes the lead. He unimaginatively carries out his temple duties, but she has exercised skilful entrepreneurship in starting and running a small shop. In spite of her obviously dominant role, when asked who was the strong one in their marriage, Motibai replied, "Oh he is, definitely." Such an answer actually bolsters her own prestige, since henpecked husbands are ridiculed and dutiful wives admired. In India as in the West, a woman cannot expect to improve her status in the community by openly belittling her husband. Motibai considers herself a perfect wife:

> A perfect wife will do what her husband asks her to do and won't answer him back or fight with him. She will have sexual relations only with her husband and with no other man. She should also become a *sati* after his death, although nobody does that nowadays. That's not so necessary now.

Widely admired as the epitome of wifely perfection, the goddess Sita remained patiently chaste and obedient to her husband Ram despite the fact that she suffered hardship and was banished by her suspicious mate. It would be most difficult for an ordinary mortal to be so devoted.

No Nimkhera woman actually treats her husband as a god, and some young women consider themselves sufficiently separate from their husbands to criticize them without fearing that the criticism will reflect on themselves. Sunalini Nayudu, my assistant, asked some women, "Should a woman think of her husband as a god? Should a wife obey her husband all the time? Do you actually obey your husband?" Motibai replied, expressing the ideal:

> Yes, a husband is a god. We touch his feet, and after he comes home from a pilgrimage, we wash his toes and drink the water. A wife should obey, but not if she is told to do a bad thing, like going to another man. I always obey my husband; I have to.

Then she added candidly, "But if he gets mad at me, I get just as mad at him." The middle-aged Barber woman replied, "I don't know. I usually obey, but when he isn't here, I do what I think is best. He also listens to me. We're equal." Kamladevi, a young Brahman wife who on other occasions had indicated a disdain for her husband, said, "Oh, no one's a god. Why should a woman obey her husband all the time? I do what I want to most of the time." Her sister-in-law agreed, "Oh, everyone says a husband is a god, but no one's a god."

Sundarbai, a high-caste mother of four, has a poor relationship with her husband. He is cold and seldom talks to her, and his mother and other members of the joint household accuse her of not doing her share of the work. Sundarbai retaliates by spending about six months of each year in her parents' home and sometimes threatening never to return. A young Thakur woman who was dissatisfied with the amount of jewellery she received for her wedding refused to return from her parents' home until she was given Rs. 3,000 worth of jewellery. She held out for two years and finally received several expensive ornaments.

Some village and urban women turn to deep involvement in religion when they cannot find satisfaction in their marriages. In North India, where a woman cannot so easily return to her parents' home, a pilgrimage may provide a needed respite from her husband and his relatives. Other women devote many hours to prayer or depend on their children for affection.

Family Living

In North and Central India a bride almost always goes to live with her husband and his parents and siblings in a joint family unit. She may live in a joint family all her life, or the group may lose members through death or division and she may find herself in a nuclear family, that is, with only her husband and unmarried children. Nuclear family living is particularly characteristic of people who do not own large amounts of land or property or who find it advantageous to move away from their homes in search of employment or both. For example, government servants who are frequently transferred are given small living quarters and usually live in nuclear families. So do landless labourers, artisans who live in areas unable to support more than one of their kind, and Westernized professionals. Some landed farmers live in nuclear families, but usually not for long. For a farmer, joint family living is usually economically advantageous, since it involves a group of kinsmen living and working together on their cooperatively farmed land. Except in some urban circles, the joint family is the ideal, and some of India's wealthiest industrialists live in large joint families. In spite of the ideal, however, brothers often quarrel and divide their property after the death of their parents.

Joint family living is frequently found among the village kinsmen of urban migrants. When a village man migrates to the city to work in a factory or as a labourer, he usually leaves his wife and children behind with his family. He lives alone or with fellow male workers in the city and may visit his family only once or twice a year.

The nature of a woman's relationships with her in-laws depends to a great extent on whether she is living with them in the same household. The wife of a government servant living away from his parents may meet her parents-in-law only occasionally, and she and her husband consequently have as much autonomy as his job allows. But a village farmer and his wife living with the husband's family must daily modify their actions to satisfy his relatives. Restraint and concern with hierarchy permeate joint family life.

For the village Hindu woman, purdah observances are important. Her respectful veiling and avoidance of her father-in-law and husband's elder brothers are ideally lifelong, but in some families a middle-aged *bahu* may exchange a few words with an aged father-in-law. The bride also veils from her mother-in-law for a short period of time and from her husband when others are present. Such veiling is an aid to harmony within the joint family, since it emphasizes the subordinate relationship of the woman to those in authority in the family and deemphasizes her tie to her husband. Veiling and seclusion in her conjugal home constantly remind a woman of her position as a *bahu* who must quietly subjugate her individual wishes to those of the group.

The fact that a woman veils from her husband in the presence of others also provides a small amount of privacy for each couple, since husband and wife converse only when they are alone and what they say to each other is not known to anyone but themselves. A young wife also finds that the veil shields her somewhat from the constant scrutiny of others in her new home.

In most Muslim families, purdah is observed not from related males but rather from strangers. A bride may be shy in the presence of her father-in-law and husband's elder brother, but if she has married a cousin, these men are her close relatives and she may be at ease with them. Muslim purdah serves to define the kindred group vis-a-vis outsiders and thus heightens the family's sense of unity. The seclusion of marriageable women from strangers also helps to ensure that a girl will marry only a man acceptable to her family. This is particularly important for Muslims of property, since Muslim women inherit and control land and other valuables.

A woman should ideally be subordinate to her mother-in-law and do as she says. In North India a bride may be expected to perform small personal services for her mother-in-law, such as massaging her arms and legs. Many *bahus,* however, resent taking orders from the mother-in-law and talk back or even quarrel openly. Gradually, a *bahu* feels more and more confident in her new home, and as the years pass, she may come to dominate her aged mother-in-law completely. Occasionally a woman and her *bahu* have a warm, loving relationship, but this is not the rule. It has been reported that a woman may even meddle in the sex life of her son, restricting his access to his wife to only once a week. But most women are eager to have grandchildren and would encourage rather than discourage sexual activity. (In a joint family household, each couple of childbearing years normally has a private room in which to sleep, although the rooms may be used by others during the day. In some regions, men visit their wives discreetly only after dark. Older couples usually sleep apart.)

Although she avoids her husband's elder brother, a woman has a warm, joking relationship with her husband's younger brother, her *devar*, to whom she is *bhabhi*. A *bhabhi* and her *devar* tease and jest openly about sex and may be confidantes. In some parts of North India it is permissible for the two to have sexual relations, but in other areas such activity would be condemned.

To a woman, her husband's elder sister may be a critical and annoying person who visits all too frequently. But her husband's younger sister may be like her own little sister, pleasant and loving, shyly confiding her own fears of marriage or her difficulties with her husband.

Other important people in a woman's marital home are her husband's brothers' wives, women brought there, like herself, as brides.

Sisters-in-law call each other "sister" and may be good friends, but they often quarrel over the division of household work and supplies. Men frequently blame quarrelling sisters-in-law for causing the division of the joint family. A young woman's first trysts with her husband may be arranged by her older sister-in-law (Luschinsky, 1962, p. 335).

After a visit with her parents, Halkibai (centre) cries bitterly as she leaves for her husband's home. Her mother and a neighbour also weep.

The oldest woman in a joint household is usually able to communicate more easily with all members of the family than can anyone else. Her children should not discuss certain matters or openly disagree with their elder brothers and father, and her *bahus* remain silent before their male elders. Thus an aged husband may rely upon his wife for communication with the younger members of his family (for example, see Madan, 1965, p. 137).

In many families, a father is expected to be authoritarian while the mother may be indulgent. Children often feel constrained in their father's presence but at ease with their mother. The closeness of a woman and her son may diminish after the arrival of the son's bride; but most sons and daughters always feel a special affection for their mothers.

A woman's love for her mother continues long after her marriage. From the loneliness of her husband's village, a girl may even idealize her mother and natal home as the epitome of love and warmth. Her father, too, takes on the aura of a saviour when he comes to escort her home on a visit.

A woman's relationship with her brother should be a special one of mutual love and concern. An older sister has cared for her brother during childhood and an older brother has helped care for a little sister. After a sister marries, her brother is expected to visit her, bring her home for visits, and bring gifts to her, her children, and her in-laws. The word "brother" is used even outside the sibling tie to denote affection. One Hindu festival, Raksha Bandhan, celebrates the brother-sister bond; a sister ties a sacred protective thread around her brother's wrist, and he reciprocates with a gift. A woman's love for her brother is communicated to her children, who accompany her on visits to her childhood home and are indulged by their mother's brother. Sisters, too, may be close, but no mutual obligations exist to ensure a lifelong bond. In North India, sisters are usually married into distant villages and may not see each other for years. First cousins who have grown up in the same household normally treat each other like true siblings, and all cousins address each other as "brother" and "sister". There is a notable lack of sibling rivalry between both true siblings and cousins (see Minturn and Hitchcock, 1966, p. 137).

Within each village, children of the same generation consider themselves "village siblings". Young people who ceremonially "hear Ram's name" together from a guru become ritual siblings. In Khalapur, women who are good friends may become ritual sisters.

The affinal relatives most important to a young Hindu woman, her husband and his mother, normally never meet her own mother. Purdah restrictions prevent these affines from interacting freely, and consequently they know each other only through what the young woman tells them about each other. The fathers-in-law may meet, but they too feel constraint in each other's presence. The formality of these relationships reflects the fact that the natal and conjugal kinsmen of a Hindu woman belong to different patrilineages and to some extent are rivals for the allegiance and services of the woman who unites them. Villagers say that an important reason for marrying their daughters to men of other villages is to insulate a woman's parents from her parents-in-law.

In Central India, a woman's happy visits to her parents' home are ended when her in-laws come to fetch her back. Since women are in short supply in this area, both groups benefit from the services of a woman and both seek her presence. A woman often feels unhappy and overworked in her husband's home, and she may hate to return.

The departure of a daughter for her husband's village after a visit is usually sad for both the girl and her parents. As she leaves her parents' home, a young woman sobs, "Oh mama, oh papa, don't think I'm of another house now. Oh mama, no one will come to get me now. I'm being sent away forever." (A woman never cries when leaving her husband's home.) The Nimkhera Barber woman once came to a women's gathering with her eyes red from crying over her daughter Halki's departure for her husband's village. Unlike other girls of her age (about twenty), Halki is allowed only short visits with her parents, and her mother-in-law is very domineering. Other women tried to console the mother. "Your poor daughter has to go to her in-laws after such short visits. Her crying is heard all over the village, she cries so loudly. Whoever hears her feels his chest burst with sorrow and pain," an elderly Brahman woman commented. As the Barber woman began to cry again, the woman continued, "A mother gives birth to her girl after bearing her burden in her stomach for nine months; then she suffers the labour pains and brings the girl up with love and care. Then she has to torture herself and marry her off to some strange person. This is all so painful for a mother." Another woman added, "Yes, but if a daughter is happy in her husband's home, then parents find some consolation in the fact. But if it is her fate to suffer miseries in her new home, then the days of the poor parents turn into hell." On another occasion, when Halki's mother was crying after her daughter's departure, a neighbour consoled her by saying, "I too suffered thus in the hands of my mother-in-law, and that old woman died soon. So Halki's old mother-in-law and father-in-law will also die; don't worry about Halki. A mother's tears are never shed in vain; they always produce results." Thus, the mother-in-law's pleasure is the mother's grief, and vice versa, even in relationships less filled with tension than Halki's.

In the parts of North India where Rajput marriages link a woman with a man of a higher-ranked subcaste, the woman and her relatives are often made to feel inferior to their in-laws. Loving her children, who are members of their father's group, expected to assimilate to her husband's family and yet loyal to her parents, a woman may feel forever torn between the two sets of relatives.

Although the two groups of relatives are to some extent united by the marriage linking them, a tension always exists between them. The hilariously insulting songs a bride's women-folk direct at her in-laws are one expression of this tension. (These songs, always expected, are never taken amiss.) Joking, respect, and avoidance relationships function to prevent the open expression of hostility, and apparent amicability is thus maintained. The key principle here is that the individual's actions must be modified to enhance harmony within the family and among kindred. This principle is also exemplified in the public negation of a special relationship between husband and wife and even between parent and child (see below).

Virtually every Indian woman looks forward to having children. Village women usually say they want "as many as God gives me" and may hope to give birth to six or seven. Some urban women who have been influenced by government family planning campaigns wish to have just two or three children. In fact, although fertility is very high in India, infant mortality is also high, and the average number of living children per mother is between three and four. In Nimkhera, most middle-aged women have given birth to five or six children, of whom three or four have survived childhood. Four-fifths of Nimkhera mothers have lost at least one child, and one-third have lost four or more children. High infant mortality is an important factor in influencing women to have as many children as they possibly can, since, as in the case of old Mograwali, a woman left without a son at home is materially worse off than a woman with sons and *bahus* in her house. Further, every cultural value stresses the importance of children.

Having a child is essential to a woman's emotional health and to ensure her status in her family and village. In giving birth to a child, a woman knows she is contributing, as only she can do, to the well-being of her family. Cradling a tiny baby in her arms, she feels a deep sense of satisfaction and happiness. Further, having a son usually gives a young wife a boost in prestige. Childless couples are much pitied, and a barren woman is an inauspicious guest at a wedding or a *Chauk* (infant blessing) ceremony. A married woman with no children is considered incomplete, even as an unmarried adult woman would be incomplete. Fear of childlessness is sometimes so overwhelming that it seems to become a self-fulfilling prophecy: childless women go in droves to visit shamans who are believed to have the power to bless them with children, and a high percentage return with babes in arms to offer gifts of gratitude to these faith healers.

Some women feel that a woman's position in her husband's household and in his heart is dependent upon or at least bettered by her production of children. A man may seek another wife if his first wife has not given birth. One young and childless Thakur woman, ill with tuberculosis, got no sympathy or kind words from her husband. He refused to give her money for medicines or hospital expenses and seemed eager to be rid of her so he could marry a young widow with whom he was having an affair. A friend of the sick woman told me,

Tulsibai's husband feels nothing for her. He told her, "If you're going to die tomorrow, you might as well die today and get it over with." You see, she doesn't have any children. Now, I have a son and little girls, and if anything happened to me, he (her husband) would worry about who would take care of his children.

Tulsibai later sold her jewellery to obtain funds and eventually married another man, by whom she bore a son, but she died shortly thereafter. But another childless woman, Jamnibai, of a low-ranking artisan caste, has lived quietly in Bhopal with her devoted husband for a dozen years. There have been no recriminations or threats of rejection, but there is an air of sadness about Jamnibai.

Contraceptives are used by a low percentage of villagers. Many villagers are ignorant of how to use such devices, and few ever visit a gynaecologist who might instruct them. Lack of easy access to contraceptives and lack of privacy also militate against their use. Many villagers are suspicious of the government family planning campaigns, since they distrust government personnel in general.

In any case, many individuals perceive no value in limiting their families. One small village in the Delhi area was subjected to an intensive family planning campaign for six months, yet no one in the village adopted contraception as a result. There, as elsewhere, pregnant young women are given special care and attention, and some consider pregnancy an inherently desirable state. Twenty women were shown two pictures—silhouettes of a pregnant woman and an unpregnant woman. All saw the pregnant woman as happier, healthier, better fed, more secure, more influential, and more respected. Most of the villagers did not believe that individual use of contraceptives would slow population pressure on limited land resources. Some thought the growth of their village would lead to the opening of new shops, tea stalls, and other facilities which would provide job opportunities (Marshall, 1971).

Nevertheless, women who have borne several children without medical attention are often anemic or suffer from other illnesses and would like to prevent pregnancy. In Nimkhera, after having four children, Sundarbai resorted to avoiding her husband as much as possible, but she recently had her fifth child. After enduring the difficult birth of her seventh child, Phulbai, a poor Weaver woman, told me, "God has been good to us; he has given us enough children. Tell me how I can stop having children." Herbal medicines for contraception and abortion are said to be available but are seldom used.

In the Gangetic area, having children too close together is frowned upon; couples are expected to avoid intercourse during pregnancy and for two years after the birth of a surviving child. There, it is considered shameful for a woman to give birth after she has a grown daughter-in-law in the house. High-caste men in Rajasthan and elsewhere in North India attempt to limit their sexual activity, since they believe loss of semen is weakening (Carstairs, 1957).

Women's conversations frequently centre around children and childbirth, and almost all women's gatherings include babies who are being cuddled and suckled. Young girls, who themselves are helping to care for younger siblings and cousins, watch and listen and grow up with the full expectation that they will become mothers. For villagers, there is virtually no alternative, but even city girls planning careers expect to have children. Girls hear of the pain of childbirth and learn in advance to accept it as part of being feminine. Still, a pregnant woman fears childbirth, not only for the pain but also because she knows she may die. Every woman has a relative or acquaintance who has died during late pregnancy or childbirth, and this knowledge perhaps increases her perception of pain. Maternal deaths are always very sad, involving as they do young women in the prime of life, many with young children. In about 1960 a Thakur woman in Nimkhera gave birth to a son, her sixth child. Her eldest daughter, about sixteen, had suddenly died the year before in her husband's village, and the family was desolate when the mother and her tiny son died four days after the baby was born. The father has never remarried but often calls his sister home to help, and the remaining four children are very responsible and cooperate in running the household. But the youngest daughter has been very troubled and often dreams about her dead mother and sister. She cries and sadly says, "My mother came to me again last night."

A child brings joy. Indians seem to truly love their children, not merely tolerate them. Family members all want to be near a baby, to look at it and to hold it. Children are included in every social event; there are virtually no separate children's functions except among the urban elite. Once two teenage village girls asked me to take their picture, and as I got out my camera, each grabbed a small child to hold. These were not their children; neither of them had any, so I asked why they were holding these children. "Because we like children," they explained.

Every mother fears that her child will die, as she has seen so many babies do. The child is guarded from contact with people who might emanate evil influences and is kept away from sick children, whose mothers might magically take good health from another child to give to their own. Ever present is the fear of the evil eye, which even a loving parent can cause to fall on his child by admiring him too much. (No child is ever admired openly.) Smallpox, typhoid, cholera, eye infections, diphtheria, whooping cough, and myriad other diseases are constant threats. In cities and towns, children are often seen by doctors and "compounders" who administer injections and other medicines. But consistent with their distrust of government officials and in response to the haughty manner of some physicians, most villagers avoid hospitals and doctors as much as possible. Illnesses are frequently treated with herbal medicines, prayer, amulets, and wishful thinking. Although many children have been vaccinated against smallpox, villagers treat the disease by isolating the patient and appealing to Sitala Mata, the smallpox goddess. In general, the quality of medical care available to a child is commensurate with his family's wealth.

A mother's love and care are considered essential to the growth of a child, and no one is surprised when a motherless baby dies. Until a child is about ten years old, women are responsible for its daily care. A mother breast-feeds her baby — usually until he is two or three years old, washes him, changes his soiled clothes, and carries him about on her hip. Almost all babies are left with bare bottoms; when a child begins to urinate or defecate, his mother holds him to one side and later wipes up the mess. Some urban mothers put diapers on their babies or expect servants to clean up the messes on the floor, and a small percentage of urban women bottle-feed their children. As the child grows, his mother prepares solid food and feeds it to him by hand. She also supervises his play, bathing, and other activities. Although his mother is primarily responsible for him, a child's aunts and grandmother may also take an active role in caring for him. The child's father, uncles, and other male kinsmen may take an interest in him, but they rarely tend to his daily physical needs.

It is considered shameful for a young mother to flaunt her relationship with her baby before her elders, and it is even more shameful for a young father to do so. A new mother feels embarrassment in nursing her baby before elders in either her natal home or her husband's home, not because she is ashamed of exposing her breasts but because the child represents absolute proof of her sexuality. When she takes her new baby with her to visit in her parents' home, a young woman lets her mother or sister care for the child, the product of her relationship with her husband, as much as possible. The baby's father does not hold or kiss the child in the presence of his elder kinsmen or fellow villagers until the child is four or five years old. This sense of shame in dealing with one's child is in accord with two important themes in North and Central Indian culture: the deemphasis of the nuclear family unit in favour of the larger joint family unit and separation of a woman's parental home from her husband's home. Young couples who live away from their parents and older and less traditional villagers openly dandle their children in public.

Children are never left alone; they are always with a parent, grandparent, older sibling, or other family member. Wealthy people sometimes engage a nursemaid to carry the child about, but most people do not allow a non-kinsman to care for a child.

Traditional Tasks

For almost all Indian women, work centres around child care, food processing, and care of the household. Some women perform other tasks both at home and outside the house, but they are still responsible for housework, which is considered woman's proper sphere.

In most of North and Central India, it is a man's job to bring home food for his family, having procured it either through sowing and reaping a crop or earning money and purchasing it. It is a woman's job to convert the raw foodstuffs — wheat, rice, millet, lentils, vegetables, tea, sugar, salt, fruits, meat, milk, and spices — into meals to serve to her family. Preprocessed or convenience foods are expensive, distrusted, and not widely available; consequently food preparation may occupy several hours of a woman's day.

The village woman must clean her grain of tiny stones and chaff by sifting, tossing in a winnowing fan, and picking through it. On sunny afternoons women gather in courtyards or on verandahs to clean grain and chat.

Wheat and lentils must then be ground, usually in a home mill. Young girls like to grind, two sitting opposite each other, turning the heavy round millstone to the rhythm of their singing. Wives also grind; turning the mill is good physical exercise for women in purdah. Grinding is time-consuming, however (it takes about twenty minutes for one woman to grind two pounds of wheat); in both cities and villages, those who can afford it have much of their grain ground at commercial mills. Rice is husked at home with a heavy wooden pestle, and salt and spices are ground by hand. Cow, goat, and buffalo milk is boiled to sterilize it and churned to obtain butter and buttermilk. Butter is clarified to produce India's favourite cooking oil, ghī, and mangoes and lemons are pickled.

Cooking may be extremely time-consuming, depending upon the elaborateness of the meals a woman's family expects. In most of the northern half of India wheat is the staple, made into flat *rotis* (unleavened bread) and served with lentil sauce or vegetables. *Rotis* are prepared fresh once or twice each day over the small horseshoe-shaped mud stove found in virtually every kitchen. Even city women who cook vegetables over small kerosene or gas burners usually make *rotis* on an earthen stove fuelled with cow dung cakes or wood. Prosperous families may dine on a number of heavily spiced dishes at each meal, dishes that are almost prepared in relatively small kitchen by the women of the family. Some well-to-do families employ cooks, but traditional families allow kitchen servants to help only in cleaning grain, grinding, paring vegetables, and washing dishes. In village families, most kitchen duties fall to the sequestered *bahus*.

After each meal the earthen oven must be cleansed with a fresh layer of yellow clay and the brass platters and tumblers scoured with fine ash and water.

For village women, fetching water is an important task. Twice daily women and girls bear heavy brass and earthen pots filled with cool well water atop their heads. Young girls learn early to balance the pots, and Hindu girls are taught to avoid contact with ritually polluting

A young Brahman wife fetches water.

lower-caste people between the well and home. Although the pots are
heavy, women like to go for water, since it is only at the well that
women of different households can meet daily to exchange news and
gossip. Women in strict seclusion, wealthy Muslims and young *bahu*
of high-status Hindu families, do not visit the well but depend upon
their menfolk or male servants to bring water.

Men are in charge of major structural additions and repairs to a house, and women are responsible for maintaining the house's cleanliness and beauty. Every day a village woman sweeps her house and courtyard to keep the earthen floors clean, and squatting, she cleans the cowshed of dung. She shapes the dung into round patties and plops them to dry in the sun. Patties prepared the previous day are added to a neat pile, the family's main fuel supply for cooking and warming fires in the winter. Every week she applies a fresh layer of cow dung paste to the floors to provide a clean, dustless surface.[11] Periodically, especially after the rainy season, house walls and courtyard floors must be patched and rebuilt with a mixture of mud and straw and then whitewashed.

A village daughter, home for a visit, plasters her porch with cow dung paste.

Many village houses in Western and Central India are decorated with fine earthen bas-reliefs around doorways and wall niches, sometimes beautifully coloured with ochre, yellow, and malachite hues. The women of Rajasthan create incredibly intricate painted mud filigree cabinets and shelves studded with tiny mirrors inside their houses, and outside walls are painted with colourful warriors and elephants. Many women paint bright flowers and figures on their walls and draw curlicue

designs in rice paste or whitewash on their doorsteps. Most urban
women, on the other hand, take little interest in home decoration,
devoting their artistic energies to decorating themselves.

A Weaver caste daughter of the village harvests wheat.

Few women are responsible for the family laundry. Village adults
usually rinse out their own clothing after bathing each day, and mothers
wash their small children's clothing. Periodically, heavily soiled

clothing is scrubbed by the village laundress and launderer, members of the Dhobi caste. City dwellers typically engage a Dhobi to wash and press all clothing. In many villages, tailors make almost all stitched clothing, but in some areas women sew baby clothes and some of their own garments. In Rajasthan and Gujarat, women spend months making cutwork and embroidered mirror-studded wall hangings, skirts, and saris. Rajasthani women also tie the knots for their colourful tie-dyed saris. Khalapur women gin and spin cotton to be made into cloth by weavers. Some middle-class urban women know how to make blouses and petticoats, but they usually depend on tailors to sew clothing for themselves and their families.

In Bengal, women of the Santal tribe work as labourers on a construction crew. © Mimi Sharma.

Many women work in their own fields or in the fields of others, but there is no agricultural task considered primarily women's work. The essential activity of ploughing, which requires driving bullocks, is considered strictly man's province. Women are particularly active in rice cultivation in areas where the crop is grown, helping with planting and doing much of the arduous weeding, harvesting, and threshing. In some areas they also take an active part in sowing and harvesting wheat and other crops. Women who belong to poor families spend many hours in the fields each year, but well-to-do women usually help only with the harvest and rely on hired men to help their menfolk with other tasks. In the Varanasi area, high-caste women do not work in the fields at all. Very poor women work as sharecroppers or hire themselves out as day labourers in the fields of others, thus contributing substantially to the family income.

A Weaver woman weaves webbing tapes for a cot.

In Nimkhera, women's assistance during the short but crucial wheat sowing and harvest periods is vital to most families, since these tasks must be completed quickly and, short-handed families must hire outside labour. It is not surprising that a woman's parents and in-laws vie for her presence at these times.

Some village women help grow and sell vegetables and fruits; others help run shops. Some make rope for household use, and a few shape earthen roof tiles for sale. Poor women gather wild fruits, vegetables, rice and *tendū* leaves, sold for use as country cigarette wrappers. Women work alongside their menfolk in cutting bales of hay for dry-season fodder and gathering firewood. A few very poor women herd goats, although animal herding is not considered safe for women, since animals graze in forest areas far from home.

Nimkhera women of all castes do at least some work in the fields, whereas high-caste women in the Varanasi area do none. This may contribute to the fact that the status of Nimkhera women in relation to men is somewhat higher than that of Varanasi women. Although virtually all women perform economically significant tasks, among peasant farmers it is feminine participation in agriculture which seems to be most closely related to female status.[12] Generally, however, Indian women who bring food and money from any source into the household enjoy greater independence than women who do not (Mandelbaum, 1970, pp. 48-50).

Very poor city women work as domestic servants for wealthy and middle-class families or labour on building and road construction projects, carrying head loads of earth and stone in the hot sun. Women of nomadic blacksmith groups work beside their husbands at the anvil. In a few areas, women work in mines and on tea plantations.

In many villages a special system of intercaste exchanges of goods and services exists. Under this system, which anthropologists call the *Jajmānī* system, service and artisan caste families have a hereditary right to provide certain services for the families of castes other than their own and in return receive traditional payments of grain, money, and other benefits. In some areas, *Jajmani* ties between families have been in force for generations; in other areas, the system is breaking down. In any case, women of these castes perform traditional caste-associated tasks in addition to their normal housework, child care, and agricultural work.

Barber women do not cut hair as their husbands do, but in some areas they deliver babies, bathe mother and baby, cut women's toenails, dress brides, and direct *Chauk* (infant blessing) ceremonies. Barber couples deliver invitations to village functions and make leaf plates for feasts.

Tailor women sew and mend garments for their patrons; Washerwomen wash them. Potter women paint white peacocks and other designs on the earthen pots their menfolk shape and help deliver them to customers. Although many are now turning to other sources of income, some Weaver women still help prepare cotton and loom fabric and webbing for cots. In some areas, Tanner women help their menfolk process leather and make shoes. The "untouchable" Sweeper women of villages and cities perform the wretched and despised task of cleaning old-style latrines, and in some cases they deliver babies. In towns, very poor women of certain groups go out to beg.

For most Indian women the day begins before dawn. Village women rise early so they can work in the cool of the early morning, but even city women are up at 5:30 to prepare sweet milky tea for their families.

After rising, the village woman goes with her tiny pot of cleansing water to the field or roadside to eliminate; then she returns to wash her hands, face, and teeth. She has a snack, fetches water, folds and hangs the bedding from the rafters, sweeps, tends to the needs of the children, cleans the cowshed, and bathes. For Hindus, daily bathing is an essential prelude to the main activities of the day.[13] The village woman squats with her sari on and pours water over her head and body. The wet sari is adroitly removed and a dry sari put on without exposing the body; thus the village woman can bathe behind an upturned cot or in public at a pond or well. Some traditional urban women also bathe fully clothed, rubbing soap through the wet cloth, but private nude bathing is now common in cities (Cormack, 1953, pp. 25-26). After her bath, the woman can begin to prepare the main meal of the day, which she serves in the late morning. In joint families, women eat after the men have finished. While a woman is cleaning the stove and dishes, her menfolk leave for the fields or office and children for play or school.

Afternoon activities vary greatly according to wealth and season. Prosperous high-caste village women at slack agricultural seasons sit around, some cleaning grain, some napping or talking. Poor women of low status go out to work in the fields, at the threshing floors, or at other income-earning tasks during busy periods of the year. Wealthy city women nap, read, or visit friends.

In the evening, village women and girls fetch water and tie the cattle returned from a day of grazing in their sheds. City women sometimes go with family members to shop at this hour in colourful, crowded bazaars. After again going to eliminate, village women light the lamps and prepare supper while men smoke and talk.

Villagers usually retire after supper, but on special nights men and women gather separately to sing until midnight or later.

It is clear that women perform a wide variety of tasks and that their services are essential to the well-being of their families and the nation. Because of the relative scarcity of females throughout much of North and Central India, there are many men who live as bachelors. These men, and those whose wives spend long periods visiting in their natal homes, complain bitterly of living without a wife to help with household and agricultural work. They fetch their own water, cook simple meals, and either hire women or impose on female relatives to grind wheat and make cow dung cakes. No single woman who desires a husband is long without one except in cities. Nevertheless, there are cultural limitations to women's activities, and women usually perceive their jobs as being less important than those of their menfolk. In fact, women consider themselves beholden to and dependent upon their fathers, brothers, and husbands. I once asked Sukkibai, a wizened and overworked Sweeper woman about her relationship with her alcoholic husband. The man had married Sukkibai when she was a girl and then brought three other women to be his wives. These women all sweep latrines and weave baskets and turn their earnings over to their idle husband, who uses a good part of the funds to buy liquor. Sukkibai said her husband would beat her if she were to buy even a set of cheap glass bangles without his permission. "Why do you stay with him?" I asked. "Oh, then where would I go?" she replied with a sigh. Women of higher caste echoed this sentiment. A Barber woman very active in agricultural and traditional caste work said, "I have to listen to whatever my husband tells me. Otherwise where would I go? He's the breadwinner." A hardworking Thakur woman once said, to the agreement of the Barber woman, "Why do you think men marry? It's only for sex."

The fact is that under the traditional Hindu inheritance and residence system still in force in villages, women are beholden to men; without dependence on a man who controls land, the ultimate source of food and the location of their home, a woman's position is most difficult. A woman alone in the world indeed lacks security.

A Hindu widow has rights to the fruits of her dead husband's land, but without sons she finds managing the land difficult. Even landowning Muslim women need men to help administer their land. A woman cannot plough herself, so must hire men to drive the bullocks. She must be vigilant to prevent cheating and stealing of her crop. With no male to take her part in court or to bribe officials, she may find even her land stolen by unscrupulous relatives.

Purdah restrictions on women's movements outside their homes add to their dependence on men in the realms of marketing and money, but women have some autonomy in these areas. Although men make almost all bazaar purchases, women buy from small village shops, from itinerant vendors, and from stalls set up at fairs. Glittering glass bangles, vegetables and fruits, sweets, combs, blouses, sweaters, and even saris are sold door-to-door in many villages. Women pay with the family cash left in their care, or — more usually — with grain, to which they have free access. Some women, in fact, residents of joint families, secretly sell grain to traders to add to their own personal hoard of money and jewellery. Some well-to-do women lend money clandestinely or openly and collect high rates of interest.

Many women feel they should consult their husbands before buying expensive items, but some women who are earning members of the household say they are entitled to spend money as they please. Generally, poor, lower-caste, and tribal women buy a higher proportion of things on their own than do wealthier and high-status women. But Birjis Jahan, Latif Khan's wife, who is in charge of the family's treasury, sends servants to make purchases for her. She once went out in a relative's jeep, veiled in her *burka*, to buy living room furniture from a private seller. Her husband was angry with her but pleased with the furniture. Birjis Jahan is also in charge of marketing vegetables grown on family land; she lets a male servant sell the produce and bring her the proceeds.

A Muslim woman has the legal right to demand her *mehr* money, pledged by her husband at her wedding, at any time. "A man has no right to complain about what his wife does with the money," Latif Khan explained to me. But normally a woman does not demand *mehr* unless her husband is squandering the family funds or divorcing her. Traditional Muslim and modern Indian courts uphold a woman's right to her *mehr*.

A woman's knowledge, cleverness, and confidence in herself greatly influence the decisions she makes. A clever woman can create her own nest egg and persuade other family members to take her point of view without arousing their antagonism. But purdah observances and

*A young Muslim woman learns to drive her family's tractor
for a short distance in the relative safety of a field.*

restrictions on her education and activities may render her ignorant of
agricultural matters, prices, bargaining, and many other things. In these
areas, many women are glad to accept the advice of informed men.

New Occupations

Traditionally, an Indian woman worked outside her home only if she
had to. The woman who earned money was pitied for her poverty and
for her husband's inability to provide for his family. In both villages
and towns, women of the lower classes have always worked in the fields
of others, as domestic servants, and carried out traditional tasks while
their wealthier neighbours performed domestic chores in the privacy of
their homes and worked only occasionally in their own fields. The
association of female money-earning and low status in society
continues in villages and in traditional urban circles, but today more and
more women of the middle and upper urban classes are working outside
their homes. Using the education they have obtained in high schools
and colleges, these women are taking an active part in the
modernization of their country.

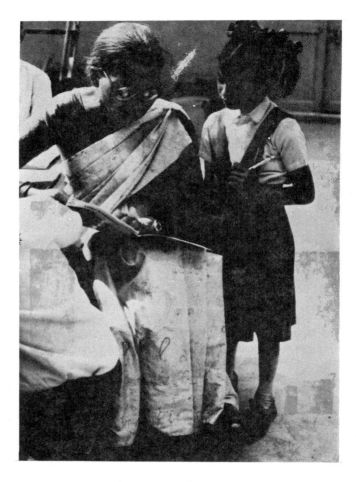

*A woman schoolteacher helps a young student
with her lessons in an urban school.*

Mahatma Gandhi, the great Indian nationalist, was partially responsible for making it socially acceptable for these urban women to come out of their homes. A man who cultivated traditional personal habits in himself and who found favour with Indians of all walks of life, he advocated women's rights and insisted that it was women's duty to come forth and work for the independence of the country and the uplift of the poor and unfortunate. Women by the hundreds demonstrated, marched, and were jailed for their anti-British activity. After independence was won, some of these women, particularly Hindus, Parsis, and Christians, continued to work outside of their homes.

More important forces bringing women into the salaried work force have been the urbanization, industrialization, and modernization of the country. Village women can still carry out economically useful tasks within the family and the small community, but if city women wish similarly to contribute to the family economy, they must seek paid employment. Further, participation in certain occupations may bring prestige to a family living in a world affected by Western values.

These three highly-educated sisters of the city of Indore teach in a primary school and a college.

Most of the occupations in which Indian women have achieved prominence are clearly related to their traditional nurturing and domestic roles. Women work as teachers at all educational levels but particularly in girls' schools and colleges. Before independence, some women actively crusaded in the cause of women's rights, determinedly working against purdah, child marriage, and for better treatment for widows. For example, Pandita Ramabai, one famous widow, founded a home and

school for high-caste child widows in Poona[*], and Sister
Subbalakshmi, a child widow herself but educated by a determined
father, founded similar institutions in Madras. Today women staff
schools of social work and institutions such as orphanages and child
welfare centres throughout the country. As village-level workers in the
National Community Development Programme, they teach village
women about hygiene, family planning, smokeless ovens, and kitchen
gardens. Many women have become nurses (particularly Christians) and
doctors. The term *lady doctor* is synonymous with *obstetrician-
gynaecologist*, since most female doctors specialize in that field and
Indian women are most reluctant to visit a male gynaecologist.

Women students develop computer skills at a New Delhi college.

Women are active in business enterprises, journalism, writing,
the theatre, cinema, art, and even law. A few women also work as
clerks in handicraft shops and boutiques and a very few as stewardesses,
but virtually none are bank tellers or waitresses. Although some
women work as office clerks, the vast majority of India's office
workers, including secretaries, are men. Government tourist information

---

[*] Poona is now known as Pune.

centres are staffed by women, and the All-India Handicraft Board has been directed by a woman.[14]*

The life of the middle-class working woman may be difficult. In conservative towns, a woman alone on the street or on a bus may be molested and annoyed by men. Discrimination against women in some fields is very great, and in virtually no field are they in the majority. Most working women could never aspire to an executive position, and, as women seek equality in pay and opportunity, they find employers refusing to hire them. Further, on a day-to-day basis, a working woman may encounter substantial opposition from her own family. In the realistic film *Mahanagar*, Satyajit Ray dramatized the conflicts in the life of a Calcutta woman of modest means and demeanor who agrees to sell knitting machines door-to-door. Although the family's finances are enhanced by her earnings, her husband's parents, with whom she lives, feel like beggars in accepting money from their own daughter-in-law. Her husband feels emasculated by her ability to earn money, especially when he loses his job and she becomes the family's sole support. He is almost crazed with jealousy when he sees her wearing sunglasses and having tea with a male associate, and their whole relationship is threatened by her venture beyond the traditional domestic sphere. In the film the couple's love for each other overcomes their difficulties, but in real life such conflicts often lead to a woman's giving up her career plans at the whim of her husband or other family members. Many working girls quit their jobs when they marry. But for upper and middle-class women who continue to work after marriage, care of children and home is greatly eased by the ready availability of domestic servants and the presence of a grandmother in the home.[15]

However, life may be extremely difficult for the domestic servants, factory workers, and other poor working women of the cities, many of whom are recent immigrants from villages. In a single crowded tenement room or shack, a woman cooks at a small stove in one corner as her children dodge clothes hanging from a line stretching across the room and her husband reclines against a pile of bedding and trunks in another corner. In the worst of the urban dwellings, the hutments, monsoon rains pour through the patchwork roofs to drench the occupants and their meager possessions and make of lanes a mire that assails the nostrils. From this environment the poor working woman

---

* Women are increasingly visible in virtually all occupations in India.

must emerge fresh each morning to travel to her job, where she earns about 30 or 40 cents a day.[*]

Religion

Religion is an important part of daily life for almost every Indian. Whether Hindu, Muslim, Sikh, Christian, Jain, or Parsi, an Indian considers his religion an important part of his identity. Others relate to him as a member of a particular religious group — so much so, in fact, that conversion to another religion is legal grounds for divorce and loss of inheritance.

Hindus worship a great many gods, goddesses, and spirits which sophisticated Hindus consider manifestations of one divine entity. Virtually all believe that souls pass through a number of existences. Although an individual's fate is "written on his forehead by God" at birth, a person is held accountable for his actions. Sinners may be reborn as subhuman creatures or untouchables, while those who fulfil the duties appropriate to their statuses in this life will be rewarded with a higher birth in the next. In the orthodox view, the ultimate reward is release from the cycle of reincarnation and union with God, but a Khalapur girl felt that the highest reward would be rebirth into one's own household (Minturn and Hitchcock, 1966, p. 70). Nimkhera women believe a woman could never be reborn as a man.

Although women are excluded from the Hindu priesthood, they participate in most important ceremonies and observances in the home and temple. In some areas, men carry out most daily temple and home rituals, while elsewhere women are responsible for daily worship. Throughout India both men and women maintain religious fasts, but more women than men fast. Women's most important contribution to religious life is performing rituals connected with the life-cycle and calendrical festivals, rituals considered vital to the well-being of the individual, the family, and the community. In Khalapur and Senapur, women are much more conservative in religious matters than are men and are the main participants in these rites (Luschinsky, 1962, p. 644 ff.; Minturn and Hitchcock, 1966, p. 65 ff.).

The number and diversity of Hindu rituals performed throughout India are astounding; an encyclopaedia could hardly catalogue them all. Rituals range from simple devotional prayers and offerings to elaborate

---

[*] Earnings are now higher, but inflation has more than outpaced increases in pay for labourers.

processions. In a town near Delhi, a woman daily lights an incense stick, places it before a colourful picture of Lord Krishna, and silently mouths a prayer for her son away at college. An Indore woman visits her special prayer room every day to place marigold blossoms, incense, and a small oil lamp before the family collection of brass images of deities. Respectfully, she garlands a framed photograph of her deceased husband. In Senapur, women gather at the shrine of Sitala Mata, the smallpox goddess, to offer food and flowers to her in exchange for her protection. In Calcutta, masses of people, including brilliantly dressed girls and women, gather to watch the annual procession honouring Durga. Elaborate images of the goddess are worshipped and, amidst a deafening din of fireworks and band music, are borne through the streets to be dumped into the river. Near Karauli, a small Rajasthani town, pilgrims congregate at a hilltop temple for the annual festival honouring Kela Devi. Far into the night women seeking to please the goddess with their devotion dance before the temple, their skirts swirling and veils covering their faces. In the morning they gather to watch the Maharaja of Karauli preside over the sword-swift sacrifice of a large goat to the goddess.

Observances like these occur every day throughout India. Even in a small village like Nimkhera, in a single year there was daily worship in the village temple and many homes, 112 festival days, and 104 days on which life-cycle rites were performed.

One festival, Divali, the festival of lights, is observed throughout much of India. In Nimkhera as elsewhere, this festival centres around the worship of Lakshmi, the goddess of wealth, and wealth in all its forms. The women of each household shape a large heap of cow dung into a recumbent man on their doorstep; this embodiment of the usefulness of cow dung is later worshipped. Men and boys bathe the village cattle in the pond, and women prepare fine festival foods. In the evening, small earthen oil lamps are lit outside each house, and several lamps are lit before a pottery figurine of goddess Lakshmi. The women of each household contribute their jewellery to a glittering pile of money and cattle ornaments before the goddess, as if to ask her to increase their wealth. In every cowshed men offer wheatcakes to the cattle, and the sound of firecrackers resounds through the village. The next morning, the cattle are decorated with bright ornaments and paints and driven out to graze. Men and women gather to sing hymns and other songs. The next day, women prepare two more cow dung sculptures, and girls ritually bless their brothers.

The spring harvest festival of Holi is celebrated over most of the northern half of India. Holi is certainly India's most colourful holiday: merry-makers throw bucketfuls of purple and red dye on each other. In many villages, Holi is the occasion for battles between men and women; women pelt men with cow dung and beat them with sticks and men fight back with hilarious verbal abuse. The opposition expressed is not between men and women in general, but between affines: only village *bahus,* never daughters, join the fray. In Nimkhera, on Holi, women stage a private session of skits, including hilariously sexy parodies and absurd situation comedies. But the festival ends on a note of utmost seriousness as all the villagers, dressed in their finery, proceed to the Mother Goddess shrine to witness the offering of coconuts and the sacrifice of a goat. Later, sounds of groups of men and women singing echo through the moonlit village lanes.

In Nimkhera, the spirit of Holi is carried over into Jhanda Torna, a semi-religious holiday celebrated at night about two weeks later. To encourage a mood of abandon, marijuana tea is served to men and women as they gather around a tall wooden pole topped with a bag of brown sugar. With flailing sticks, a group of low-caste wives vigorously defend the pole from the attack of a large number of men of all castes. The men protect themselves with T-shaped shields as they advance and retreat to the sound of rhythmic drumming. High-caste women and Muslims are fascinated spectators. The uproarious battle eventually terminates with the men's victorious uprooting of the pole and seizure of the sugar, but not before several have suffered painful blows. Later, a professional dancing girl performs.

Participation in ritual activities brings happiness and a sense of importance to most Hindu women. Although belief in the divine is strong throughout India, women perhaps even more than men are devout believers in the supernatural. Only through proper performance of rituals can deities and spirits be placated and persuaded to bring benefits of good health and wealth to a woman and her family. In carrying out these rituals, a woman feels she is doing something important to benefit her family. In Nimkhera, the young Brahman woman Kamladevi had lost three babies. Even before she became pregnant again, she began to diligently worship a goddess said to help women have healthy babies. Kamladevi is now the mother of a healthy little boy, named after the goddess.

During the Jhanda Torna festival, low-caste wives wage a
raucous battle against the village men of Nimkhera.

Further, Hinduism provides opportunities for recreation and
emotional release. The many worship services, rituals, ceremonies, and
pilgrimages that are part of the religion are not only occasions to
worship God but also entertaining and fun. Participation in religious
activities is a socially and morally acceptable reason for a sequestered
woman to leave her house to enjoy a trip to the Ganges or other holy
place. In fact, failure to perform prescribed rituals outside the home
could bring divine retribution.

The proportion of religious activity carried out by Hindu women
seems to be correlated with their status vis-a-vis men. In Central India,
where women are not always subordinate to men, both sexes participate
actively in rituals and festivals. In contrast, the women of Senapur,
who seem to be of significantly lower status than their menfolk, are
responsible for nearly all religious ceremonies. There, men can easily
satisfy their needs for recreation, sociability, and emotional catharsis
outside religion. Further, "men make many decisions which affect
women, and women sometimes have very little, if any, voice in the
decisions. Aside from household work, religious activities provide the
only opportunity for women to take initiative in major endeavours"
(Luschinsky, 1962, p. 718).

For those who do not find complete satisfaction in their family life, religion provides an acceptable outlet in the form of lengthy prayer, worship, pilgrimage, and even spirit possession. In the village of Shanti Nagar near Delhi, Daya, a bride of the Tanner caste, became ill through spirit possession. In interviews with Ruth Freed, Daya revealed that she was having difficulty adjusting to her new role as a wife and veiled *bahu*. Her spirit-induced illness allowed her to draw attention to herself, express hostile feelings, and to otherwise act in ways that would not normally be socially acceptable. In Senapur, veiled *bahus* who visit spirit-possessed male shamans sometimes themselves become possessed and writhe and shake so much that their clothes fall from their shoulders (Freed and Freed, 1964; Luschinsky, 1962, pp. 694-704). Such performances provide important emotional outlets for these young women. Among some tribal peoples, woman act as shamans (Elwin, 1958, pp. 210-211). Through religion, family conflicts can often be skirted or resolved without hostility or confrontation.

Religious activity is not only psychologically beneficial but may also help cure physical disability. Many sick worshippers report cures following pleas to the divine.

Starkly monotheistic in doctrine, Islam provides fewer religious activities for women. Religious Muslim women may fast during the month of Ramzan and pray five times each day to Allah (at home rather than in a mosque as their husbands do), but most women do not pray that often. Muslim festivals are few and unelaborate, but women participate in all of them. The most important holiday is Mithi Id, celebrating the end of Ramzan. After prayers, dressed in bright new clothing, separate groups of men and women visit neighbours and relatives to exchange Id greetings. Holiday food is prepared and eaten. On other occasions women visit famous Muslim saints' tombs to seek boons. Shi'ite Muslims, in the minority in India, observe Muhurram, commemorating the martyrdom of the Prophet's grandson. Women gather to hear a priest read a traditional text telling of Hussein's demise; an occasion that has been described as follows:

> A few hundred women arrived, dressed in deep mourning, sat on the rush mats with tears coursing down their cheeks and listened to the priest. While they beat their breasts in delicate anguish, they gazed slyly at the marriageable girls of the community out of the corners of their eyes (to find matches for their sons and nephews). The older women, however, were more sincere. They

thumped their chests so violently and wept so copiously that they sometimes fainted.

. . . [The women next to me] were behaving strangely. . . .Tears rolled down their red, agonized faces; the knuckles of their fists beat a violent tattoo on the floor. They writhed uncontrollably and from time to time their heads fell back against the wall on which we leaned with a resounding whack. (Ishvani, 1947, pp. 99 and 102).

Ideally, every Muslim should read the Koran in Arabic at least once. Even otherwise illiterate girls are guided through the sacred book by a teacher. Thus religion may provide an uneducated girl with her only contact with reading and add to her sense of dignity.

Amusements

In recreation as in so many others aspects of Indian women's life, restraint is a key principle. Women find most of their pleasures and relaxation in the course of their daily lives in their homes and local communities in the company of other women. For most, life is far from hedonistic, and young wives confined to their courtyards often complain of boredom.

One small pleasure can be enjoyed daily by most women: chewing the mildly intoxicant betel nut and leaf, mixed with a pinch of tobacco or a pungent cardamom seed. In some parts of North India, village women also smoke the hookah (water pipe) or an occasional cigarette. On Holi, some village women drink a marijuana tea that makes them feel giddy. But even in castes which permit the drinking of alcohol, women rarely do so.

Some women enjoy handicrafts. Nimkhera women decorate their housefronts with mud bas-reliefs, and some also create elaborate earthen grille-works around the shelf on which water jars are kept and around the sacred basil plant which stands before most homes. Girls visiting their parents make prettily shaped papier-mâché bowls, and some weave small baskets and make beadwork chokers and patchwork fans. It is to women that almost all of India's traditional non-professional art work is attributable (Untracht, 1968, p. 149). In cities, educated women knit sweaters, paint pictures, read books and fashion magazines, and write letters. They may also find amusement in visiting sari and bangle shops.

Halkibai shapes a papier-mâché bowl.

Among traditional villagers, women almost never gather merely to enjoy each other's company, and they have no formal associations. Neighbours chat about village events and occasionally tell stories as they clean grain, make rope or huddle around a warm fire on a winter night. Larger parties are held to sing in celebration of a religious holiday, a wedding, or a birth. These events are so frequent that village women gather to sing scores of times each year. Clustered together on a dimly lit verandah, women and girls of all ages talk and sing traditional songs appropriate to the occasion. The night-time songfest goes on for hours, ending only when the hostess passes out sweets or boiled grain. Clutching their little bundles of refreshments, their bracelets and ankle ornaments softly jingling, the sari-draped figures walk through dark and quiet lanes to their homes. City women, too, enjoy singing at weddings and at special gatherings devoted to singing hymns.

*To welcome the gods to her home, Motibai draws
auspicious designs on her porch.*

*Enjoying the freedom of their mature years, women gather
in Junagarh, Gujarat, at a Hindu religious fair.*

Middle and upper-class urban couples sometimes go together to Western-style dinner and tea parties, but even there women tend to gather in one room and men in another.

City women also attend movies — escorted by a brother, father, husband, or son. They enjoy the lengthy dramas featuring religious themes, famous heroes of the epics, never-ending singing and dancing, and involved romance. D.P. Mukerji has written, "Indian films are, in fact, one long exercise in wish fulfilment and offer tempting avenues of escape from the drudgery of family life and disappointments in the love that-might-have-been" (1951, p. 797). The lilting film songs are very popular throughout India.

Throughout most of North and Central India, women who value their reputations do not dance except under certain limited circumstances. Typically, the "dancing girl" is also a prostitute; to traditional villagers, the image of the completely debased and public woman of no morals is best conjured up by the phrase "dancing naked in public." Even prostitutes are well dressed when they perform their public dances. Film stars who dance in scanty clothing in movies may amuse urban viewers, but they scandalize most villagers. Village women who allowed me to photograph them extracted a promise that I would not sell their pictures to Bombay cinema producers who would "make the photo dance in a movie." In Nimkhera, women and girls celebrate Holi by performing slow-moving walk-through reel dances and some women perform brief but energetic dances to bless a groom at a wedding or *gauna* ceremony, but no men other than the groom may watch these hurried performances. In contrast, men publicly join in a vigorous stick dance many times during the rainy season. Once or twice a year prostitutes or female impersonators visit the village; women and girls stand in the dark shadows behind the enthusiastic male viewers to watch the dancing performances.

In some educated urban circles, girls are taught classical dancing by a dance master. Young schoolgirls give singing and dancing programmes, but after puberty they usually perform only within the family circle, if at all. In her autobiography, Ishvani wrote of secretly indulging a passion for dancing, all the while fearful that her stepmother would catch her at this "shameless" pastime (1947, p. 67). But the women of Mathura, Lord Krishna's birthplace, are famous for their devotional dancing, and at not-too-distant Karauli women dance before the goddess. Gypsy women sometimes join in a circle dance. Only among tribal peoples do men and women openly dance together. On moonlit nights unmarried young people gather together to drink toddy and dance with their arms around each other in long lines to the sound of drumming and beautifully haunting singing. Among the Muria of Bastar District, young couples then retire to the dormitory where all teenagers sleep.

Neighbour women sometimes play pachisi, but village females do not normally play vigorous sports or games. Their most energetic play is during the rainy month of Savan, when girls don bright clothes and frolic on swings to celebrate the promise of fertility of the land — and themselves. City schoolgirls play volleyball and table tennis, and a few years ago a team of young Indian women attempted to scale Mount Everest. In some cities a few women ride bicycles. Well-to-do women of the larger cities also belong to sports clubs where they can meet to swim, play tennis, and have soft drinks or tea. Anglo-Indians have been particularly active in organized sports.

Itinerant entertainers visit many villages to amuse and amaze spectators with trained monkeys and bears, magic shows, sword-swallowing acts, devotional songs, and hand-cranked peep shows.

Dating is severely disapproved in most circles, and even a married woman should never publicly admit that she enjoys sex. However, making love is an extremely common amusement. In some villages it is assumed that any healthy young woman not living with a vigorous husband will find a lover, and this has certainly happened in many cases. It is for this reason that the parents of a Nimkhera Brahman man who died tragically in his early twenties did not object when his young widow remarried. "She was very young; it would have been hard for her to bear it," her former father-in-law explained to me. If she had become promiscuous, the entire family would have been shamed.

In the Himalyan village studied by Gerald Berreman, it is assumed that any man and woman who have ever met alone in the jungle have had sexual relations (1963, p. 173).

Although most women say a man's sexual desires are always stronger than a woman's, Tejibai, a young Thakur mother, once told me jokingly that she was looking forward to her husband's return from a pilgrimage, "so we can do it day and night." One Nimkhera man and his wife happily admit to having sexual relations twenty-five nights of every month.

Few women travel just for pleasure: outings and journeys are undertaken only for specific, approved purposes. Males have much more freedom to gallivant, although they ideally combine errands with pleasure.

Women often visit relatives, either for long stays with their parents or cousins or, in cities, for just an afternoon. Groups of village women sometimes walk to neighbouring villages to pay ceremonial calls or gather for religious picnics near a shrine. Virtually the only events village Hindu women admit to attending "just for fun" are the country fairs; yet these fairs, too, are centered around religious dramas. Groups of men and women go on pilgrimages to distant holy cities, but it would be almost unthinkable for a group of village women to go to a nearby town just to see a movie.

For most Indian women, visiting holy sites remains the most delightful recreation. Sunalini Nayudu, my former assistant, now in charge of training women to work in villages as social workers, recently wrote of an educational tour on which she led her students to visit social welfare institutions in North India:

Practically all our trainees are married women; some are even grandmothers, having been married at the age of 10, 12, 13 — by the time they reach the age of 30 to 35 they have become grandmothers. Except for three Christian girls, all are Hindus. Taking all these mothers and grandmothers to Allahabad and Varanasi (holy cities on the sacred Ganges River) on an educational tour was really difficult. We-visited more temples than social institutions. It was more like a pilgrims' trip, with everyone consulting the holy men and having huge *tikas* [auspicious red marks] put on their foreheads. Forty-three such charges were on our hands, and having just three days in each place to visit many social institutions at the appointed time was really too much for us four teachers. All these trainees are village girls who have lived all their lives in an orthodox atmosphere, fearing God and the devil to a great extent. They were singing religious songs the whole time. We vowed never to choose a holy place for an educational tour again (1971, personal communication).

Latif Khan and Birjis Jahan occasionally travel with their children to visit relatives in Bombay. There, far from conservative Bhopal, Birjis Johan doffs her *burka* (cloak) and, in the company of a sophisticated cousin or her husband, visits shops and cinemas. Many middle and upper-class urban families travel together on trains and buses to visit relatives in distant areas and even to vacation in beautiful Kashmir or the foothills of the Himalayas. The very wealthy even travel abroad. But for many the enjoyment of such a trip is enhanced if it can be combined with visits to holy pilgrimage sites.

The Older Woman

Rambai's mother-in-law, Hirabai, is now over sixty years old. Her beauty has long since faded, and she wears little of the jingling jewellery that once signalled her presence — her silver and gold are now worn by her granddaughters-in-law. She considers it a great misfortune that she is a widow, since every woman hopes to die before her husband. The very word *widow* (*rānd*) connotes inauspiciousness and sorrow. But she does not regret being old; she takes pride in her position as the senior member of a large and reasonably prosperous joint family. She has enjoyed years as a mother and a grandmother, with her sons, *bahus,* and grandchildren living with her. Sometimes she remembers with sorrow the deaths of two baby sons and a daughter decades ago, but more often she proudly contemplates the joy her living descendants have brought her. She has been fortunate enough to welcome great-grandchildren to her family. Now older than most men in the village, she rarely needs to veil her face. She is free to attend all festive and social events denied her as a young *bahu*, long ago. Now she seldom cooks, leaving kitchen work mostly to her *bahus*, but she continues to help care for the small children and perform other household tasks. Further, she is in charge of keeping the family funds safe and telling her sons what to bring from the bazaar each week. She is a useful and needed member of the family.

Not so prosperous is Santibai, an old woman of the Daroi Gond tribe, who lives but a few lanes from Hirabai. Santibai is a wizened widow, living with her son and his wife and child. Labourers on Latif Khan's land, Santibai and her family work long hours in the fields— planting, weeding, and harvesting — while the baby plays beside them. In the evening they return to their small house of sticks and mud to cook a simple meal. Santibai keeps the family treasury, but there is usually very little in it. Years ago she lost four little sons and a daughter, and her young *bahu* has already lost three babies. But the old woman is blessed with a son and *bahu* who respect and love her. Her daughter, married in a nearby village, visits five or six times a year.

Srimati Parvati Misra lives comfortably in a town near Delhi with her husband, a school principal, and her youngest son and his wife and children. She enjoys her quiet domestic life and spends much time in the kitchen preparing foods she knows her husband and son will enjoy. Most of the rest of the housework is taken care of by her *bahu* and a servant girl. Srimati Misra looks forward to receiving letters from her eldest son, a lecturer at a college in England. A few years ago when he and his wife had a new baby, they invited her to stay with them for a year. She went, but after only a few months she returned home because her husband and younger son wrote of how much they missed her in the household.

All these women have in common the fact that they have never seen a retirement village or an old people's home. In the final years of their lives they are surrounded by their families and are busily performing tasks useful to themselves and to others, never doubting their roles as loved and needed women.

Throughout her life the Indian woman may encounter unhappiness and frustration: poverty, illness, painful separation from her parents and her daughters, the death of a child, a dictatorial husband or a domineering mother-in-law. But with rare exception, she has a clear sense of what she is and what she should be doing. When, as a child, she grinds a bowl of grain into soft flour; as a *bahu*, she shyly presents her newborn son to her husband; or, as an adult woman, she sees her demure daughter properly married to a boy of a respectable family, she receives no overt expression of praise or gratitude. But she knows that she is doing what is expected of her and feels a deep sense of achievement. Except for the most unfortunate — the very ill, homeless beggars, or women deprived of near kinsmen — Indian women are reasonably happy and fulfilled. Every woman complains, for to pride oneself on one's good fortune would be to tempt the fates, but few women would trade places with anyone else.

Notes

1. I wish to express my gratitude to the National Institute of Mental Health for supporting my research in India from 1966 to 1967 and to the American Council of Learned Societies for a postdoctoral grant. I also wish to express my appreciation to Kumari Sunalini Nayudu, my assistant in the field, and to the people of "Nimkhera."

    I am indebted to Suzanne Hanchett, Jerome Jacobson, Mildred Luschinsky, Sunalini Nayudu, Mimi Sharma, and W.G. Sheorey for their helpful comments on an earlier draft of this chapter.

    All the personal and village names in this paper are pseudonyms. In this chapter, diacritics are used only at the first appearance of each Hindi word.

    All photographs in this volume are © Doranne Jacobson, with the exception of the photographs of Ellora statuary and of the former Queen Mother of Jaipur, which are © Jerome Jacobson, and the photograph of Santal women, which is © Mimi Sharma.

2. Helen Gideon has written a warm and intimate account of the birth of a Sikh baby at his mother's home in the Punjab (Gideon, 1962).

3. *Melia azadirachta.*

4. Dietary restrictions vary greatly from caste to caste and are an essential element of caste identity. Generally, vegetarian castes rank higher than meat eaters, although the high-ranking former warrior castes (Rajputs and Thakurs) are non-vegetarian. Many Indians find the thought of eating meat, especially beef or pork, disgusting. In Khalapur, Rajput women are vegetarian; when their menfolk want meat, they cook it themselves, away from the kitchen (Minturn and Hitchcock, 1966, p. 44).

5. There are a few low castes in Western and Northern India which lack clans, and in a few areas and among certain low-caste peoples of North India, marriages within the clan are acceptable

(Mandelbaum, 1970, pp. 144-148; Mimi Sharma, personal communication).

6. For further information concerning legislation affecting Indian women, see Luschinsky, 1963.

7. In the Dehra Dun area of the Himalayas, brothers share their wife or wives and divorce and remarriage are frequent. A woman works hard in her husband's village but is allowed much freedom in her parental home. In the Jaunsar-Bawar sector, she is free to have love affairs and even become pregnant in her natal village (Majumdar, 1960, pp. 124-132; Berreman, 1963, pp. 171-173).

8. For detailed information on women in ancient and medieval India, see Altekar, 1962, and Thomas, 1964.

9. In Nimkhera, a young divorcee of tribal descent became promiscuous. The village elders warned her father to control her behaviour, but when the girl continued her sexual activities, a group of irate men attacked and beat her father. Clearly, the villagers faulted the father for not exercising his paternal authority.

10. In a paper about an alternately benevolent and malevolent goddess of South India, Brenda Beck has shown that the goddess's vacillation is linked to her ambivalent position as unmarried and chaste yet attended by a would-be lover. Only the married goddess (for example, Parvati, the wife of Shiva, whose power is transferred to her husband, is completely benevolent (Beck, 1971).

11. Village women of all castes handle cow dung as a matter of course. Cow dung is considered a purifying and cleansing agent, although adult human fecal material is regarded as filthy and polluting. Cow dung is in fact a very valuable substance, providing India's major source of fuel and fertilizer. Westerners sometimes wonder why Indians tolerate so many aged and skinny cattle in their villages and cities, but until they die these cattle are capable of converting otherwise useless scrub grass and vegetable garbage into useful cow dung (see Harris, 1966).

12. In a survey of forty-six peasant communities around the world, Michaelson and Goldschmidt found that of six societies in which women did much of the agricultural labour, male dominance was inconsistent or absent in five. Of thirty-seven peasant communities in which the female contribution to agriculture was relatively small, male dominance was strong in thirty-four. Feminine control of other significant economic activities such as sericulture, marketing, or the collection and sale of shellfish did not appear to diminish male dominance (Michaelson and Goldschmidt, 1971, p. 333).

13. Indians who are aware of the fact that Westerners do not always
     bathe daily and use toilet paper to cleanse themselves are disgusted
     by these habits. Traditional Hindu parents who send their children
     to missionary schools where they come in contact with "dirty
     Christians" insist that the children bathe when they come home
     from school.

14. For a history of the women's movement and a survey of modern
     women's activities in India, see Baig, 1958. For all their hard
     work, relatively few women have achieved eminence. In "Who's
     Who In India", published in the *Times of India Yearbook* for 1971,
     only 18 of some 600 entries are women — or 3 per cent. (This
     roster was presumably compiled by men.)

15. Several factors in Indian society supportive of the educated
     working woman have been outlined in a paper by Karen Leonard.
     Some of these factors are:

     1) Adolescent Indian girls of educated families are
         encouraged to concentrate both on schoolwork and on
         household and religious duties rather than to establish
         relationships with boys, as American girls do.
         Anticipating an arranged marriage, the Indian girl does
         not need to divide her attention between her education
         and attempts to find a husband for herself, and she avoids
         the "sex object" aspects of western female adolescence
         which often prove dysfunctional for a career woman.

     2) The earning power of an educated and employed bride
         may be an important asset in arranging her marriage.

     3) The separation of sex and family life from the white
         collar working world seems to mitigate sexual
         competition and conflicts in the Indian occupational
         context.

     4) Separation of the sexes in educational facilities is
         largely responsible for the high number of women
         academics of all ranks in India today, just as feminine
         modesty and sex segregation have encouraged the
         training of large numbers of women doctors (Leonard,
         1973).

Bibliography

Altekar, A.S.: *The Position of Women in Hindu Civilization*, Motilal
     Banarsidass, Delhi, 1962.

Baig, Tara Ali (ed.): *Women of India*, The Publications Division, Government of India, Delhi, 1958.

Basham, A.L.: *The Wonder That Was India*, Grove Press, New York, 1959.

Basu, Tara Krishna: *The Bengal Peasant from Time to Time*, Asia Publishing House, Bombay, 1962.

Beck, Brenda E.F.: "Mariyamman: The Vacillating Goddess," unpublished ms., 1971.

Berreman, Gerald D.: *Hindus of the Himalayas*, Oxford University Press, Bombay, 1963.

Carstairs, G. Morris: *The Twice Born: A Study of a Community of High-Caste Hindus*, The Hogarth Press, London, 1957. (1967 ed., Indiana University Press, Bloomington, Ind., and London.)

Cormack, Margaret: *The Hindu Woman*, Teachers College, Columbia University, New York, 1953.

Elwin, Verrier: "Tribal Women," in Tara Ali Baig (ed.), *Women of India,* The Publications Division, Government of India, Delhi, 1958.

————:*The Kingdom of the Young*, Oxford University Press, London and Bombay, 1968. (Abridged from *The Muria and Their Ghotul,* 1947.)

Freed, Ruth S.: "The Legal Process in a Village in North India: The Case of Maya," *Transactions of the New York Academy of Sciences*, series II, vol. 33, no. 4, pp. 423-435, 1971.

Freed, Stanley A., and Ruth S. Freed: "Spirit Possession as Illness in a North Indian Village," *Ethnology*, vol. 3, no. 2, pp. 152-171, 1964.

Gideon, Helen: "A Baby is Born in the Punjab," *American Anthropologist,* vol. 64, pp. 1220-1234, 1962.

Harris, Marvin: "The Cultural Ecology of India's Sacred Cattle," *Current Anthropology*, vol. 7, pp. 51-66, 1966.

Ishvani: *Girl in Bombay*, The Pilot Press Ltd., London, 1947.

Leonard, Karen: "Educated Women at Work: Supportive Factors in Indian Society". Paper presented at the Annual Meeting of the Association for Asian Studies, Chicago, 1973.

Lewis, Oscar: *Village Life in Northern India*, Vintage Books, Random House, Inc., New York, 1965.

Luschinsky, Mildred Stroop: *The Life of Women in a Village of North India*, Ph.D. dissertation, Cornell University, Ithaca, N.Y., 1962.

————:"The Impact of Some Recent Indian Government Legislation on the Women of an Indian Village," *Asian Survey*, vol. 3, no. 12, pp. 573-583, 1963.

Madan, T.N.: *Family and Kinship: A Study of the Pandits of Rural Kashmir*, Asia Publishing House, Bombay, 1965.

Majumdar, D.N.: *Himalayan Polyandry*, Asia Publishing House, Bombay, 1960.

Mandelbaum, David, G.: *Society in India*, 2 vols., Univeristy of California Press, Berkeley, 1970.

Marshall, John F.: "What Does Family Planning Mean to an Indian Villager?" Paper presented at the Annual Meeting of the American Anthropological Association, New York, 1971.

Mayer, Adrian C.: *Caste and Kinship in Central India*, Routledge and Kegan Paul, Ltd., London, 1960.

Michaelson, Evalyn Jacobson, and Walter Goldschmidt: "Female Roles and Male Dominance among Peasants," *Southwestern Journal of Anthropology*, vol. 27, no. 4, pp. 330-352, 1971.

Minturn, Leigh, and John T. Hitchcock: *The Rājputs of Khalapur, India,* Six Cultures Series, vol. 3, John Wiley and Sons, Inc., New York, 1966.

Mukerji, D.P.:"The Status of Indian Women," *International Social Science Bulletin*, vol. 3, no. 4, pp. 793-801, 1951.

Thomas, Paul: *Indian Women through the Ages*, Asia Publishing House, Bombay, 1964.

Untracht, Oppi: "Ritual Wall and Floor Decoration in India," *Graphis*; vol. 24, no. 136, pp. 148-178, 1968.

Women and the Hindu Tradition

Susan S. Wadley

Introduction

Most of the world views Hindu women as degraded, downtrodden slaves. Yet the percentages of Indian women in the professions compare favourably with those of the West: Indian women comprise 7.1 per cent of the doctors, 1.2 per cent of the lawyers and 10.9 per cent of the scientists, in spite of incredibily low literacy rates for the over-all female population (18.4 per cent of Indian women are literate). Clearly, Indian women present a paradoxical situation for the interpreter of South Asian society. The view of the Hindu woman as downtrodden represents one behavioural reality; her participation in the highest political and social arenas is another undeniable reality.

This situation cannot be fully explored in one short paper and this paper is concerned only with Hindu ideology and practice relating to women and their roles: the aim is to suggest factors of Hindu belief and practice which may affect changes in women's secular roles in South Asia. I am concerned first with Hindu definitions of femaleness. For this discussion the primary source materials are both ancient and modern scriptures and mythology. Although the village practitioner of Hinduism may not be consciously aware of the sophisticated textual statements sometimes referred to, he/she has command of myths and folk beliefs which restate many classical statements. Part I continues with a discussion of Hindu norms and expectations for women's behaviour. Again, the sources are primarily literary traditions. In Part II, I turn to a consideration of women's actual place in Hindu practice. Here I draw primarily on anthropological descriptions. Last, in Part III, I suggest some factors of Hindu orthopraxy which affect or may affect changes in women's secular roles in South Asia.

Part I

HINDU IDEOLOGY AND WOMEN

In discussing women in Hinduism, one must first consider how the nature of femaleness is portrayed in Hindu ideology.[1] Beliefs about what a female is underlie both the role models religious figures present and advocate for women and the place of women in Hindu religious practice. These beliefs about the nature of femaleness also affect the potential for change in the roles of women in Hindu South Asia.

Femaleness: The Hindu Perspective

The concept of the female in Hinduism presents an important duality: on the one hand, the woman is fertile, benevolent — the bestower; on the other, she is aggressive, malevolent — the destroyer. A popular statement characterizes the goddess in all her manifestations: thus, "in times of prosperity she indeed is Lakshmi, who bestows prosperity in the homes of men; and in times of misfortune, she herself becomes the goddess of misfortune and brings about ruin."[2] In a similar vein, Brenda Beck discusses the name of the South Indian goddess, Māriyamman, noted for her dual character. Using Sanskrit and Tamil etymologies, *māri* means death or rain while the folk etymology has *māri* meaning "to change", while *amman* means "lady" or "mother"[3] so that the goddess is in fact recognized as the "changing lady"— a clear acknowledgement of her dual character. Both goddesses and women — for there is no differentiation of superhuman and human in Hindu belief[4] — reflects these characteristics of the female as both benevolent, fertile bestower and malevolent, aggressive destroyer.[5]

Two facets of femaleness relate to this duality, and perhaps provide a cultural logic for it. The female is first of all *śakti* (energy/power), the energizing principle for the universe. The female is also *prakṛti* (Nature) — the undifferentiated Matter of the Universe. I shall examine each of these in turn, elaborating their role in illuminating the dual character of the Hindu female.[6]

In Hindu cosmology, the universal substratum from which all being arises is known as *brahman*: "Invisible, inactive, beyond grasp, without qualifications, inconceivable, indescribable...ever aloof from manifestation."[7] From this unmanifest substance, beings are made manifest through the tension created by the opposition of cohesion (Viṣṇu) and disintegration (Śiva).[8] This tension defines *śakti* — the manifesting power, the creative principle. The Hindu notion of divinity rests upon that of *śakti* (power)[9]: greater power is what distinguishes gods from men. So, *śakti* underlies both creation and all power in the Hindu world is based on femaleness — there would be no being without energy/power.

Although without the female there would be no energy in the universe, in fact all beings contain their share of *śakti*, their share of power and energy, with which they are endowed by birth along with their defining qualities (*guna*) and actions *karma*).[10] Furthermore, the *śakti* that is part of an individual at birth can be increased or decreased through later actions. For example, a woman by being a true and devoted wife (*pativrat*, literally "one who fasts for her husband"), increases her *śakti*. Various austerities, particularly sexual abstinence, also increase a person's *śakti*. But even though both men and women have *śakti* as a personal attribute, the woman embodies *śakti*, the original energy of the universe.

A common metaphor is that woman is the field or earth into which man puts his seed. "By the sacred tradition the woman is declared to be the soil, the man is declared to be the seed; the production of all corporeal beings (takes place) through the union of the soil with the seed."[11] The image of field or earth also symbolizes a second facet of femaleness: woman is *prakṛti* (Nature). Nature is the active female counterpart of the Cosmic Person, *puruṣa,* the inactive or male aspect. Moreover, Nature is Matter; the Cosmic Person is spirit. But whereas *prakṛti* represents the undifferentiated matter of Nature, *puruṣa* provides the Spirit, which is a structured code. Thus, *puruṣa* (Cosmic Person) is code (differentiated Spirit), as opposed to *prakṛti*, which is Nature (undifferentiated Matter). The union of Spirit and Matter, code and noncode, inactive and active, leads to the creation of the world with all of its differentiated life forms. No life exists without both Matter and Spirit; *prakṛti* and *puruṣa* are in all beings. This relationship can be represented diagrammatically (Figure 1).

The unity of *puruṣa-prakṛti* underlies the beliefs regarding biological conception. Here we find that the male contributes the hard substances: the bones, nerves, and structuring elements of a child. The woman contributes the soft substances: the flesh, skin, blood, and unstructured parts of a child.[12] Whichever partner dominated at the time of conception determines the sex of the child. The *Laws of Manu* speak on this point: "On comparing the seed and the receptacle, the seed is declared to be more important: for, the offspring of all created beings is

Figure 1.

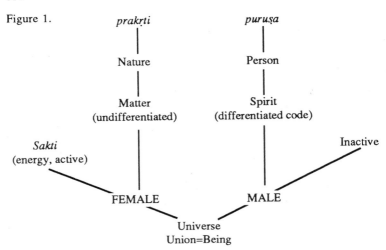

marked by the characteristics of the seed."[13] The hard substance (seed) is structure (culture?) as opposed to the soft substance which is non-structure (Nature?). Women, then, are automatically more Nature than men. The Nature and non-structure in them dominates over coded Spirit and structure.

Uniting these two facets of femaleness, women are both energy/power and Nature;[14] and Nature is uncultured. In fact, the Aryan vernacular languages of ancient India are called Prakrit ("Uncultured" or "Natural"), as opposed to the priestly religious language Sanskrit (literally, "Cultured"). Uncultured Power is dangerous. The equation "Woman=Power+Nature=Danger" represents the essence of femaleness as it underlies Hindu religious belief and action about women. The equation summarizes a conception of the world order that explains the woman/goddess as the malevolent, aggressive destroyer.

As we saw above, however, the Hindu view of woman is not only one of danger —Woman is also the benevolent, fertile bestower. Fertility is easily comprehended, for woman is the necessary receptor of man's seed: she, like the closely conjoined images of cow and earth, represents growth, prosperity and fertility. Benevolence and goodness, however, are more complex. One possible explanation of female benevolence is that woman is capricious, therefore she sometimes uses her Uncultured Power for human benefit. Recent studies have provided a sharper insight:[15] "good females—goddess or human—are controlled by males; that is, Culture controls Nature."

A popular myth presents the male controlling dangerous, female Power, thus rendering that Power positive and benevolent. Kali the Black One, one of the many wives of Śiva, was sent by the gods to oppose a giant and his army when the gods could not control him themselves. Kali defeated the demons. Delighted with her victory she performed a savage killing dance so furiously that the earth trembled beneath her weight and its destruction appeared imminent. The gods, frightened and unable to stop her, sent Śiva, to induce her to desist. Entranced in her bloody rampage and not noticing him, Kali continued killing and dancing. So Śiva lay down at her feet. When eventually Kali was about to step on him, she realized that it was her husband upon whom she was placing her feet — an inexcusable act for the Hindu wife. She stopped her rampage and the earth was saved — because her husband had regained control over her.[16]

The benevolent goddesses in Hindu pantheon are those who are properly married and who have transferred control of their sexuality (Power/Nature) to their husbands. Symbolically, a woman is "a part" of her husband, his "half-body". Rules for proper conduct mandate that she transfer her powers, as they accumulate, to her husband for his use. Mythology is replete with stories of the properly chaste wife who aids her husband in winning his battle by virtue of her proper behaviour and ensuing transfer of power (it is probable that females, in the last analysis, win all battles). In the following two myths the gods' triumph depends on the control of female power.

1. There was once a continuous twelve-year war between the gods and the demons. The gods were losing badly and Indra felt that there was no way to avoid losing his life. At this time, Indrani said to her husband, "Don't be afraid. I am a faithful wife. I will tell you one way by which you can win and protect yourself." After saying this much, Indrani bound the *rakhī* (a bracelet, literally "protection") on the wrist of her husband. After she bound the *rakhī*, Indra again went to war and defeated all the demons.[17]

2. There was a demon named Jalandhar. He had a very beautiful and faithful wife name Branda. Because of the power accruing to him from the faithfulness of his wife, the demon conquered the whole world. The gods were in trouble and arrived at this solution: changing a dead body into the shape of Jalandhar, Viṣṇu threw it into the courtyard of Branda's family. Then Viṣṇu gave life to the body and, in this way, Branda embraced another man and marred

her faithfulness. Owing to her loss of faithfulness, Jalandhar's power was weakened and Viṣṇu killed him in a big war.[18]

According to Hindu cosmology, if a female controls her own sexuality, she is changeable; she represents both death and fertility; she is both malevolent and benevolent. If, however, she loses control of her sexuality (Power/Nature) by transferring it to a man, she is portrayed as consistently benevolent. There are two images, then, of the woman in Hinduism, linked by the basic conceptions of the nature of femaleness: the fact that the female is both *śakti* (Power/Energy), and *prakṛti* (Nature).

As Power and Nature, and controlling her own sexuality, the female is potentially destructive and malevolent:

KALI (the Black One): "Bearing the strange skull topped staff, decorated with a garland of skulls, clad in a tiger's skin, very appalling owing to her emaciated flesh, with gaping mouth, fearful with her tongue lolling out, having deep-sunk reddish eyes and filling the regions of the sky with her roars..."[19]

With the control of her sexuality transferred to men, the female is fertile and benevolent:

LAKSHMI (the Goddess of Fortune): "She who springs forth from the body of all the gods has a thousand, indeed countless, arms, although her image is shown with but eighteen. Her face is white, made from the light streaming from the lord of sleep (Śiva). Her arms made of the substance of Viṣṇu are deep blue: her round breasts made of *soma*, the sacrificial ambrosia, are white. . . . She wears a gaily coloured lower garment, brilliant garlands, and a veil. . . . He who worships the Transcendent Divinity of Fortune becomes the lord of all the worlds."[20]

The Ideal Hindu Woman

Understanding the dual character of the Hindu female's essential nature (her *śakti* and *prakṛti*), provides a backdrop for understanding the rules and role models for women in Hindu South Asia. A central theme of the norms and guidelines for proper female behaviour, especially in the male-dominated classical literature, is that men must control women and their power. But whether in classical texts or folk traditions, the dual character of the Hindu female emerges definitely, and is seen most clearly in the roles of wife (good, benevolent, dutiful, controlled) and mother (fertile, but dangerous, uncontrolled).

I draw on a variety of material to explicate these roles. Rules for proper conduct are explicitly laid down in Hindu lawbooks, collectively known as the *Dharmaśāstras* (the Rules of Right Conduct). Mythology, written and oral, in Sanskrit and in the vernaculars, provides many examples of female behaviour and its consequences, thus setting up explicit role models for the Hindu woman. Folklore yields yet other beliefs about female behaviour. Finally, social organization and structure mesh with, allow for, and reinforce these beliefs about the proper conduct of women.[21]

The dominant norms for the Hindu woman concern her role as wife. Classical Hindu laws focus almost exclusively on this aspect of the woman. Role models and norms for mothers, daughters, sisters, etc., are less prominent and are more apt to appear in folklore and vernacular traditions. In addition, in most written traditions, the emphasis is on woman's behaviour in relationship to men: wife/husband; mother/son; daughter/father; sister/brother. Role models for female behaviour concerning other females (mother/daughter; sister/sister) are almost non-existent in any of the literature. In contrast, two female/female relationships — mother-in-law/daughter-in-law and husband's sister/wife — are common themes in folklore and oral traditons but not in the more authoritative religious literature. These two relationships are vital to the well-being of woman, but of little concern to men.[22] That they do not occur as important themes in the male-oriented and written literature of the Sanskrit tradition is not surprising. Rather, they surface in the popular oral traditions of women themselves. The male orientation in classical literature is also apparent in differing depictions of the husband/wife and brother/sister relationships. With these factors in mind, let us examine norms for female behaviour in Hindu South Asia.

The basic rules for women's behaviour are expressed in the following passages from the *Laws of Manu*, written early in the Christian era. These passages stress the need to control women because of the evils of the female character. The first set is excerpted from a section dealing with the duties of women.

> By a young girl, by a young woman, or even by an aged one, nothing must be done independently, even in her own house.

In childhood a female must be subject to her father, in youth to her husband, when her lord is dead to her sons; a woman must never be independent....

Though destitute of virtue, or seeking pleasure (elsewhere), or devoid of good qualities, (yet) a husband must be constantly worshipped as a god by a faithful wife....

By violating her duty towards her husband, a wife is disgraced in this world; (after death) she enters the womb of a jackal, and is tormented by diseases, (the punishment) of her sin.

She who controlling her thoughts, words, and deeds, never slights her lord, resides (after death) with her husband (in heaven), and is called a virtuous (wife).[23]

The following set is excerpted from the section regarding the duties of wife and husband.

Day and night, woman must be kept in dependency by the males (of) their (families), and if they attach themselves to sensual enjoyments, they must be kept under one's control. . . .

Considering that the highest duty of all castes, even weak husbands (must) strive to guard their wives. . . .

Women do not care for beauty, nor is their attention fixed on age: (thinking) "(it is enough that) he is a man," they give themselves to the handsome and the ugly.

Through their passion for men, through their mutable temper, through their natural heartlessness, they become disloyal towards their husbands, however carefully they are guarded in this (world).

Knowing their disposition, which the Lord of creatures laid in them at the creation, to be such, (every) man should most strenuously exert himself to guard them.[24]

Thus, women, because of their evil inclinations and birth, are to be kept under the control of men at all stages of their lives. The ideal women are those who do not strive to break these bonds of control. Moreover, the salvation and happiness of women revolve around their virtue and chastity as daughters, wives and widows.

These themes are not relegated merely to laws in ancient Sanskrit texts. They continually reappear in later Sanskrit and vernacular writings as well as in oral traditions. One of the most popular religious texts in India is the *Rāmāyana*, found in Sanskrit and most vernaculars.

This text tells the story of Rama, an incarnation of Viṣṇu, sent to earth to destroy the menacing demon Ravana as he was on the verge of upsetting the right moral order of the earth. In the *Rāmāyana*, Rama's wife Sita exemplifies the behaviour of the proper Hindu wife, devotedly following her husband into forest exile for twelve years, and eventually, after being kidnapped for a time by the evil Ravana whom Rama finally destroys, proving her wifely virtue by placing herself on a lighted pyre. When she remains unscathed by the flames, the gods above pour flowers down upon her. In a happy ending her husband accepts her back into his household.

The story of Rama and Sita is well known to most Hindus and is enacted yearly, with greater or lesser splendour, in villages and cities all over India. Pictures of Sita following her husband to the forest, of Sita being kidnapped by Ravana, of Sita on the pyre, are found in a great many homes, on the walls of shops and even in government offices. Famous cinema stars portray Rama and Sita in gargantuan film epics. The message of the *Rāmāyana* is clear, and remarkably similar to that of the more esoteric and inaccessible lawbook written years before.

Sita is to most Hindu women the epitome of the proper wife. She represents the ideal towards which all should strive. Other wives in the Hindu tradition also provide popular role models. Women who have committed *satī* (burning themselves on their husbands' funeral pyres), are acclaimed as goddesses and are honoured with shrines and rituals. The theme of the devoted wife also recurs in connection with calendrical rites. Throughout North India, the women yearly worship Savitri, a goddess whose renown emanates from her extreme devotion to her husband, through which she saves him from the god of death. The story of Savitri is held up as a prime example of the length to which a wife should go in aiding her husband. The good wife saves her husband from death, follows him anywhere, proves her virtue, remains under his control and gives him her power.

These aspects of wifely behaviour and norms are also found in oral traditions, with one crucial addition: the wife's desire for her husband and her dismay at his absence. The theme of love between husband and wife is minor in the classical written literature, whether Sanskrit or vernacular; rather, devotion and dutifulness dominate.[25] However, the traditions of women, those created and perpetuated by women alone, continuously reiterate the longing for a husband's return and their mutual love as these examples illustrate:

> One seer of wheat I will eat for one year,
> > eat for one year,
> (But) I will not allow my husband to go.
> I will keep him before my eyes, (and) I
> > will not allow my husband to go.
> > Or,
> I will not allow you to go for the whole night,
> O beautiful wife, I will not allow you to go
> > for the whole night.[26]

The above discussion emphasizes, as does the literature, the wife's regard for and duties to her husband, not his towards her, though this theme does emerge partially in the oral traditions. The textual traditions contain few injunctions for husbandly behaviour beyond stating that a man must marry to procure sons who are needed for his salvation. One passage from Manu is critical, however, stipulating that men should treat their women well or women will destroy them:

> Women must be honoured and adorned by their fathers, brothers, husbands, and brothers-in-law who desire (their own welfare). . . . The houses on which female relations, not being duly honoured, pronounce a curse, perish completely, as if destroyed by magic. Hence, men who seek (their own) welfare, should always honour women on holidays and festivals with (gifts of) ornaments, clothes and (dainty) food.[27]

Thus, women ideally have some recourse when ill-treated — using their power, they can destroy. But, as we saw above, the best of wives (Sita) will worship their husbands even when abused.

The wifely role is pre-eminent in Hinduism. There are other roles but they are not generally considered normative patterns. Rather, they provide expectations for possible behaviour. The woman as mother is the most critical of the other female roles.

The norms for mothers are less explicit than those for wives. Whereas mythology and lawbooks provide endless examples of the good wife, there are no prime examples of the good mother. However, it is the goddesses as mothers rather than as wives who are village guardians, who are worshipped regularly for their protection and aid, and who are feared. A common name for many goddesses is "Mother"; a goddess is never called "Wife".[28] The wifely role is one of subordination, of devotion in any circumstances, of dutifulness. It is the mother who gives, who must be obeyed, who loves, and who sometimes rejects.[29] Although there are no popular and well-known role models of the mother treating her children well, the mother as a giving, loving individual, although sometimes cruel and rejecting, is present at a sub-conscious but critical level in Hindu thought.[30]

It is the mother transformed into the mother goddess whose devotees are her "children", who is both the bestower and destroyer. Mothers and mother goddesses represent clearly the dual character of Hindu females. They can give and take away, whether from children or devotees. As such, the mother role is not acclaimed as proper or ideal behaviour; rather, her danger is accepted because she is necessary. The mother, also, more than the wife, represents the polluting aspects of the Hindu female as well as representing the purifying milk. In her very biology — a biology necessary for motherhood but not for wifehood — the mother is a contradiction.[31] Last, mothers and the mother goddesses are in control of their sexuality; wives are not. Again, we find the opposition of Lakshmi the wife and Kali the mother.

Hinduism also includes women who are totally malevolent, who never change from an evil maliciousness. These figures, primarily ghosts of women who died in childbirth or in other inauspicious ways, but also witches, are the antithesis of the wife. Beck has suggested that they themselves have lost control of their sexuality and cannot channel their actions towards any positive end.[32] If this interpretation is correct, we obtain the following model of women's roles in Hinduism:

Wife	Mother	Ghost
Culture via male control	Nature but in self control	Nature but out of control
Good	Good/bad	Bad
Subordinated	Worshipped	Appeased

Expectations for other female behaviour can be summarized briefly. The daughter obeys her father and the sister is under the protection of her brother (and fervently desires his protection as he is her primary link with her natal home, especially in North India). The husband's mother is threatening and the husband's sister is an unreliable ally in the husband's home. The expectations for these latter three come mostly from women's oral traditions and reflect women's concern for their day-to-day welfare.

Norms for women in Hinduism derive from two separate, though related, sources. First, the male-dominated literature prescribes control and subordination of the woman. Second, folk and oral traditions, often created and propagated by women, yield norms that are concerned with women's welfare and emphasize the behaviour of crucial male kin (the husband as lover, the brother as protector, the son as security) as well as female kin (the mother-in-law, the husband's sister). In both these realms we find the mother — not merely as the bearer of children, but also as the mother of the devotee — given extreme importance. The wife is the woman under male control; the mother is the woman in control of herself and her "children". These two figures dominate Hindu thought about women.

Part II

WOMEN IN HINDU RELIGIOUS PRACTICE

Women are active religious practitioners, but they have little religious authority—legitimate, textually sanctioned religious power—which is limited to a small group of men. Paradoxically, however, at the popular level, women are prominent religious participants, both as specialists and non-specialists.

To comprehend the place of women in Hindu religious practice, a brief summary of Hindu social organization is necessary. As is well known, India is a society based on hierarchies, including not only that of caste but also that of kinship and others. The many thousands of castes in India are grouped into five broader social classes: The four varna that originated in ancient times (Brahman, priest; Kṣatriya, warrior; Vaiśya, tradesman; Sudra, worker) and the untouchable. One's membership (via a specific caste) in a particular varna is of little importance most of the time.[33] However, religious activity is sometimes based on varna membership. Specifically, only male members of the first three varna have access to the sacred texts of the *Vedas*, the earliest and most authoritative of the Hindu scriptures. Women, Sudras and Untouchables are not allowed to know, or sometimes even to hear, the *Vedas*. Further restrictions dictate that only Brahman men are to use the *Vedas* in approaching the gods, i.e., in rituals. Thus, men of the top three varna are "Twice Born" (i.e., can wear the sacred thread after a ritual second birth and can know the scriptures). And only Brahman men can perform Vedic rituals. Women, therefore, are no worse off than a great many men in terms of access to the principal authoritative sources of religious power.[34]

Women's access to the *Vedas* and other authoritative texts apparently underwent revision sometime around 600 B.C. Previously, women had been able to undertake fasts for themselves, to hear and learn the *Vedas*, etc. By the time of Manu, women were no longer allowed to hear the *Vedas* or to be major participants in rituals. During this time, perceptions of women as dangerous were developing among the Aryan population. Most probably, these redefinitions of the nature of femaleness affected women's positions in ritual activities.[35]

Fortunately, Hindu religious activity is not based solely on Vedic rituals. The dominant form of ritual activity today is that of *bhakti*, or devotion to a deity. Stemming from the *Bhagwad Gītā* and gaining strength from an anti-Brahman, anti-Vedic movement which started in about 700 A.D., *bhakti* (devotion) and associated ritual forms do not require the services of a priest to approach one's chosen deity.[36] One result is that women have direct access to the gods, and thus to salvation. Today, *pūjā* (devotional ritual) is the principal form of ritual activity in India. Vedic rituals are reserved for life-cycle rites and other male-dominated occasions, such as the opening of a new temple.

Although women may approach the deities directly through *bhakti* rituals, men continue to be recognized as legitimate religious specialists.[37] Males are temple priests; males conduct life-cycle rites; males are the leaders of most public rituals. To understand the female as religious specialist, we must first understand the varying roles of male specialists. Table I summarizes the following discussion of Hindu religious specialists and their social characteristics.

The best-known Indian religious specialists are the priests — the care-takers of temples and the family priests who conduct life-cycle rites. Priests are called by various terms: in North India, two (*pandit, purohit*) refer only to Brahmans; the third *pujārī*) often refers to a lower-caste priest/caretaker of a temple. Normally, *pandits* are temple priests. *Purohits*—family priests—serve their patrons whenever called—sometimes daily, sometimes only for major life-cycle rites. Both must be Brahman males. *Pujārīs* are often lower-caste males who function as priests at the temples of local deities who lack scriptural sanction. In addition, the wives of Brahman priests often act as specialists for life-cycle rites or on other ritual occasions. Generally, they are experts in oral tradition, knowing the songs or stories associated with a particular rite or the unwritten rules for women's correct ritual behaviour. Their husband's role has scriptural sanction; theirs does not.

Table I
Religious Specialization in Hinduism

| | Sex | | Textually |
Specialist	Male	Female	Sanctioned
Priest:			
Pandit	x(B)	(wife)	x(not wife)
Purohit	x(B)	-	x
Pujāri	x	-	-
Actor as God	x(B)	-	?
Shaman	x	x	-
Exorcist	x	-	-
Client in jajmānī	x	(wife)	-
system			
Yogi/Sadhu	x	Seldom	x
Personality	x	x	-
cult-leader			
Devadasī		x	x(South
			India only)

Explanation: "x(B)" means, "must be Brahman".

"wife" in parenthesis indicates "plays role by virtue of wifehood."

A related specialist, often also called *pandit*,[38] is the astrologer — the expert who provides essential information and advice at the time of marriages and births and fixes auspicious dates for journeys and other undertakings. The astrologer is also Brahman and male.[39]

Brahman men dominate still other forms of public ritual. For example, various forms of religious folk operas and plays are found throughout India: in these, the actors portraying a deity are all male — whether the deity be male or female. In fact, the actor *is* the deity, is worshipped as a manifestation of the deity, and because worship of the actor as deity is required, the actor must usually be a Brahman.

Less legitimate participants in public rituals are more likely to be non-Brahman males. Possession rituals, which are not textually sanctioned, appear to be male-dominated; many exorcists and shamans are non-Brahman.[40] Occasionally, a shaman will be female. Shamans and exorcists are religious power figures who lack textual sanction; their power comes from oral traditions and societal recognition. As such, they provide access to religious power for those normally forbidden such access: non-Brahman males and all females.

Other ritual specialists must also be considered, particularly those who are specialists by virtue of their position in the *jajmānī* system, a system of inherited patron-client ties found throughout most of South Asia. Several of the clients (workers who provide services in return for payment) have primarily ritual connections with their patrons. One such client is the barber and his wife, who are necessary figures in most life-cycle rites. In addition to providing services (hair cutting, bathing the new infant, bathing the groom, etc.), they instruct and guide their patrons through the proper ritual forms. The midwife is another such ritual guide. None of these have textual sanction for their roles as religious specialists *per se*, and the instruction they provide is usually based on local traditions.[41]

Other specialists are the sadhus and yogis. Many play no vital role in Hindu religious practice beyond that of a "presence", while others are important lecturers and teachers. Occasionally, a woman will be a yogini. Both male and female yogis are sanctioned by various textual traditions. However, the yogi is considered to be outside the society and its structures. All members of society can thus opt for being non-members. These non-members lacking caste *and* sexual distinctions, are sanctioned by the classical texts.

Popular, non-classical religious specialists in Hinduism can be either male or female—the "personality cult" leader such as Guru Maharajji or The Mother. Women are less often the figureheads of such movements than men; nevertheless, female leaders do recur regularly and are sanctioned by society if not by textual tradition.

Traditionally, only one religious specialist so far as I know was always female — the *devadāsī* (votary of God). Found in South India, the *devadāsīs* were nominally married to the god of the temple, but allowed mates. Their offspring were legitimate: the girls were often, in turn, dedicated to the temple: the boys might become professional musicians. The *devadāsī* was always felt to be distinct from the 'dancer'; her role was definitely religious. Outlawed by the British, the institution of the *devadāsī* fell into disrepute, although its traditions of dance still exist with some descendants and as "dance" are having a revival in both East and West. Traditionally, the *devadāsī* was a religious specialist who had textual sanction only in South India.[42]

These facets of religious specialization are summarized in Table I. Textually recognized specialists are, with one exception, Brahman men. Women and non-Brahman men are religious specialists, but are only rarely sanctioned by authoritative traditions. Thus, women, like low caste men, have religious power in Hinduism, but non-legitimate, non-authoritative power.

Clearly, then, Hindu women have considerable religious involvement. Women as non-specialists are "invisible" religious practitioners, since most of their observances are performed non-publicly (in the home or "domestic" sphere) and their role is not textually sanctioned; indeed, the *Laws of Manu* forbid a woman to fast or participate in rituals without her husband. Yet, if we look at folk religious practices rather than the Hinduism of the texts, women, along with low caste men, are the primary actors.

Women alone perform a large number of the yearly calendrical rituals in both rural and urban India and are essential to most others.[43] In Karimpur, a village in North India, women are the instigators and prime participants in twenty-one of the thirty-three annual rites.[44] Women also dominate nine of the twenty-one annual rites in the village Mohana near Lucknow[45] and are apparently the sole participants in nine of the twenty-two festivals in the annual cycle of Rampur, a village north of Delhi.[46] The exact "great tradition" status of the rites of women — which are all based on *pūjā* (devotional ritual) rather than on Vedic fire sacrifices — has yet to be determined. However, most festivals which can be easily identified as having no great tradition ties are women's festivals. I suspect the if the rituals of women do have textual sanction, their performance varies widely and reflects manifold local differences.

Women's participation in life-cycle rites is definitely part of the little tradition. Women surround these rituals, in which they are mere accessories, with local folk practices. During actual ceremonial time, women's practices clearly dominate: taking a marriage or a birth ceremony as a whole, men's rites take very little time, although the men's rites are a crucial subsidiary (to women).[47]

Much of India is a society with strict sexual segregation. Purdah is generally associated with sexual division of labour and existence in separate worlds.[48] As a corollary, women's concerns are very different from those of men. This separation is found also in religion: the many folk practices of women focus on the prosperity and well-being of the family. Women's rites seek the protection and well-being of crucial kinsmen (especially husband, brother and son), the general prosperity and health of family members, and "good" husbands. This emphasis is found in both calendrical and life-cycle rites. Men's rites do not seek "good" wives or ones who will have a long life; rather, they are concerned with a good wheat crop, ridding the village of disease, etc.[49] It is not surprising to find this religious division of labour in the sexually-segregated purdah society of traditional India.

Women's religious practices are influenced in part by conceptions of the female: her danger provides a justification for her not being an active participant in the most authoritative rites; yet within the domestic sphere women are vital religious practitioners who have developed a subsidiary religious realm of largely folk, or local, non-textual traditions. The sexual segregation of Hindu society also articulates with the role that religion plays in drawing women together: female solidarity is continuously reinforced through religious practices. Moreover, many women's rites relate to their dual roles as wives and mothers. But females, such as the mother goddesses, who protect most villages in India are, nevertheless, frequent objects of worship by both men and women.

Part III

THE POTENTIAL FOR CHANGE

There can be no doubt that Hindu perceptions of femaleness are powerful and pervasive: women are threatening; their sexuality is destructive to men, whose energy they sap, yet their fertility is needed for bearing their sons. One result is deep-seated fear of women aligned with a recognition of their power. Women are thus banned from the dominant sources of religious power and authority, but in fact they obtain power and prosperity through their own religious practices. Moreover, social practices and religious ideology seem to be mutually reinforcing: for example, a woman worships her brother, who is indeed her protector, and she is secluded (and kept in need of protection) because it is believed that she can be dangerous.

Yet India, a country where Hindus constitute 83 per cent of the population, was ruled by a woman. This fact initially appears disconcerting and contrary to most outsiders' impressions of South Asian and Hindu women. Indeed, it contradicts the image of the properly behaved wife given above. But Mrs. Gandhi's role apparently was not a contradiction to the residents of India. A brief look at some Indian impressions of Mrs. Gandhi illustrates an important aspect of the potential for change for Hindu women.

During the height of Mrs. Gandhi's power, a famous Indian artist had completed a portrait of her as Durga riding on a tiger.[50] Durga is one of the goddesses considered to be a wife of Siva. However, she, like Kali, has a vast potential for aggression — and destruction. She does not remain under her husband's control and controls her own sexuality. Yet Durga is generally beneficent (especially in contrast to Kali)[51] and is worshipped as a mother goddess throughout India. We are being told by the artist, I suspect, that Mrs. Gandhi was the mother as epitomized by the goddess—a mother who is generally kind, but one who repulses her children (devotees, citizens) at times.

Similarly, the Hindu villager was apt to describe the Prime Minister as *devī*, the goddess. And in a poem dedicated to Indira Gandhi published in a popular English language magazine just after the Bangladesh war, we find these phrases: "Presiding deity of our country's fate" and "Of noble grace and looks and yet defiant, thunder in her eyes. . . "[52] Mrs. Gandhi is the goddess—not Sita of the *Ramayana*, the devoted wife who obeys her husband's every wish,[53] but the Mother, the goddess who epitomizes the dual character of the Hindu female. As such, she is easily comprehended in Hindu terms. The Hindu female can be aggressive: her essential nature makes her exactly that. Thus, Hindu conceptions of the female place the Hindu woman in a position opposite to that of the American woman who is generally believed to be passive by nature. Hindu women need only take advantage of their defining characteristics whereas American women must overcome theirs. As a result, when the Hindu woman does act as "Durga" (or as Mrs. Gandhi), there is a ready explanation for her behaviour and acceptance of the woman in a dominating role (after all, Durga does save the world). Thus, Hindu beliefs about the nature of the female and corresponding religious role models (but not the ideal type— the wife), do contain an ideology that can and seemingly does provide a meaningful code for women actively involved in non-wifely roles.

Until recently, Hindu ideology has been Brahman (high-caste) male dominated. Even today, almost 80 per cent of India's population is rural, and literacy rates remain low. But this situation is rapidly changing. Women, through schooling and mandatory learning of Sanskrit in many states, can now study the scriptures, forbidden to them for the past two thousand years, although a female pandit (as novel as a female Catholic priest would be) is yet to be seen. With the relaxation of purdah restrictions in both urban and rural areas, women are not as sexually segregated as previously; their freedom of movement allows them more opportunities for forming alliances with other women, and women's participation in public rituals is enhanced. Since the early nineteenth century, many Indians have agitated for reform of traditional religious-based rules for women. Practices such as *satī*, bans on widow remarriage, and prepuberty marriage have already been outlawed, and divorce and abortion are legal, although social practice lags behind the laws. Other social practices based on Hindu orthopraxy continue to impede women's secular status. Purdah is still rigidly followed in some rural areas and aids in denying women economic equality. Daughters are not desired because of economic liabilities with regard to hypergamous marriages and dowries, both aspects of Brahmanical orthopraxy, especially in the North. The sex ratio continues to decrease — from 972 females per thousand males in 1961 to 930 females per thousand males in 1971 — suggesting that female mortality is high. A recent study suggests that Brahmanical practices are one aspect of discrimination against females and they contribute to the benign neglect of female children, resulting in juvenile female deaths.[54] The Hindu-based desire for sons forces women into unwanted pregnancies and denies them control of their sexuality.

Many questions remain. Manuals for the proper conduct of women are now popular. These include material ranging from how to guarantee the birth of a son, to the necessary yearly rituals, to decorating the house. The content of these needs to be examined. The recent popularity of a "new" goddess, "The Mother of Peace" (*santoshi māta*), in both rural and urban North India needs investigation, including the phenomenon of a sellout film featuring this goddess and her all-abiding concern with family, but particularly with the husband/wife tie. Are these phenomena signs of change or a reaffirmation of traditional, male-dominated values?

There is potential for further change. Hinduism provides a conception of the world in which women are necessary but powerful and dangerous. Traditionally, this power and danger has been controlled through religious laws prescribing women's proper behaviour as being under the control of men. Yet women (and the mother especially) do control others; the mother in Hindu thought becomes the Hindu woman in control of herself. As such, she provides an alternative role to that of the dutiful wife. Women's religious practices, meanwhile, are not authorized by the religious authorities but do provide for female solidarity and for alternative sources of religious power. Women's ritual practices, however, emphasize kinship and family relationships, reinforcing the view of woman as wife. Thus, despite the ideology of the powerful aggressive woman, most Hindu women probably will continue to be motivated by the Hindu conception of the woman as dutiful wife, and will perform their yearly rituals for their husband's long life, the presence of many sons, and so forth. But, as women take more powerful positions

in India's changing society, they will find validation for their new roles
in long-standing Hindu textual traditions.

> The fearful goddess (Caṇḍika), devoted to her devotees, reduces to
> ashes those who do not worship her and destroys their merits.[55]

Yet,

> For those who seek pleasure or those who seek liberation, the
> worship of the all-powerful Goddess is essential. She is the
> knowledge-of-the-Immensity; she is the mother of the universe,
> pervading the whole world.[56]

Notes

1. Hinduism is a classical religion, with ancient and established tex-
    tual and authoritative traditions. But it differs from Christianity,
    Judaism, and Islam in that it lacks a single authoritative text:
    rather, it has thousands, produced over a 3,000 year period. In
    general, the *Vedas*, written over a period of a thousand years, are
    the ultimate source to which Hindus refer. However, most Hindus
    are themselves unfamiliar with the contents of the *Vedas*, and
    Hinduism as it is practised today is more non-Vedic than Vedic. In
    addition, within the geographic space of South Asia, Hinduism
    assumes varied forms and often appears more diversified than
    unified. Thus, any particular practice or belief found among a
    group of Hindus may, in fact, be contradicted elsewhere or denied
    by Hindus of other groups or regions. Clearly, not even the
    textually-based but varied "great traditions" of Hinduism could be
    fully explored in a brief paper; further, the "little traditions", or
    local practices that are not based on written texts, provide endless
    complications of interpretation and acknowledgement of belief
    and practice. As a further complication, Hinduism is a way of life;
    most actions, whether cooking or ploughing, have religious ele-
    ments. In this paper, I attempt to be faithful to the Hindu tradition
    in its multiple forms. If I have not succeeded, I apologize.
         As a guide to the reader, I use "textual", "authoritative", or
    "great tradition(al)" to refer to written texts or material from writ-
    ten texts, usually in Sanskrit. "Non-authoritative" implies prac-
    tices without written scriptural sanction, although they may be
    equally authentic in the minds of their practitioners.
2. Jagadisvarananda, *The Devi-mahatmyan or Shri Durgā Saptashatī*,
    Sri Ramakrishna Math, Maylapore 1953, Ch. XII, line 40 as
    quoted in Lawrence A. Babb, "Marriage and Malevolence: The Uses

of Sexual Opposition in a Hindu Pantheon," *Ethnology*, vol. IX, 1970, p. 140.

3. Brenda E.F. Beck, "Māriyammaṇ: The Vacillating Goddess," unpublished manuscript, the University of British Columbia, 1971, p. 2.

4. Susan S. Wadley, *Shakti: Power in the Conceptual Structure of Karimpur Religion*, The University of Chicago Studies in Anthropology, Series in Social, Cultural and Linguistic Anthropology, no. 2, Chicago, 1975, pp. 53-61.

5. Without detailing the historical development of Hindu beliefs about women, some crucial factors of this duality must be noted. Early Vedic literature (pre-600 BC, brought by the Aryan migrators from the North) emphasizes the prosperity and benevolence of female figures. Later developments in Hindu literature introduce the dangerous image of females. Women are the source of sacred power — frequently bad or dangerous sacred power. This developing emphasis on female power, including its potential danger, probably reflects an incorporation of Dravidian beliefs (already existing in India prior to 600 BC) into the Aryan religious complex. The earliest available Dravidian literature (specifically, Tamil literature) refers frequently to dangerous female power, a theme not found until later in the Sanskrit literature of the Aryans (see George L. Hart, III, "Women and the Sacred in Ancient Tamilnad," *Journal of Asian Studies*, February 1973, pp. 233-250.

    The modern Hindu, however, does not know about historical developments but only their result: the dual image of femaleness as simultaneously bad and dangerous, good and fertile.

6. The following discussion is abbreviated and generalized, due to the necessities of space. Hopefully, no injustice is done to the Hindu tradition. I wish to thank Barbara D. Miller and Bruce W. Derr for their many readings and helpful suggestions. In addition, H. Daniel Smith aided in clarifying points from the great traditions.

7. *Māndūkya Upanisad*, 1.7, quoted in Alain Danielou, *Hindu Polytheism*, Pantheon Books, New York, 1964, p. 21.

8. The beings of the universe are necessarily manifest or they could not be known; they are not necessarily a total representation of *brahman*; for, each god, goddess and being represents a part of the Unknowable that is *brahman* itself.

9. See Danielou and Wadley, op. cit.

10. McKim Marriot and Ronald B. Inden, "An Ethnosociology of South Asian Caste Systems," Paper read at the American Anthropological Association Meetings, Toronto, 1972.

11. G. Buhler (trans.), *The Laws of Manu*, Sacred Books of the East, vol. XXV, Motilal Banarsidass, Delhi, 1964, IX. 33, p. 333. The initial numbers in this reference indicated chapter and verse. The page number refers to this translation. *The Laws of Manu* were supposedly written by the first man Manu. While most Hindus are not personally familiar with the laws of Manu, the laws do express a corpus of beliefs about women which are still prevalent in India.

12. See Ronald B. Inden and Ralph W. Nicholas, "A Cultural Analysis of Bengali Kinship", Paper presented at the Sixth Annual Conference on Bengal Studies, Oakland University, May 1970.

13. Buhler (1964), op. cit., IX.35, p. 333.

14. This argument is strongly influenced by Sherry B. Ortner, "Is Female to Male as Nature is to Culture?" in Michelle Zimbalist Rosaldo and Louise Lamphere (eds.), Woman, Culture and Society, Stanford University Press, Standford, 1974.

15. See Babb (1970) and Beck (1970), op. cit.

16. It should be noted that there are also destructive and malevolent male deities in Hinduism. The goddesses alone do not cause all the trouble of the world. However, there seems to be a basic difference between male and female destructiveness. Male deities and demons appear to be logical in the trouble which they cause. Unlike Kali, they do not get carried away with the idea of mere killing. In discussing this matter with Guy Welbon, we came up with the distinction of plotted versus plotless action. Male destruction has an end goal; female destruction often does not. The logic (and Culture?) of the male dominates his actions; the non-logic (and Nature?) of the female dominates her actions.

17. This myth is excerpted from Wadley (1975), op. cit., p. 135.

18. This myth is excerpted from Wadley (1975), op. cit., p. 131.

19. Jagadisvarananda (1953) Ch. VII, lines 7-9, as quoted in Babb (1970), op. cit., p. 140.

20. Karapātrī, "Sri Bhagavati Tattva", as quoted in Danielou (1964), op. cit., p. 262.

21. See, for example, Susan S. Wadley, "Brothers, Husbands, and Sometimes Sons: Kinsmen in North Indian Ritual," Eastern Anthropologist, Spring 1976.

22. In what is essentially a sex-segregated society, women's primary day-to-day interactions are with other women, often in a joint family setting.

23. Buhler (1964), op. cit., V. 147-165, pp. 195-197.

24. Buhler (1964), op. cit., IX. 2-16, pp. 327-330.

25. This is not to say that the written traditions provide no examples of wifely love. However, the emphasis switches as we move from written (men's) to oral (women's) traditions. Moreover, there is one notable example of male/female love in the written traditions in the pairing of Radha and Krishna. In many parts of India, this pair is not believed to be married. And Radha is seldom recognized as an ideal. She does provide a possible role model, but not one which is advocated.

26. S.L. Srivastava, Folk Culture and Oral Tradition, Abhinav Publications, New Delhi, 1974, p. 28.

27. Buhler (1964), op. cit., III. 55-59, p. 85.

28. As one of the complications of this facet of motherhood, the goddesses who are said to have children are seldom called mother; rather, it is the goddesses who do not have children per se (Durga, Kali, Santoshi, Sitala) who are known as "Mother".

29. Susan S. Wadley, "Women, Wife and Mother in the Ramayana", unpublished paper.

30. The imagery and psychology of the "Mother" in Indian thought presents complications in interpretation and meaning far beyond the potential and scope of this paper.

31. The woman is especially impure and inauspicious just before and during childbirth. Yet her milk is a most pure substance. Her monthly menses are polluting, but not equalled by the pollution of childbirth. To what extent Hindu perceptions of the female are based on biological functions, it is hard to say. I have not attempted to deal with the relationship between female biology (pollution/purity) and perceptions of the female in Hinduism. Others have suggested that they are closely intertwined, with which I would agree. However, purity/pollution and femaleness presents another set of problems which must be dealt with elsewhere. I should note, however, that Hindu mythology does explicitly relate the low ritual status of women to (a) her monthly periods (b) her ability to bear children.

32. See Beck (1971), op. cit.

33. Many people cannot name their varna, though Brahmans generally know theirs. Aside from religion, it appears to have been of minor importance until recently when varna is regaining popularity both as an urban classification scheme and for political purposes.

34. Untouchables, both men and women, are generally the most maligned members of Hindu society: higher caste men and women can enter temples, until recently Untouchables could not enter many temples. (Untouchability is outlawed in the Indian constitution, but is still practiced in many parts of India.)

35. See Mildred Pinkham, *Women in the Sacred Scriptures of Hinduism*, Columbia University Press, New York, 1941.

36. Priests are still found in most temples; however, temple worship is not necessary for the followers of *bhakti* (and the early *bhakti* movement was anti-temple as well as anti-Brahman).

37. By the term religious specialist, I mean (a) someone who is paid for religious/ritual services, and (b) someone who conveys religious instruction, or is a guide in ritual practice, or performs rituals for others. People who provide essential ritual services (such as the flowergrower or washerman), but not religious instruction or guidelines, are not considered religious specialists.

38. "Pandit" is also an honorific used for any Brahman male, including those who do not perform priestly functions.

39. Modern astrologers are sometimes female — you find their ads in English language newspapers or big hotels. To what extent traditional astrologers might have been female is unknown. I have not seen any reference to them in the literature.

40. Exorcists and shamans come from any caste and from either sex, although female shamans are rarely mentioned in the literature and female exorcists may be non-existent. Some authors have claimed

that the shamans/exorcists (the two are often confused) are the non-Brahman counterparts of priests. I believe that the situation is vastly more complicated than that — Brahman shamans are common, for one thing. I should mention that there are also possessions related to illness where a religious specialist is not possessed; rather, a victim is (especially young women facing the tribulations of their husband's home).

41. Other clients in the *jajmāni* system have connections which are the provision of ritual services often based on conceptions of purity/pollution. Here we find the washerman, sweeper and leatherworker. However, like the flowergrower mentioned in note 37, they are not considered religious specialists as they provide no religious instruction and play no role in rituals *per se*. (On the other hand, all activity by a Hindu can be considered religious, in which case everyone is a specialist.)

42. See Ragini Devi, *Dance Dialects of India*, Vikas Publications, Delhi, 1972, pp. 45-50.

43. The evidence in the following discussion comes from rural North India. Comparable evidence is lacking for most of the rest of India. Urban data come from my personal experiences in Delhi and Agra.

44. See Wadley, "Brothers..."(1976), op. cit.

45. D.N. Majumdar, *Caste and Communication in an Indian Village*, Asia Publishing House, Bombay, 1958, pp. 252-276. Majumdar lists more than twenty-one yearly rites, but provides no descriptions of the others. Identification of the participants by sex could only be made for these twenty-one.

46. Oscar Lewis, *Village Life in Northern India*, Vintage Books, New York, 1965, pp. 197-248. The available evidence on these festivals in the three villages suggests that there is some variation in which festivals are organized and run by females versus males, with only a few always being male or female. This variation in local practice needs further investigation. Also, most authors list caste variation in participants; sexual variation must be culled from descriptions.

47. In some regions, men make fun of and laugh at the women's rites and generally put up with them in a condescending fashion.

48. Hanna Papanek, "Purdah in Pakistan: Seclusion and Modern Occupations for Women," *Journal of Marriage and the Family*, August 1971.

49. See Wadley, "Brothers..."(1976), op. cit., for some of this material. I would also like to thank William Houska for his insights into male-female orientations in North Indian rituals.

50. J. Anthony Lukas, "India is as Indira Does," *The New York Times Magazine*, 4 April 1976.

51. If Mrs. Indira Gandhi has been portrayed as Kali, the implications probably would be vastly different.

52. J.N. Dhamija, "The Rising Star," *The Illustrated Weekly in India*, 30 January 1972.

53.   It should be mentioned that Mrs. Gandhi did play on her image as
       the "proper Hindu woman", — looking meek, with covered head
       and mild manners on many public occasions.
54.   Barbara D. Miller, "A Population Puzzle — Does the Desire for
       Sons in India Increase People...or Sons," unpublished paper read
       at the New York State Conference on Asian Studies, Albany, 1976.
55.   *Devi Māhātmya*, quoted in Danielou (1964), op. cit., p. 257.
56.   Karapātrī, "Sri Bhagavati Tattva" quoted in Danielou (1964), op.
       cit., p. 257.

Golden Handprints and Red-Painted Feet: Hindu Childbirth Rituals in Central India

Doranne Jacobson

The cry of a newborn child sounds faintly from within the thick mud-plastered stone walls of a house in an Indian village. Barely audible in the night air, this tiny cry gives evidence of a major event in the lives of those who dwell within the walls of that house.

While this birth is but one of about 58,000 that occur each day in India (21 million every year), it is the focus of much concern, some of which is manifested in a set of rituals performed by women before and after the arrival of the baby. Centering on the infant and its mother, these rituals involve kinswomen of the baby, other women of the village, and, tangentially, some men. The rituals serve a number of purposes: they announce the baby's arrival to the world, magically strengthen and protect mother and child from evil influences, mark the passage of mother and infant from one stage of life to another, provide the new mother with approval and support, contribute to women's sense of solidarity with other women, and publicly recognize women's vital roles in perpetuating and enhancing the prosperity of the family and the larger community. In a culture in which women typically enjoy fewer privileges than men, the rituals serve to remind women—and men—of the fact that women, after all, produce children, the one thing without which no kin group or society could long exist.

This paper discusses the Hindu practices and rituals surrounding pregnancy and childbirth that are observed in Nimkhera, a village in Madhya Pradesh State, Central India.* These rituals, summarized in

From *Unspoken Worlds: Women's Religious Lives,* edited by Nancy Auer Falk and Rita M. Gross. Reprinted by permission of the publisher.
© 1989 by Wadsworth, Inc.

Table 1, are primarily life-crisis rites, or rites of passage, centering on a major transition in the lives of the newborn infant, its mother, father, and other kin. Typically, in all cultures rites of passage—ceremonies marking birth, coming of age, marriage, and death—note momentous changes in the lives of individuals. Rites of passage are remarkably similar the world over. Those undergoing a major transition are formally separated from their old status and routines, and they assume their new roles, often in isolation. Finally, a ceremonial reintegration into the larger society recognizes their changed status and resulting changes in social relationships.

In Indian childbirth ceremonies, although the infant is important, most of the ritual focuses on the parents, especially the mother. Childbirth rituals are unique in the degree to which they are the domain of women in a culture where men often seem to dominate. The contrast is seen, for example, in a Hindu wedding; when the bride is given to the groom and his family, a male Brahman priest chants Sanskrit verses and directs the rites, while veiled women sing on the sidelines. In childbirth rituals, however, men play only minimal supporting roles. Giving birth is a skill in which no man can claim expertise. This is the heart of the domestic sphere, the women's domain par excellence. In dramatizing one of women's most vital roles, the rituals contribute to harmonious cooperation among women brought together to live in the patrilineal joint family, the key social unit in rural India.

Nimkhera Village and the Cultural Setting

Nimkhera village is in Raisen District, about 50 miles east of Bhopal, the capital of Madhya Pradesh, India's largest state. The village is similar to hundreds of others in the region. The population of the village was 621 in 1974, approximately 80 per cent Hindu and 20 per cent Muslim. The villagers belong to 21 different ranked Hindu castes and 5 Muslim caste-like groups. A few of the village men work outside Nimkhera, but most villagers derive their support from the abundant wheat crop grown on the village fields.

Table 1. Summary of Childbirth Rituals and Practices in Nimkhera Village

Pregnancy	Minimal restrictions on food and activity	Gradual separation of pregnant woman from group
Delivery and 3-day pollution period (*Sor*)	Strong restrictions on food and activity	Definite separation of mother and child from group; recognition of their lineage membership
Day of birth	Placement of the *charua* pot; special foods for the new mother	Psychological support for the new mother
Evening after birth	*Charua* songfest	Announcement to village of the birth; tacit public recognition to new mother; symbolic sharing of her fertility
3 days after birth	Lifting of 3-day pollution period (*Sor*); ritual cleansing	First step in reintegration of mother and child into group
7-10 days after birth	*Chauk* ceremony: blessing of mother and child; worship of sun and water pots; ethno-birth control	Recognition and support of the new mother; introduction of mother and child to outside world; symbolic extension of her fertility
	Chauk songfest	Announcement to village of infant's successful completion of most dangerous period of life
	Grass Celebration (*Duba Badhai*): celebration of first son; gift distribution	Display of generosity; averting of envy

Contd

Occasion or Timing	Ritual and Practice	Sociological Interpretation
About 40 days after birth	Well Worship	End of postpartum pollution period; final reintegration of mother into group; symbolic extension of her fertility to village water supply
$2^{1}/_{2}$ or 5 months after birth	First feeding of solid foods	A milestone in the child's growing individuality
No set time	Pach gifts from mother's natal kin	Recognition of importance of kinship ties with maternal relatives
No set time	Head shaving	Final separation of child from physical attachment to mother; acknowledgment of importance of mother's care for child's survival; introduction of child to life outside the home

Occasion or Timing   Ritual and Practice   Sociological Interpretation

Raisen District is almost completely rural, and most of its villages are small. The district has a relatively low population density and is underdeveloped agriculturally and educationally. Fewer than 8 per cent of district women can read. As in many other parts of India, there are fewer women than men (900 to 1,000), reflecting the special physical hazards to which women are subject in a region where good medical care is difficult to obtain. The rate of infant morality is declining but remains high.

Hindu parents arrange the marriages of most girls before puberty and most boys before age twenty-two. The young couple—usually strangers to each other—do not normally begin living together until after the consummation ceremony, about three years after the wedding. Dressed in fine clothes, ornamented with glistening jewelry, and modestly cloaked with a white shawl, the weeping bride is led from her parental home and borne in a bullock cart or taxi to her marital home, usually in a village one to forty miles distant from her parent's home. There she meets alone with her husband for the first time. She begins to spend much of her time in her husband's home as the lowest-ranking member of his joint family. However, most women enjoy long, refreshing visits in their natal homes until late in life.

In most joint families the young wife is expected to observe purdah: she stays inside the house most of the time and veils her face from elders. She is usually responsible for cooking and other time-consuming chores. Some women—usually not the youngest brides—go to the village well twice daily to bring back heavy pots of water atop their heads. Women's duties also include plastering and painting the house and courtyard. Many women work in the fields and perform myriad other tasks.

But in the eyes of all, a woman's prime role is to be a mother, particularly a mother of sons. Every girl receives early training in child care, and girls love to carry young children about. A young woman is brought as a bride into her husband's family to produce children for the family. Through bearing children she finds social approval, economic security, and emotional satisfaction. Every young bride knows of old women who lack children; with houses empty of sons and grandchildren, they have no young hands to depend upon for support and aid. Even having daughters is not enough, for daughters marry and go to live with their husbands' kin. Adoption is possible only under very limited circumstances. Fortunate women are those who are fed from their sons' earnings and cared for by daughters-in-law. The message is clear: to be barren brings grief; to bear children brings joy. Thus every bride looks forward to becoming pregnant. Even women with several children are usually happy about new pregnancies. Contraception and abortion are very rarely practiced. Given the high infant-mortality rate in the region and the advantages of having children, the lack of enthusiasm for birth control is not surprising.

Childbirth rituals are almost the same for a baby boy as for a baby girl, but the greater enthusiasm surrounding rituals for boys shows a strong bias in favor of sons. Women say they love boys and girls the same; after all, they suffer equally painful birth pangs for both. "But we feel great pleasure if a son is born," one woman said. "A son remains part of our family. A daughter will belong to others."

Throughout the birth rituals certain materials appear again and again as symbols, expressing cherished values and desires. Cow dung is commonly used for cleaning and purifying. Produced by the sacred cow, dung is used daily in the form of dried cakes for cooking fuel; as a paste that dries to form a resilient film, it is used to plaster earthen walls and floors. Only women make cow dung cakes and apply cow dung paste.

Golden turmeric, used in many Hindu rituals, is especially noticeable in ceremonies involving women. Wet turmeric is used to help effect transition from one state to another, and in childbirth rituals it also symbolizes female generative powers. Items of red and russet hue are often part of women's rituals along with the turmeric; these, too, symbolize female fertility. Wheat and objects used by women to produce wheat foods appear frequently—hardly surprising in this area where wheat is literally the staff of life. Chilis, pulse, and salt, classic accompaniments to a meal of wheat breads, are also evident. Brown sugar and the more expensive puffed white sugar candies are highly desired treats used in many rituals and also distributed at births and weddings to express the joy of the family. Water is a key symbol signifying both purification and fertility. In this region the water supply is limited throughout much of the year, and the vital link between water and survival is keenly felt by the villagers. Since one of women's particular duties is to bring water into the house, women and water are often connected in ceremony and symbol.

Pregnancy

Since women's overriding concern is to produce offspring, no effort is spared to encourage pregnancy. Brides who remain childless too long are given every opportunity to be with their husbands by night and to worship Matabai, the village Mother Goddess, by day. The childless wife also offers special oblations to Lord Shiva or fasts every week in honor of the Goddess Santoshi Mata. Concerned relatives may take her to visit the shrines of other deities of the region, particularly the temple of the Goddess Narbada Mai. Silently begging the Goddess for a son, the woman wets her hands with cow-dung paste and makes inverted handprints on the base of the Goddess's temple. If her prayers are answered, she gratefully returns to make upright handprints in golden turmeric on the temple and to make other offerings to the Goddess. The childless woman may also visit a shaman, or medium, who will divine the cause of her problem and seek to cure it. The shrines of such mediums are thronged by worshippers, many of whom return to express their thanks for newly born offspring. A few villagers also consult women gynaecologists.

Generally, failing to conceive is regarded as a feminine defect. A childless daughter-in-law is criticized, and may be replaced. Barrenness may be seen as punishment for sins committed in a past life or as the result of educating a girl too highly. Husbands are virtually never blamed for childlessness, despite the fact that most villagers believe that a baby grows out of the man's seed alone, developing like a plant's seed in the fertile field of the womb. On the other hand, a woman is not blamed if she gives birth to babies that die; people say that it was not her husband's fate to have living children.

Once she suspects that she is pregnant, the happy young woman shyly refrains from mentioning the joyous news to anyone. She delicately leaves it to others to notice that she has not observed the usual monthly pollution period, is sometimes nauseous, or is widening at the waist. Her husband and other relatives gradually recognize the situation, and she begins to receive special treatment.

The pregnant woman is advised not to eat certain foods that are regarded as possibly harmful to the baby, and she may be given special delicacies. A major concern is shielding the expectant woman and her unborn child from malevolent magic and spirits. The pregnant woman is encouraged to remain home as much as possible. She is not allowed to wander about after dark, for fear of evil spirits. The woman may wear a tiny jackknife on her belt: a sharp iron object wards off ghosts and spirits. She also does not wear the usual auspicious substances with which women paint themselves, for fear that they may attract an evil spirit. A pregnant woman stays shut up inside her house during an eclipse of the sun since her appearance would be an "offense to God," and the child would be born

To thank the Goddess Narbada Mai for the gift of a son, a woman makes upright handprints in golden turmeric paste at the base of the goddess's temple at Hoshangabad, Madhya Pradesh. Handprints in cow- dung paste, pointing downward, have been left by women asking the goddess for a son.

with a defect. Conservative villagers feel that sexual relations should be avoided for the latter months of pregnancy. These protective practices serve to gradually set the pregnant woman apart and to inform others of her special and valued condition. Particularly for the first birth, the woman must be at her husband's rather than her parents' home for delivery. If a woman bears her first child in her parental home, it is strongly believed that misfortune or tragedy will befall her relatives. For example, one young woman bore her first child in her natal home, and villagers shook their heads knowingly when her teen-aged brother suddenly died the next day. Furthermore, a woman giving birth is almost never attended by her mother but by her female in-laws.

Delivery

When labor begins, the prospective mother is suddenly and radically separated from others. In Hindi, the language of the region, a woman who is in labor or has just given birth is called *jachcha*. A *jachcha* is in a highly polluted and polluting state, similar to that of the lowest untouchable castes. Anyone who touches her or her newborn infant becomes ritually polluted and must take a bath before contacting others. Therefore, when labor begins, the *jachcha* retires to a little-used room or curtained-off area, separated from all other members of the household. A man of the family is sent to call the midwife.

The midwife who delivers most babies in Nimkhera lives in a nearby village. Like traditional midwives in much of India, she belongs to a very low-ranked caste, because of the ritually defiling nature of her work. Four generations of women in her family have been midwives. She has received some training in modern methods and sterile technique at the district hospital, but she completely ignores this training in her practice. A non-traditional nurse, trained in midwifery and employed at a government health station in a nearby village, is also available. This post is usually filled by a Christian woman from the southern state of Kerala, to whom ritual pollution concepts are relatively unimportant or even irrelevant. The traditional midwife's fees are lower than the government nurse's, and her methods are more familiar, so most villagers call the nurse only in a very difficult case.

During labor some women undo their buttons, braids, knots, and trunk locks to "open the way" for the baby. The *jachcha* may be fed water in which the idols in the village temple have been bathed. The sacred water is said to alleviate labor pains and bring about a speedy delivery.

Inside the dimly lit birth room, the *jachcha* squats on the cow-dung-plastered earth floor and clings to a rope or house post. If delivery is difficult, the midwife or nurse may encourage her to lie on her back. One woman from her marital family and the midwife are with the *jachcha*. The assisting relative hands things to the midwife and watches to make sure that the midwife does not perform magic on the *jachcha*. No matter how great the pain, the *jachcha* is expected to endure the pangs of labor stoically. Silence is ideal, low moans are tolerated, but shouting or crying are strongly disapproved of and ridiculed.[1] One woman who had been in labor for nearly twenty-four hours was seen crying and clutching her husband in a desperate embrace. The village women gossiped for weeks about this shameless indiscretion. Furthermore, the woman giving birth is expected to retain her modesty as much as possible by draping her sari adroitly, and she should take care not to soil any garments or bedclothes, since the Washerwoman[2] objects to laundering cloth defiled with uterine blood. In childbirth, as in other facets of life, restraint is the keynote.

Finally, the baby emerges. No exclamations or cries of delight are heard; only a quiet statement is made: "It's a boy" or "It's a girl." Emotions are kept in check; to compliment or admire the baby would surely draw the evil eye.[3] A man with a watch is asked the time, so that an accurate horoscope can be prepared later. Otherwise, no announcement is made.

The midwife lays the slippery babe on a rag on the floor and waits for the placenta. Then, without care for aseptic technique, she ties a string or bit of rag around the umbilical cord and cuts it with a sickle (or, in recent times, sometimes an old razor blade). The act of cutting the umbilical cord is considered to be extremely polluting and is done only by the midwife. Even if the midwife's arrival is delayed for hours after the birth, the cord is left uncut until she arrives.

After the mother and child are cleansed, the newborn baby is placed for a moment in a winnowing fan along with a sharp metal object and a handful of uncooked wheat, lentils, salt, and red chilis "to make the child's mind sharp." The midwife then digs a shallow hole in the earthen floor near the mother's cot and buries the placenta and severed umbilical cord there to keep them safe from the clutches of malevolent magicians. (A bit of placenta, manipulated magically by a childless woman, could help the woman produce a healthy child but would cause harm to the original baby.) The midwife scrapes up the other remnants of the birth from the floor and later discards them. Then she plasters over the area with a new layer of purifying cow-dung paste. A broken earthen pot is put beside the mother's bed for a urinal, as she will not leave the birth room for several days. The birth sari is given to the Washerwoman to be laundered (and thus purified). The midwife may give the new mother an oil massage. Still in a very polluted state, not to be touched by anyone other than the midwife and assisting relative, the sequestered mother and child rest. Outsiders are not invited to see the baby, and even when the midwife makes follow-up calls on the mother, the baby is covered with a cloth to avoid the evil eye (and, unknown to the villagers, extra germs). The fear of illness or death striking the baby is so strong that no visitors, and not even the parents, ever openly admire the child. Instead they exaggerate complaints about the baby's health.

Ceremonies Following Delivery

On the day of the birth, a small ceremony is held for the new mother. At an auspicious time selected by the family Brahman priest, an herbal tea is ritually brewed for the mother. Only women of the extended family are invited to this event. The sister of the baby's father purifies an area of the floor with cow dung, and, using wheat flour, draws an auspicious design (*chauk*) on it. Then a special new pot, called a *charua*, is decorated with red paint, cow dung, turmeric, and grass. It is then filled with water, special herbs, and fruits and set on the design. After that, five or seven women from the family carry the pot into the kitchen, where the sister of the child's father places it on the stove. The reddish herbal tea that results is the *jachcha*'s main drink for many days. The new mother must also be fed other special foods that are very expensive but that miserly in-laws can hardly balk at providing.

That evening a women's songfest is held at the home of the new infant. These songfests bring women together as women to celebrate a uniquely female achievement and to honor the new mother. Women and girls from the neighborhood—or the whole village—are invited by the Barber woman on behalf of the host family. As darkness settles over the village, the women gather in the *jachcha's* courtyard to talk, spread news, reminisce about other pregnancies and other births, and sing special childbirth songs. The *jachcha* and the infant remain hidden and unheard in their polluted isolation, but they can hear the sounds of the gathering. Most of the birth songs refer to the *jachcha* and the pain she has suffered, as well as to tensions between the new mother and the in-laws with whom she lives. A typical song is the lament of a woman in labor, with her husband away, and her mother-in-law and husband's sister providing her with no help or sympathy. None of the songs center on the child, presumably to avoid the evil eye, but in a few songs the child is referred to as "jewel-like." In one song Lord Krishna's adoring mother is singing a lullaby to her beautiful divine infant. Thus, indirectly, women can express the joy they feel in holding their own precious babies—their one great consolation for having to live among unfamiliar and often unloving in-laws. Listening to the conversation and to the songs, young girls at the songfest receive early training in what to expect when they reach childbearing age. As refreshment the singers receive sugar candies and also swollen boiled wheat, suggestive of the *jachcha*'s formerly swollen body and hence symbolically extending her fertility to the other women.

For three days after the birth the new mother and child are in an especially great state of pollution, "because nine months' menstrual blood comes out at a baby's birth." During these three days, called *Sor*, no one but the midwife touches the mother and infant. All members of the father's family are also polluted though less so than the mother and child. Even if the child is born away from its paternal home, members of the patrilineage are still polluted. This pollution observance emphasizes to kinsmen the significance of the arrival of a new member of the kin group. At this time, the father of the baby may glimpse it but not hold it. Any contact whatsoever between husband and wife is forbidden during these three days. They may not have any intimate contact for forty days.

During *Sor* mother and child are given sponge baths and oil massages each day by the midwife. Then, on the third day after the birth, a ritual ends this state of greatest impurity. The midwife breaks the mother's old glass bangles, polluted by the birth, off her wrists. She rubs the mother with an ointment of turmeric, wheat flour, oil, and water to cleanse her skin. The baby is rubbed with a ball of turmeric and dough and given an oil massage. Then the midwife gives both mother and child complete purifying baths (the mother's first real bath since the birth), and they don clean clothes. Other family members also bathe. The bedding and dirty clothes are either washed by the Washerwoman or thrown away. The midwife purifies the birth room by applying cow-dung slip to the floor and up onto the base of the walls.

After *Sor*, since the new mother has moved a step closer to her normal state, the untouchable midwife no longer takes care of her. Instead, the middle-ranking village Barber woman now takes over. The Barber woman cuts the new mother's nails and applies another layer of cow dung to the floor of the room. If the new mother wants to become pregnant again soon, she asks the Barber woman to apply the cow-dung slip so that it covers only a narrow band at the base of the walls. But if she wants to postpone her next pregnancy, she asks the Barber woman to smear the slip higher on the wall. Women members of the family apply cow dung to the other floors of the house, and all earthen water pots (which are absorbent and hence polluted by the birth) are replaced with new pots. The sickle used to cut the umbilical cord is purified with fire by the blacksmith.

After this purification, the members of the kin group, as well as the infant, emerge in a clean and renewed state. The new mother can now enter the main room of the house and be touched by others, but she is still not pure enough to engage in normal household tasks. In particular, she avoids cooking and any jobs involving contact with dampness; in fact, she should not even wash her own baby, for fear of her catching cold. Also, she still avoids eating certain foods. Not until forty days after the birth will she achieve a completely normal state.

The *Chauk* Ceremony

The major ritual following childbirth is the *Chauk* ceremony, held about a week to ten days after the birth. The exact time is selected by the Brahman priest according to astrological calculations. The *Chauk* takes its name from the four-sided design drawn in wheat flour to mark the central location of the ritual.

The infant's paternal aunt, who should be present for the occasion, plays an important role in the *Chauk*. Through that role she reaffirms her involvement in the home of her birth and the importance of her continuing bonds with her parents' family. If she is not available, another female relative—usually a young girl—can substitute. If the child is a boy, the aunt makes two designs out of wet cow dung, one on each side of the house's main door. Otherwise, the *Chauk* ceremonies are the same for boys and girls. In the late afternoon, after the designs have been made, the Barber woman arrives to prepare the mother for the *Chauk*. She bathes her, cuts her nails, does her hair in fresh braids, and fits new mirror-studded lacquer bangles on her waists. The baby too is bathed.

The *Chauk* ceremony itself takes place at dusk, around 6 or 7 P.M It is a private ceremony, normally attended only by women and girls of the household and by the Barber woman, who physically guides the new mother through the ceremony. Boys and men are usually excluded.

The aunt uses cow dung to cleanse a spot on the floor in the center of the main room of the house, just in front of the door, and then draws the *Chauk* design in wheat flour on the spot and arranges other ritual paraphernalia. The new mother appears, her face covered by a veil, and sits down on a wooden platform, which has been placed over the design, facing the door of the house. She is wearing all her fine jewelry and best clothing, over which she wears a white cover-all shawl. Held in the crook of her right arm and completely covered with her sari and shawl is her

Dressed in fine clothing, a new mother sits on a small wooden platform over a chauk *design, as a Barber woman paints her feet with auspicious designs. Cradled in the mother's lap is her infant daughter, completely covered with a new cloth to protect her from evil influences. The baby's father's sister blesses the mother and child with auspicious symbols and gestures.*

baby, dressed in new clothes that were blessed by having a maiden step on them.

The Barber woman rubs the mother's feet with wet turmeric and, using red paint, draws an auspicious design on them. Garbed in finery, modestly cloaked in white, with only her ornamented hands and gold-and-red-painted feet protruding, the new mother looks as she did when she first arrived at the door of the house as a bride on the occasion of her consummation ceremony. Then she stood outside the door, facing the house, with her white veil tied to her new husband's shawl, while he stood on the wooden platform. Now, holding her baby, she sits on the platform inside the door, facing out. In her new role as mother she is fulfilling the promise that was inherent in her role as bride.

Guided by the Barber woman, the sister of the baby's father holds a platter filled with ritual paraphernalia and stands before the veiled mother and child. With her finger she carefully paints a turmeric swastika (an ancient Hindu auspicious design) on the white cloth over the woman's head and on the cloth over the baby. The swastika on the mother's head is said to help ensure that she will enjoy a long married life. The swastika over the baby is intended to "keep her lap full of babies." The aunt then slowly swings the brass platter back and forth over the woman's head, in an arc from one shoulder to the other, five or seven times. As she moves the platter, she puts her hand over the glittering oil lamp and then onto the mother's shoulders and the baby, blessing them. The gesture, called *arti*, is a key feature of the worship of deities by their devotees and in addition to being an act of adoration may also provide protection from the evil eye.

Carrying her baby, the mother rises from her seat over the auspicious design on the floor and goes out the door. She quickly turns and hands the baby back in through the door to a relative who puts the baby in a wheat-filled winnowing fan and covers it with a cloth. Out in the dark courtyard, the Barber woman guides the new mother through several additional rituals, one of which is believed to determine how long it well be before the new mother conceives again. She herself makes the determination when she throws lumps of food eastward "as an offering to the sun." The farther she throws them, the longer it will be before her next pregnancy. In another part of the rite, the new mother worships and blesses the family water supply by placing her own golden handprints—symbols of her fertility—on the family water pots. She then re-enters the house.

The entire *Chauk* is performed without any particular verbal expressions or prayers. Formalized ritual utterances are the province of the male priests; women's rites involve doing, not talking, except for their songs.

In the *Chauk*, the woman clearly emerges in her new role as mother of a child and as a woman who has fulfilled her duty to her marital lineage. Leaving the door of the house with her baby, both mother and child make a formal entry into the outside world. The *Chauk* stresses the beneficent and creative powers of the female. In her new role as a child-producing member of the household and lineage, the mother is reminded that she upholds the strength of the family group through chaste behavior and devoted motherhood. Much depends on her.

Although the *Chauk* has brought them a step closer to normal life, the mother and child are still in a state of vulnerable transition. They are shrouded by layers of cloth and darkness throughout the ceremony, and the child must not even glimpse the lamplight. They remain sequestered for the rest of the forty-day postpartum period. The infant is not yet individualized to the point of being given a name. Although it has survived the most dangerous days after birth, its grip on life is still not deemed to be a sure one.

That night, after the *Chauk* ritual itself is over, many women are invited to a *Chauk* songfest. If the family is prosperous and high ranking, a drummer is hired to announce the start of the event, and a crowd of perhaps forty women and girls gather in the courtyard to sing childbirth songs. The mother and child are still not seen or heard from. Here too, as in almost all other situations involving childbirth, the new father is not at home and is nowhere to be seen. The women sing the usual songs, many of which stress a woman's alienation from her conjugal kinfolk. One song, about Bemata, a goddess who gives babies to women, declares:

As a scorned basket is useful in carrying cow dung,
A scorned daughter-in-law is useful in producing sons.

The birth of a first-born son in a prominent and prosperous family may be marked with a special celebration, to which all the villagers are invited. This celebration, held on the night of the *Chauk* festival, is called *Duba Badhai* (Grass Celebration) in reference to the sacred *duba* grass that the village Barber sticks in the turbans of the male guests as a kind of blessing. The men sit and chat while the women, sitting separately, sing. Guests may give money or clothing to the Barber to be presented to the baby.

To the sound of beating drums, the celebrating family distributes gifts — clothes and money to the family Brahman priest and his wife, the family guru (religious teacher) and his wife, the village temple priest and his wife, the Barber and Barber woman, the Sweeper woman, the Potter woman, and even the Tanner woman. Sisters and daughters of the family often receive clothing. All the male guests are given brown sugar lumps or sugar candies, and the women receive sweets and boiled wheat. In the privacy of the courtyard, away from the eyes of the men, women guests may dance in celebration. In addition, women of the higher castes may be feasted as special guests on the *Chauk* day. The family head may also present cows to the village tailor, the Barber, the Sweeper, and, as an act of religious merit, to a poor maiden. All of this largesse reaffirms the family head's position as a prominent and generous person and suggests that the new born infant may follow in his footsteps. The generosity also helps to fend off envy, as the good fortune of the family in having a new male member is shared with others.

After the *Chauk*, the mother can again eat most normal foods; in addition, she may continue to eat the special foods that are prescribed for new mothers. She can now do many routine household tasks, such as cleaning grain and sweeping. But she should still refrain from fetching water or touching wet cow dung, for fear she might catch a chill. For the same reason, she does not take a full bath again until the forty days are over. Because she is still somewhat polluted, she does not enter the kitchen or cook, except sometimes for herself on a small stove outside the kitchen. Grinding flour, too, is usually avoided. She does not participate in any worship services for Gods or Goddesses or touch the household's holy images. Except for going out to eliminate at the edge of the forest or fields, she stays home. Very poor women, however, may not be able to afford so many days of idleness and may return to their jobs in the fields much earlier.

Finally, the postpartum pollution period ends about forty days after the birth. The exact date is set by a Brahman. The mother bathes, her room is cleansed with cow dung, and her clothes and bedclothes are washed again. She is now ready to resume normal life. The return to normalcy is marked in some castes with a ritual called Well Worship. In some of the middle castes, women perform the Well Worship ceremony after the birth of a first child, and Brahman women perform it after the birth of every child. Women of other castes may perform a tiny ceremony at the well side before drawing water for the first time, or they may not bother with any ceremony at all.

For her Well Worship, the bejeweled and white-shrouded Brahman mother goes at night to the village well, preceded by a drummer and accompanied by the Barber woman, a few women members of her household, and a few relatives and neighbors. After a fairly complex ritual in which the new mother makes auspicious diagrams at various points around the well's rim, she pushes all the ritual offerings into the well, draws some water in the household water pots, and carries it home. Women who have gathered there sing and receive sugar treats. The new mother has thus symbolically extended her fecundity to the village water supply. The woman's transition to her new status as the mother of her child and her reintegration into the normal life of her family and community are now complete.

The Continuing Cycle of Ceremonies for the Child

The ceremonies following the Well Worship center on the child, its gradual achievement of individuality, and its relationships with others. In the *Pach* ceremony, held at any convenient time within the first few months after the birth of a first child, members of the mother's natal family arrive at her marital home with gifts of clothing, jewelry, toys, and perhaps even a fancy cot for the baby. The visitors also ceremonially present clothing to the child's parents and other men and women of the child's paternal household. Thus, the bond between a child and its mother's parents, its mother's brother, and other maternal relatives is acknowledged and strengthened. At the same time, the importance of the link between a woman's natal family and her conjugal kin is recognized. When they leave, the visitors take the new mother and the baby home with them for a lengthy stay. Most children and their mothers visit their maternal kin often, and some children live in their maternal uncle's home for years at a time.

A small ceremony is held when the child is fed solid food for the first time—generally, at two and one-half months for a girl and five months for a boy. Tiny portions of wheat breads, fritters, sweet milk-and-rice pudding, or other foods (ideally, thirty-six varieties of food) are fed to the child from a silver rupee coin by the child's paternal aunt or a stand-in. The aunt then receives a present from the baby's father. The child usually continues to suckle until it is about two years old, gradually increasing the amount of solid food it consumes.

At some time in the first year or two of life, a child's head must be ritually shaved to remove the polluted "birth hair". Among many high-caste families in Nimkhera, the Head-Shaving ceremony is held near the Matabai (Mother Goddess) shrine. The mother and child are dressed in good clothes; accompanied by female relatives, neighbor women, and the Barber couple, they parade to the shrine in late morning. An auspicious design is made on the ground in front of the shrine. The mother sits on a wooden platform over the design, with her baby cradled in her lap. A worship service (*puja*) is performed; then the Barber shaves the baby's head with a wicked-looking straight-edged razor, and the baby's head is anointed with turmeric, usually by the mother. The hair cuttings are collected to be thrown into a sacred river as an offering.

The hair-cutting is the first public ceremony involving the child and serves to introduce the child to the village Mother Goddess and to the village. While the earlier rites are performed in dark protective privacy, the hair-cutting ceremony takes place in open sunlight. Here, for the first time, a male (the Barber) representative of the world outside the home, acts as the child's attendant. The simple *puja*, with offerings put into a small fire, is typical of scores of other rituals involving male participants. This ceremony mediates between the dangerous period of infancy and the less dangerous period of childhood. With the removal of the birth hair, the child is finally separated physically from the mother and achieves individuality. Offering the hair to the divine may act to consecrate the child and help protect him or her from harm. The mother's anointing the child's head with turmeric is a blessing, a visible symbol of a belief often stated by village women: "A child needs his mother's hand over his head; then he grows fast, sustained by her love." Not until the child's wedding, when he himself steps on the path to parenthood, will he again be rubbed with turmeric. Then the child—bride or groom—will be anointed with the golden ointment by young women of the family, while the mother protectively holds her hand on the child's head.

Conclusion

During the total of thirty-seven months I spent in Nimkhera, at least seventy-six Hindu babies were born, sixty-seven of whom survived the first two weeks of infancy. Thus, Hindu childbirth rituals were performed at the rate of about twenty-two complete sets per year, involving the women of the village again and again in the rites and practices surrounding initiation into motherhood. Childbirth rituals are certainly the most frequently performed life-cycle ceremonies; among all Hindu ritual observances in Nimkhera only the short daily worship services held in the temple and at some homes and shrines outnumber them. In a situation in which modesty and fear of unseen evil forces militate against public discussion of childbirth, these ceremonies provide public recognition to women as they contribute their procreative capacity to the family and to society. Indeed, except for her wedding, there is virtually no other situation in which a woman can legitimately achieve recognition at all. Ideally quiet and—in her marital home—veiled and secluded, the woman is the center of attention only in new motherhood. The never-ending sequences of childbirth ceremonies continually tell her that, above all, women should be mothers and that only in motherhood will she find satisfaction.

Within the family-oriented village society, there is little room for following individual preferences; all must work together for the family's strength. Women must dutifully carry out their assigned tasks in the home and in the fields and, most important, make their unique contribution of new members for the group. As anthropologists Yolanda and Robert Murphy have written, "The woman remains the custodian and perpetuator of life itself. Those who would question the worth of this trust must first ask if there is anything else in human experience that has an ultimate meaning."[4]

Notes

* The data on which this chapter is based were collected during three years of field research in India (1965-67, 1973-75). I am grateful to the American Institute of Indian Studies and the U.S National Institute of Mental Health for supporting the research. A grant from the National Endowment for the Humanities supported the writing of the article. For their essential assistance, I wish to thank the residents of "Nimkhera" village and Ms. Sunalini Nayudu, Dr. Leela Dube , Dr. Suzanne Hanchett, and Dr. Jerome Jacobson.

1. No painkillers are used. Indian women could benefit greatly from knowledge of Lamaze childbirth techniques, in which a series of breathing exercises direct the pregnant woman's mind away from feelings of pain or discomfort.

2. The terms "Washerwoman" and, later, "Barber woman," have been capitalized in this paper because they designate the women's caste rank as well as the service that they perform. The term "midwife," however, designates only a service; the woman who performs it may performs it may come from a number of different caste groups.

3. Excellent sociological and ecological analyses of the evil-eye beliefs found in many parts of the world are presented in Clarence Maloney, ed., *The Evil Eye*, New York: Columbia University Press, 1976.

4. Yolanda Murphy and Robert F. Murphy, *Women of the Forest*, New York: Columbia University Press, 1974, p. 232.

Hindu Women's Family and Household Rites in a North Indian Village

Susan S. Wadley

Slap! Slap! The sound of the winnowing fan being beaten reverberates through the house and courtyard as Jiya, the mother, rids the family living quarters of evil spirits and chases away poverty. It is late on a dark night, the no-moon night of the month of Kartik (October-November), and everyone else is asleep. Earlier in the evening the entire family has celebrated Divali, the Hindu festival honoring Lakshmi, the goddess of prosperity. Divali is also known as the Festival of Lights because Lakshmi is called to homes throughout India by lighting rooftops and windows with clay lamps. It is a joyous festival, also celebrated with fireworks and special foods. But even though the main celebration is over and the family is sleeping, Jiya performs this one last task. As is the case for many other women's calendrical rituals in north India, she, as the eldest female in the family, has to protect her family's health and welfare.

Whereas men's rituals are aimed primarily at general prosperity or good crops and at the world outside the house itself, women's rituals focus more specifically on family welfare and prosperity within the walls of their homes. In this paper I will examine how women deal with these concerns by discussing the calendrical cycle of rituals practiced by the high-caste Hindu women of Karimpur,[1] a village of North India.

Karimpur is located approximately 150 miles southeast of Delhi. In 1968 it had a population of 1,380 divided among 22 hierarchically ranked castes. Jiya belongs to the highest-ranking group, the Brahman

From *Unspoken Worlds: Women's Religious Lives,* edited by Nancy Auer Falk and Rita M. Gross. Reprinted by permission of the publisher.
© 1989 by Wadsworth, Inc.

caste. In Karimpur members of this caste, though nominally priests, are actually farmers. They dominate the village ritually and economically. Most people in Karimpur live by farming. The men work the fields with their bullock-drawn plows, while the women process the food through winnowing, husking, grinding, and cooking. Women work in the fields only rarely, and it is a sign of a family's low status if the women work outside of the home.

Most Karimpur families are joint families—families in which sons, sons' wives, and grandchildren all live with the parents. Married daughters live with their husbands' families in other villages and only periodically visit the home of their birth. Most of the women in Karimpur, especially wealthier and young married women, follow *purdah* restrictions. In north India *purdah* requires that females should be secluded in their family courtyards and houses. When outside these quarters, they must cover their heads and faces with their saris or shawls. Even inside they must cover their faces before their husbands and husbands' older male relatives—fathers, uncles, and older brothers.

Essentially, men and women in Karimpur occupy separate worlds. For the most part, women live and work in their homes and have little mobility outside of them. The physical structure of Karimpur houses is important in understanding women's activities. Most homes are built of mud bricks and have an outer room with a verandah adjoining the village lanes. Behind this room is an open courtyard with one or more rooms attached to it. This courtyard and the rooms around it form the women's world. Men must cough or otherwise announce their presence before entering it. Within the confines of their homes, women cook, clean, care for children, visit with neighbors (who come by crossing over rooftops rather than by using the "public" lanes), weave baskets, knit, and celebrate their rituals. Men use the courtyard primarily for eating and bathing. They entertain their guests on the front verandah or in the outer room. Much of the time the men sleep there as well.

In many aspects of life, even in the content of songs and the way they are sung, men and women express their separate worlds. It is not surprising, then, that women's desires, as expressed in their rituals, are those of their world—the household—while men's concerns are focused primarily on the outer world. Since the world affects women differently than it does men, women's symbols of hope and prosperity are also different from men's symbols. On a more theoretical level, we could say that the calendrical rituals of Karimpur express women's most vital moods and motivations. Whether by beating the winnowing fan on Divali night or by worshipping a banyan tree during Marriage Worship or by offering milk to snakes, women in Karimpur symbolically, yet very powerfully, state the longings and ideas that are vital to their women's world. They express these longings and concerns in the twenty rites they perform every year.

Of these twenty rituals performed by women, three involve the direct worship of male relatives. In these rituals the male relative is actually the deity worshiped, and offerings are made directly to him. Four rituals involve the worshipping of a deity for the protection of a particular family member. Another four annual rituals are concerned with obtaining protection for one's family in general. Nine more rituals seek household prosperity. (See Table 2 for a complete list of these rituals.)

Before going on to examine these rituals in detail, three points should be clarified. First, living human beings can be, and often are, deities in Karimpur, as are plows, snakes, bullocks, and wheat seedlings, in addition to the normally recognized pantheon of mythological gods and goddesses. The basic rule is that any being that a person considers more powerful than himself or herself in any particular realm of life can become an object of worship. Thus for any given individual the religious pantheon of Karimpur is potentially enormous, since it could consist of all other beings. Moreover any action that is undertaken because of another being's power (*shakti*) is religious action. The implication of this point for women's religion will become clearer later.

Table 2. Women's Rituals in Karimpur

Deity Worshipped	Name of Festival	Purpose	Date*
Worship of Kin			
Brother	Tying on Protection (*raksha bandan*)	Obtaining his protection	Savan 2:!5 (July-Aug.)
Husband	Pitcher Fourth (*Karva chauth*)	Obtaining his protection	Kartik 1:4 (Oct.-Nov.)
Brother	Brother's Second (*Bhaiya duj*)	Obtaining his protection and his long life	Kartik 2:2 (Oct.-Nov.)
Worship on Behalf of Kin			
Savitri Banyan tree	Marriage Worship (*barok ki puja*)	Long life of husband	Jeth 1:15 (May-June)
Gauri	The Third (*tij*)	Brother's welfare	Savan 2:3 (July-Aug.)
Devi	Nine Nights (*neothar*)	Happy marriage for girls	Kuar 2:1-9 (Sep.-Oct.)

Contd.

Deity Worshipped	Name of Festival	Purpose	Date*
Siyao or Sihayo Mata	Lampblack Mother (*siyao or sihayo mata*)	Having sons; children's welfare	Kartik 2:1 (Oct.-Nov.)

Worship on Behalf of Family

Devi	Goddess Worship (*Devin ki puja*)	Protection for family	Chait 2:9 (Mar.-Apr.)
Snakes	Snake's Fifth (*nag panchmi*)	Deliverance from snakes	Savan 2:5 (July-Aug.)
Krishna	Cow Dung Wealth (*gobardhan*)	Protection for family	Kartik 2:1 (Oct.-Nov.)
Devi	Goddess Worship (*Devin ki puja*)	Protection for family	Chait 1:8 (Mar.-Apr.)

Worship for Prosperity

Grain	Grain Third (*akhtij*)	New crops, shelter	Baisakh 2:3 (Apr.-May)
Vishnu			
Devi	Asarhi (*asarhi*)	Protection from rains	Asarh 2:!5 (June-July)
guru			
Hanuman	Eternal Fourteenth (*anant chaudas*)	Protection	Bhadon 2:14 (Aug.-Sep.)
Lakshmi	Elephant Worship (*hathi ki puja*)	Wealth, fruits	Kuar 1:8 (Sep.-Oct.)
Lakshmi	Festival of Lights (*divali*)	Wealth	Kartik 1:15 (Oct.-Nov.)
Vishnu	Awakening Gods (*deothan*)	Prosperity	Kartik 2:11 (Oct.-Nov.)
Vishnu	Full Moon of Kartik (*Kartik purnamashi*)	Wealth	Kartik 2:15 (Oct.-Nov.)
Shiva	Shiva's Thirteenth (*Shiva teras*)	Protection	Phagun 1:13 (Feb.,-Mar.)
Holi Mata Krishna	Holi	Crops, removal of evil	Phagun 2:15 (Feb.-Mar.)

*The religious calendar in India is reckoned by lunar months, with each month divided into a dark half (full to new moon) and a light half (new to full moon); this column specifies the date by month, then half (1=dark half; 2=light half), then day within the half (1-15).

Second, all the rituals listed in Table 2 are performed by women and/or girls. None of these rites requires the services of a priest or other religious specialists (who are almost exclusively male). All the rules for proper worship and all the stories and songs that accompany worship are orally transmitted from women to women for women's use.

Third, women in Karimpur practice three major forms of religious activity: *vrat* (fasts), puja (worship), and *bhajan* (devotional singing). Fasting implies greater devotion than that associated with mere worship. Worshipping means honoring the deity as one would a guest: food is presented, the image may be bathed and perfumed, and new clothes are given. To further symbolize her humble subordination to the deity, the worshipper then eats the god's leftover food (*prasad*). The third ritual form, devotional singing, is both entertainment and serious religious activity. Women's religion in north India is primarily devotional. The deities are worshipped with love and respond with boons for the devotees. Devotional singing accompanies the worship.

I will examine in detail five of the twenty rites practiced by women. I will also look in depth at those aspects of the women's world that give meaning to their ritual actions. The five rituals to be discussed are Brother's Second, Marriage Worship, Lampblack Mother, Snake's Fifth, and the Festival of Lights. Male kin—brothers, husbands, and sons—are the focus of the first three; general family health is sought in the fourth; and family prosperity, in the fifth.

Brother's Second

Brother's Second occurs in the fall, two days after the Festival of Lights. On this day women worship their brothers, if the brothers are present in the village, or images of their brothers, if they are not present. To understand the ritual significance of brothers, we need to learn why brothers are important to Karimpur women. To do this, we shall focus on the roles and activities of women, for it is what women are and do that makes their brothers so important.

Two crucial factors in the lives of Karimpur women affect their relationships with their brothers. First, all girls must marry out of the village of their birth (village exogamy); second, they must marry into families considered to have higher ranks than their own (hypergamy). As a result of becoming a part of her husband's family and hence "taking on" his higher status, a married woman has higher status than her own brothers, father, and other natal kin. Because of his lower status, her father does not visit her new relatives or receive any hospitality from them. Yet, since women of north India may not travel alone, some male relative must fetch her from her husband's home when she makes her annual visit to her natal home. Normally, brothers are entrusted with this task. Hence a woman's brothers symbolize her links to her natal village. They bring her back for her first visit after her marriage, and they come at times of distress or bring gifts when a child is born or married. This cultural rule makes a great deal of sense. Given the Indian life span of approximately forty-four years for males, it is the brother and not the father who will more likely live to carry out these tasks; only rarely would a woman's father be alive into her middle age.

Conditions of life in a husband's household, as well as stereotypes about it, add to the brother's significance. In rural north India all marriages are arranged by the male kin of bride and groom. Neither the girl or the boy will have ever seen the other before the wedding day itself, and even then *purdah* restrictions require that the bride be cloaked in heavy shawls. The wedding takes place in the bride's home. Afterward the groom and his male relatives (no female relatives can take part in the journey from one village to the other) remove the bride from the family that she has known since birth and take her as a complete stranger to her new family. Here she is a *bahu* (wife), and is subordinate to all until either she has a child or a yet younger "wife" is added to the family. As a servant to her elders, locked into strict *purdah*, and under the tyranny of a mother-in-law, the woman sees her husband's home as a trying and often lonely and unhappy place.

In contrast, the time spent in her father's home, ideally at least one month a year, gives a woman joy, happiness, and a feeling of being loved and cherished. While she is again a daughter, not a wife, *purdah* restrictions are lifted, childhood friendships are re-established, and freedom is gained from imprisonment in servile relationships with everyone above her. Thus the emotional tone of a woman's life undergoes a complete turnabout when she moves from one house to the other. Many women's songs recognize this fact, particularly those of Savan, the rainy-season month when daughters should return home. Swings are hung in trees, and daughters of all ages gather to sing of swinging in the cool air of the monsoon, gazing at the green of the fields, and listening to the peacock. Many of the Savan songs lament the fate of women whose brothers did not bring them home.

A brother's importance is further enhanced by his gift-giving role. Beginning with engagement gifts and ending only when she dies, a woman's natal family is expected to give gifts to her husband's family. Gifts should be given yearly and also on special occasions, such as the birth of a child and children's marriages. For example, the mother's brother provides his sister's children with their wedding clothes. Gifts are especially important during the first years of marriage, when gifts from the bride's family, given via the brother, are almost like bribes to ensure that the bride will be well treated in her new home.

Brothers are necessary for women's long happiness. A girl without a brother is considered only slightly better off than a widow. A girl with many brothers is most fortunate. Brothers shelter their sisters from afar. Thus, in the rituals called Brother's Second, The Third, and Tying on Protection, women work to ensure the health and welfare of their protectors.

In the fall, after the Festival of Lights, sisters worship their brothers by putting an honorific *tika* (auspicious mark) on their foreheads and by offering them food, especially sweets, and water. The brother responds by giving his sister gifts of money or clothing, symbolizing his protection for the coming year. When the brother is not present, his sister draws a figure of him in flour paste on the courtyard floor and offers food and water to the image. Some women also make a figure out of cow dung that represents their brothers' enemy. They crown this figure with thorns, take it to the door of the house, and smash it with a rice pestle. Having thus demolished their brothers' enemies for the year, the women conclude their ritual.

Although ritual actions during Brother's Second suggest that the sister seeks the brother's protection, stories told in connection with the rite emphasize that in fact the sister protects the brother. She destroys his enemies for him and thus ensures him a long life. There are two common stories.

Once upon a time, a brother came to his sister's house to take her to his marriage. She made food for him in the middle of the night; but by accident she ground a snake into it. When later she discovered that the cakes she had prepared were bad, she promptly replaced them. Having saved him from the poisonous food, she learned of a thorn (*sahe*) that would rid him of all misfortunes. So, when he got married, she put *sahe* thorns on all the offerings and used them at all the ceremonies, thus giving everybody the impression that she was mad. She even insisted on sleeping in the same room as the bride and groom. When a snake sneaked into the room and tried to bite her brother, she killed it and saved him and his bride. Thus, she shielded her brother from many troubles. When she told her story, she was highly praised. So all sisters worship their brothers and ask for their brothers' long life.

Yamuna and Yamraj were sister and brother. Every day Yamuna went to her brother's house and gave him food. One day Yamraj came to Yamuna's house instead. This day was the second day of the light half of Kartik (the day of Brother's Second). Seeing her brother, Yamuna greeted him with reverence and great happiness. After worshipping him, she gave him food. Yamraj was very pleased by her signs of respect and gave her gifts of ornaments and clothes. When he left, Yamraj said "Sister, I am very pleased with you. Ask any boon; I will fulfill all your wishes." Yamuna said, "Brother, if you are truly pleased with me, come every year on this day and I will feed you. And may a long life be given to those people who go to their sisters and take food on this day." Saying, "It shall be this way," Yamraj left, and Yamuna's every wish was fulfilled.

These stories highlight the main elements of a brother's importance to a Karimpur woman. In the first story, the brother has come to fetch his sister, and she in turn seeks his long life. In the second, the brother not only visits his sister but also gives her gifts. We have seen how important both these elements are to Karimpur women.

Marriage Worship

However important a brother may be, the husband is even more important to a woman's general happiness. A variety of factors, both religious and social, contribute to a husband's importance.

According to Hindu teachings, a good woman is devoted to her husband. The ideal wife is Sita, heroine of the Ramayana, an epic widely read and known throughout India. In the Ramayana, Sita follows her husband Rama into twelve years of exile in the forest. She is kidnapped by a demon, whom Rama eventually destroys. When Sita's virtue is questioned, she mounts a lighted pyre to prove her continued chastity. The gods recognize her purity, and the flames do not burn her. The Ramayana's message is explicit, as illustrated by this quotation from the version commonly read and recited in Karimpur.

[A sage's wife speaks to Sita]

> Though a husband be old, diseased, stupid, or poor, deaf, bad-tempered or in great distress, yet if his wife treats him with disrespect, she will suffer all the tortures of hell. This is her one religious duty, her one vow and observance—devotion in thought and word and deed to her husband's feet.... The wife who honestly fulfills her wifely duty wins salvation with the greatest ease; but she who is disloyal to her husband, wherever she be born, becomes a widow in her early youth.[2]

Thus a woman's hopes for salvation also depend on her marriage.

Traditional Hindu teachings also deal with women who are widowed. Ideally, the widow should commit *sati* by throwing herself on her husband's funeral pyre; this actually occurred quite rarely even in the past. However, by committing *sati*, the widow eliminated two problems: her own inauspicious presence and potential charges of unfaithfulness. Upper-caste widows traditionally were not allowed to remarry, and the sad status of widowhood was displayed for all to see. Widows could no longer wear jewelry, they had to wear plain cotton saris, and their heads were shaved. They could not attend marriages, childbirth celebrations, or other auspicious occasions. In fact, even today, widows are often considered to be witches or carriers of the evil eye.

The conditions of the extended family also make a husband vital to a woman's happiness. Although a husband should not intercede with his mother on his wife's behalf, having a husband around to note mistreatment is considered crucial for a woman's protection. A popular myth associated with the goddess Santoshi Mata iterates this theme. According to this myth, the husband has gone to a foreign land to make his fortune. Meanwhile his wife is abused by her mother- and sisters-in-law. The goddess herself intervenes on behalf of the wife, but fair treatment is meted out only when her husband returns.

Since Hindu women believe that husbands are necessary for their own religious salvation and for a better day-to-day life, it is not surprising that women direct much of their yearly religious activity toward them. Three rituals directly concern husbands. *Barok ki puja* (Marriage Worship) seeks the husband's long life. Young girls perform *neothar* (Nine Nights) in order to secure a future good husband. Performing *karva chauth* (Pitcher Fourth) makes the husband protect his wife, while incidentally asking for his long life. These rites differ from rites honoring brothers in that the two performed by married women (Marriage Worship and Pitcher Fourth) are deemed absolutely necessary. They are part of wife's duty (*dharma*). In order to be a *pativrat*

(worshipful wife)—a state requiring chastity, virtue, and the worship of
one's husband—these two rites must be performed.

In Marriage Worship, which occurs during the hot season, women
seek long lives for their husbands. The Hindi name for this ritual is
revealing—*barok ki puja. Barok* literally means "the gifts given to the
groom's family by the bride's relatives at the time of marriage." In this
ritual the gift given to the groom's family is his long life. And only a
faithful, worshipful wife can give this gift. On this day, women fast and
worship the goddess Savitri and a banyan tree in order to ensure a long
married life, health for their husbands, and many sons.

The well known story of Savitri captures the essence of this important celebration. I give a summary here.

A daughter, Savitri, named after the goddess, was born to a wise
king. When the time came for her marriage, her father told her to
choose her own husband. She selected Satyan, son of King Dumtsen,
who had lost his kingdom and his eyesight. Satyan cared for his
parents by collecting firewood in the jungle. Later, a great sage told
Savitri about Satyan's fate. He said that Satyan was a very great man
but that he would live only one year. Nevertheless, Savitri married
him and served him and his parents well. Three days before he was
due to die, she started fasting, and on the third day she insisted on
accompanying him to the forest. There, under a banyan tree, he died
and Yama (God of Death) came to take him. Savitri followed.
Eventually Yama noticed her and tried to send her back, but she
refused to go. Noting her devotion, Yama allowed her one wish—
anything but her husband's life. She asked for King Dumtsen's
kingdom and eyesight. Her wish was granted. Again she followed,
and again she received a boon—a hundred brothers—because she
was a true and faithful wife. Yet another boon was given—one
hundred sons. Still Savitri followed. Yama again stopped her, and
she said, "Having a hundred sons without a husband is not right.
How can I, a true and faithful wife, have a hundred sons if I have no
husband?" Outwitted, Yama conceded defeat and returned Satyan
to life. His father's kingdom was restored, and eventually Savitri
gave birth to one hundred sons.

By worshipping Savitri, the women honor their marriages and
claim recognition as loyal and faithful wives. As they well know, those
who worship their husbands and worship on behalf of their husbands will
be rewarded. The truly devoted wife can even save her husband from the

arms of the god of death. Wifely duties and worldly happiness are intertwined in this ritual.

Lampblack Mother

In their worship of Lampblack Mother (Siyao Mata), women seek the welfare of a third set of important kin—their sons. Having sons is considered vital by women for several reasons: sons are needed to perform the ancestral rites, they provide "insurance" in one's old age (especially crucial if a woman should be so unfortunate as to become a widow), and they also make up the family labor force. Equally important is the emotional support that sons provide. Daughters marry and leave home, but sons remain. And whereas in rural India husbands and wives are not supposed to have close emotional attachments, mothers and sons have the strongest emotional affinity of any kinship pair. It has been noted that Indian women's devotion to their sons surpasses that to their husbands.

> For a young [Indian] wife, her son in a quite literal sense is her social redeemer. Upon him she ordinarily lavishes a devotion of an intensity proportionate to his importance for her emotional ease and social security.... Even when a woman has several sons, she cherishes and protects and indulges them all to a degree not usually known in the Western world.[3]

This joy in sons is reflected in the songs women sing to honor their sons' births:

> Jasuda gave birth to a son, bliss spread in Gokul.
> Came outside the call for the midwife;
> The midwife cut the cord, bliss spread in the palace.
> Now the queen gave birth to a son, bliss spread in Gokul.

Women's desire for sons is expressed in the ritual known as Lampblack Mother, in which women express their desire for sons and also seek their sons' continued welfare. At dawn on the morning following the Festival of Lights, women rise early to perform their rites before beginning the day's work. Mornings are chilly in October. While everyone else sleeps, the married women gather, shivering, at designated spots felt to be auspicious to their family—most often the site or doorway of the ancestral home. They make a rough figure of a cow with a heap of fresh cow dung. Then a lamp is lit, and a silver coin is immersed in the lamp's oil. Finally a spoon is held over the lamp to collect the soot (lampblack), which is applied around the eyes of children to ward off evil spirits. Symbolically Lampblack Mother is the cow mother, who in this case is clearly related to women's fertility. After these preparations the women in turn take a bunch of sacred grass and, while "sweeping" it behind them with one hand, say, "Give me wealth. That which is bad, run away." They then each take a *puri* (fried bread) and, while holding it under their saris at the womb, say, "Siyao, don't give daughters, give sons. Keep all well in the next year." Or, if they already have sons, they say, "Keep my sons alive and give them many children." After each woman in turn has sought the goddess's favor, the rite ends with a short session of devotional songs.

Stories told during this ritual are about women who have no sons. In the stories someone tells the unfortunate woman about Lampblack Mother and how to worship her. She does so and has many healthy children. To the Karimpur women having many healthy sons is extremely important. Equally important is their belief that the goddess will give them sons and will help them keep their sons healthy.

Snake's Fifth

On *nag panchami* (Snake's Fifth) women ask the snakes to keep away from their families. This ritual takes place in July during the monsoon season. Because of flooding, snakes often seek refuge on higher land—in many cases inside someone's house. As a result, snake bites increase.

Early in the day, women draw a picture of snakes on the wall of the house. These symbolic snakes are offered milk (believed to be a favorite food of snakes) and flowers. The oldest woman in the family usually makes these offerings. The snakes are asked not to harm family members. The rite itself is brief, and generally no songs and stories are associated with it. Similarly, the request itself is less weighty than those made to other deities.

Festival of Lights

I have already described how Jiya concludes the Festival of Lights; it is enlightening to put her activities in a larger context. The Festival of Lights is widely celebrated throughout India. Preparations are made for several days. Houses are repaired and freshly whitewashed, new clothes and ornaments are bought, and sweets and special foods are cooked. Most of the day itself is spent in further preparations. The potter has brought numerous tiny clay lamps that must be filled with oil. The cotton brought by the cotton carder is made into wicks. The courtyard is cleansed once more with a fresh layer of cow dung.

Finally darkness descends. While the women and children arrange the unlit lamps on an auspicious square marked on the courtyard floor, the head of the household, with his wife at his side, worships Lakshmi, the goddess of prosperity. This ritual takes place in the small walled space forming the family "kitchen". This area is the heart of the home physical structure, and family heads often conduct their rituals in it. Here, in sacred space, Lakshmi is entreated to visit the household during the coming year. To encourage Lakshmi's arrival, clay lamps are then lit and placed around rooftops, in windows, and on or near items that could benefit from Lakshimi's gift of prosperity, such as the cattle yard, a student's books, or the granary. Where a lamp burns, Lakshmi's way is lit. To spell out the invitation to her, fireworks, rockets, sparklers, and pinwheels are set off. Men dominate these activities. But men cannot deal with the spirits of the house—the women's world. Hence, when all other activity ceases, Jiya bangs her winnowing fan and shouts, "Get out, poverty" as she roams the courtyard and rooms where her family sleeps. This act, dealing with the immediate family and house, is women's work. Her husband and sons have sought Lakshmi's protection, but she must ensure that evil spirits are chased from the nooks and crannies of *her* house.

Conclusion

Hinduism is nominally a male-dominated religion. According to the Sanskrit scriptures, women cannot study the most sacred texts or engage in rituals without their husbands. Furthermore, the most important rituals should be performed by a male religious specialist—the Brahman priest. Yet, as the evidence from Karimpur shows, women are very actively religious. Devotional religion does not require priests. The rites of Karimpur's women are all devotional in character; therefore, they can be conducted by women.

By studying these rituals, we can see which ones are most important to Hindu women. Only in the case of three rituals performed for specific relatives does each woman perform her own ritual herself. The female head of the family conducts two more general rites for all the other

women. Two of these five rituals involve fasting—Brother's Second and
Marriage Worship. The fast for Marriage Worship is longer and more
rigid. Ritual preparations, including the making of special foods, are more
demanding for Brother's Second, Marriage Worship, and the Festival
of Lights. Thus, it is clear that Marriage Worship is given the greatest
weight, followed in order by Brother's Second, Lampblack Mother, and
Snake's Fifth. The Festival of Lights is an anomalous case, because it is
actually a family ritual in which men also play an important role.

In all these rituals, women, who should ideally be submissive and
passive, become instead active. Such rituals may give psychological
support to the women themselves, because they allow women to have
active control of events rather than depend completely on their male kin.
Ritually, only a wife or a sister can really save a husband or brother from
death; only Jiya can in fact finally chase poverty out of her house. The
rituals performed by Karimpur's women clearly reflect the women's
social world—the world of the family and household. Their attempts to
have active control over these most important facets of their lives may
in fact be most critical for our understanding of Karimpur women's
rituals.

Notes

1.   Karimpur is a pseudonym. The village has been described in William
      Wiser and Charlotte Wiser, *Behind Mud Walls*, Berkeley: University of
      California Press, 1972, and in Susan S. Wadley, *Shakti: Power in the
      Conceptual Structure of Karimpur Religion*, Chicago: University of
      Chicago Department of Anthropology, 1975. I conducted the research
      on which this paper is based during 1967-1969 and 1974-1975 and was
      supported by grants from the National Science Foundation; the South
      Asia Committee, the University of Chicago; and the American Institute
      of Indian Studies. I also wish to thank my colleagues Barbara D. Miller,
      William Houska, and Bruce W. Derr, whose insights and suggestions
      aided me in writing this paper. Last, the women of Karimpur deserve the
      most thanks. I can never repay them for their hospitality and kindness;
      I only hope that I do them justice.
2.   W. Douglas P. Hill, *The Holy Lake of the Acts of Rama,* London: Oxford
      University Press, 1952, pp. 297-298.
3.   David Mandelbaum, "The Family in India," in *The Family: Its
      Function and Destiny*, New York: Harper and Brothers, 1949, p. 104.

Women and Jewelry in Rural India

Doranne Jacobson

ABSTRACT. In Madhya Pradesh, as in other parts of India, the ornamented woman symbolizes auspiciousness and prosperity, while a woman naked of jewelry represents poverty and sorrow. In India, jewelry has long been invested with elaborate symbolic associations which have served to provide ideological support for the acquisition and possession of jewelry in social settings in which precious ornaments fulfil significant economic functions. Jewelry ownership has been paricularly important for women denied ownership of more valuable forms of property. A woman's rights in the jewelry she wears differ according to her relationships with its donors: jewelry is divided into categories over which a woman has different degrees of control. This paper analyzes the importance to individual women, to couples, and to joint families, of jewelry ownership and conversions of wealth over which a woman has little control to jewelry over which a woman has complete control. The relationsips of jewelry to economic power within the community and the kin group and the economic power of men vs. women are explored.

> Noble women with graceful gait...went forth with happy hearts to perform the lustral rite; all fair of face as the moon and with bright fawn-like eyes...dressed in fine robes of many hues and decked with every kind of adornment, wearing on every limb auspicious ornaments, they sang their songs more sweetly than the sweet-voiced cuckoo; bracelets and anklets tinkled and bells upon their girdles...
>
> The marriage of Rama and Sita, in Hill, 1952:140

Jewelry and personal ornamentation have been part of India's cultural tradition from prehistoric times until the present day. Invested with aesthetic, ritual, social and economic significance, treasured by countless generations and decried by modern economists, elaborate jewelry has been inescapably visible on the the Indian sub-continent for millennia. This paper briefly explores the importance of jewelry in India in ancient and modern times and, in a more detailed way, examines data partaining to jewelry in one area of India today.

Jewelry is today worn primarily by women in India; consequently this paper focuses on women's ornamentation, although men's jewelry is also discussed.[1]

Indian jewelry has long been invested with elaborate symbolic associations, particularly with states of well-being, and is also of considerable economic significance. That Indian jewelry has many symbolic associations is well known (see, for example, Coomaraswamy, 1964:154; Russell and Hiralal, 1916 (IV): 517ff; Bhushan, 1964: 2-20, 88), and the notion that ornaments are of economic importance has been advanced by several writers (e.g.Bailey, 1958: 76-80; Basham, 1959: 212; Bhushan, 1964: 20; Fuchs, 1966: 27,342), but few have expressly stressed its importance for women (e.g. Altekar, 1962: 303-4). I am not aware of any detailed study bringing together data from a single region on the ideological, social and economic aspects of jewelry and jewelry ownership, particularly as these relate to women and their kinship and residence groups. It is intended that this paper be such a study, albeit incomplete.[*]

It is hoped that examining jewelry within a specific cultural context will enhance understanding of its economic significance, its attendant symbolic and social associations, and the cultural forms of which it is an integral part.

In this paper I will argue that the positive associations of jewelry have served to provide ideological support for the acquisition and possession of jewelry in social settings in which precious ornaments fulfil vital economic functions. Culturally reinforced desires to own jewelry contribute to the well-being of individuals and families in several ways. As a form of savings, jewelry is in some respects better than cash, and as a source of liquid capital, preferable to land. For women, ownership of jewelry is often especially important, since traditionally, most Indian women have been conspicuously denied ownership or full control of immovable property. At the same time, cultural norms sanction and even require that women be decorated with valuable ornaments, frequently the only form of wealth they control or can manipulate without opposition from others. Jewelry often serves its wearers as a vital source of capital providing some measure of security and crucial freedom of action.

I will also attempt to delineate some important relationships between jewelry ownership and power. In general, members of privileged and prosperous groups own more jewelry than members of poorer groups. But *within* each kin group, jewelry is owned by those who control the fewest other economic resources, particularly young brides. Conversely, within each household, those who have most control of other material assets tend to own the least jewelry.

Given the present Hindu and Muslim systems of inheritance and property control, the cultural reinforcement for jewelry ownership can be seen as contributing to the economic well-being of women. At the same time, however, the positive symbolism and prestige associated with jewelry ownership may tend to divert attention from the reality of women's less favored economic position relative to that of men. In modern India emphasis on jewelry ownership is diminishing, while at the same time opportunities for women to achieve financial security by means other than ownership of ornaments are increasing.

JEWELRY IN INDIA

The Tradition

Evidence of the importance of jewelry can be found in the artistic and textual heritage of every epoch of Indian civilization. For example, some early Harappan figures, otherwise unclothed, wear many bangles and other jewelry, and several ornaments are mentioned in the *Rig Veda*. Important officials of Aryan courts were known as "jewel bearers" (*ratnins*), from their important roles in royal ceremonies in which jewels were offered to the gods (Basham, 1959: 23, 36b, 42; Apte, 1951a: 397, 1951b:436). Indian sculpture of later periods portrays male and female figures decorated with lavish ornamentation. Basham has written of ancient India:

> If clothes were simple and few, ornaments were complex and many. Gold, silver and precious stones of every available kind were always in demand for personal adornment. Women wore jewelled ornaments on their foreheads, and along the partings of their hair. Earrings were worn by both sexes, and the ears were stretched by heavy and large ornaments.... Ornate necklaces were worn, and wide girdles of linked gold with hanging ropes of pearls. Bangles and armlets... and anklets, often set with little tinkling bells, or with their hollows filled with rattling pebbles, were... popular.... The few surviving pieces of jewellery, and the representations of jewellery in sculptures and painting, show that the Indian jeweller attained very high standards in his art.... Even the poorer people, who could not afford gold or gems, loaded

themselves with jewellery of silver, brass, glass and painted pottery, and all classes adorned their hair, ears and necks with the beautiful flowers which India provides in abundance (Basham, 1959: 212).

A multitude of different ornaments are mentioned in ancient texts and depicted in art works, including more than half a dozen different pieces for the head and forehead, a gauzy pearl ornament over the breasts, several types of large shoulder ornaments, and even a bejeweled thigh decoration (Altekar, 1962: 298-99). Virtually absent in earlier periods, nose ornaments became significant after the Muslim conquest (Basham, 1959: 212 ; Altekar, 1962: 302). The Moghul rulers were lovers of precious stones and ornamented themselves with fabulous arrays of diamonds, emeralds, rubies, pearls, and other jewels. The Moghul princesses of the sixteenth century were plentifully and beautifully ornamented, as were Hindu princesses of the period (Bhushan, 1964: 74ff). Sources of the seventeenth and eighteenth centuries pertaining to Rajasthan mention more than 40 differently named pieces of jewelry to adorn virtually every part of the female form [Sharma, 1968: 154-58,(26)]. Classical Indian poetry makes constant reference not only to the jewelry of gods and of human beings, but also to the jeweled decoration of horses, cattle, elephants, carriages, beds, palaces, and cities. Even ships were garlanded with pearls and gold (Coomaraswamy, 1964; 151-53).

Jewelers of the past created elegant and finely made pieces that were clearly appreciated for their aesthetic value; indeed, the presence of jewelry on virtually all ancient Hindu sculpture suggests that ornaments were considered important assets to personal beauty. Since most sculptures depict divine beings or their worshippers, it is to be expected that jewelry had ritual significance as well. The Code of Manu commands the wearing of ornaments on certain occasions, and the coffers of India's great temples are filled with jewelry offered by devotees of the deities. Crowns and diadems signified divinity as well as terrestrial sovereignty. Various designs came to symbolize particular deities and astrological signs. Many traditional Hindu ornaments were embellished with religious figures, and some pieces provided their wearers protection from evil influences. Rosaries of various substances have long been in use among Hindus, Buddhists, Muslims, and Christians (Bhushan, 1964: 6, 9, 15). Hindus attached sanctity to gold itself, particularly to "pure gold"; that is, gold of a fineness of 20 carats or above (Russell and Hiralal, 1916 [IV]: 523; Stern, 1970: 21).

The association of personal ornamentation and auspiciousness so widespread in India today is doubtless of long history. It is apparently an ancient tradition that the Hindu bride be decorated with jewelry and receive at least a token ornament at her wedding (Bhushan, 1964:9). Attesting to a long tradition is the widespread distribution throughout India of bangles, toe rings, and marriage necklaces worn by women to signify the married state.

The amount of jewelry worn by an individual was clearly related to his or her wealth and power, and in recent historic times, in some areas the wearing of jewelry was restricted by caste and rank. In the princely state of Udaipur, for example, gold could be worn on the feet only by those of high rank. As a man rose in courtly rank, he was permitted to add to his foot ornamentation. In parts of South India members of certain low-ranking castes were forbidden to wear jewelry of particular kinds and materials (Bhushan, 1964: 15; Hutton, 1963; 85-86, 205-6).

Jewelry apparently served as an important form of investment for its possessors, both male and female. For women, jewelry was probably of particular practical importance, since it was the primary form of property which women could own. Post-Vedic lawgivers denied or severely limited women's right to inherit and control immovable wealth, except in certain matrilineal communities. Some lawgivers included inherited real estate in women's wealth (*stridhana*), but most denied women the power to alienate such property. The only property over which women had apparently undisputed rights of ownership and disposal was jewelry and clothing presented to her by her natal kinsmen at any time, by her husband after the marriage, or by others at the time of the marriage or departure for her husband's home (Manu, in Altekar, 1962: 220). According to most traditional sources, husbands had no legal rights over such *stridhana*, except in dire emergency.[2]

Jewelry in Modern India

Much of the traditional importance of jewelry continues in India today, although the inflation of gold prices in recent decades and various modern influences have contributed to a diminishing emphasis on ornamentation. Among western-educated Indians and most urban dwellers, jewelry is less weighty and plentiful than it was a generation ago. It would be rare indeed to see a modern Indian male laden with jewels, but by the same token, it would be difficult to find a man not wearing at least a few items of decoration, such as a ring, a watch, an amulet, or even earrings. Virtually all women wear jewelry at all times, either in modest or lavish proportions, and in most social groups, jewelry is an essential part of dowry and dower. On the streets of any Indian city one can see on women passersby an abundance of glass and gold bangles, gold neckchains, gold and enameled earrings, diamond nose ornaments, and rings of many designs. In sophisticated circles, costume jewelry is sometimes worn. Among rural women pieces of jewelry characteristic of each region are worn in abundance: ponderous silver head and neck ornaments in the Himalayan areas, lighter silver and gold pieces on the Gangetic plain, heavy silver, ivory, and mirrored lac jewelry in Rajasthan, very wide cuff-like silver bracelets in Gujarat, gold and pearl nose rings in Maharashtra, fairly heavy gold jewelry throughout South India, bell metal, brass, beaded, and silver spiked jewelry among the tribals of Bastar and Orissa, ornate and filigree gold pieces in Bengal, and many more unique fashions throughout the land.[3]

Jewelry designs differ not only from region to region but also between different communities and ethnic groups within a region. Distinctive ornaments may be worn by members of particular groups and, in conjunction with other items of apparel, serve as identifying markers. For example, among the little-ornamented working women of Maharashtra near whom they live and work, women of the Lambāḍi group, of Rajasthani origin, are conspicuous in their large earrings and mirrored clothing. Members of most tribes in India adorn themselves with items of jewelry and dress unique to each group.

Many of the designs worn today echo those of centuries ago, and several designs seem to have survived intact since ancient times. The names and designs of some ornaments seem derivative of the ancient and still current practice of wearing garlands of fresh flowers and seeds (Bhushan, 1964: 10, 49; Basham, 1959: 212; Coomaraswamy, 1964: 149). Indian films portray heroines of epics in a almost incredible array of metallic and petrous ornamentation, many pieces apparently modelled after those carved on ancient statuary. In modern representations, goddesses are always plentifully ornamented. The covers of nationally distributed magazines commonly feature young women bedecked in the traditional clothing and jewelry of particular regions and communities. These female figures clearly personify enduring standards of Indian beauty.

The important place of jewelry in the lives of the people is recognized by the compilers of the Indian census monographs, a series of small village studies prepared in conjunction with the national census. Many of these publications include a section on jewelry, sometimes illustrated with drawings and photographs of the pieces. The titles of modern popular novels frequently refer to gold and gold ornaments.

The attachment of the India public to jewelry has had important national consequences. Because gold is in high demand but short supply in India, the price of gold within the country is generally more than twice the price of the metal on the international market, thus encouraging the smuggling of gold into India. It was estimated in 1962 that gold worth perhaps 40 crores of rupees ($84 million, at the rate of exchange in effect at that time) was smuggled into India annually. Smuggling led to the loss of foreign exchange and weakened the rupee. During the 1962 hostilities with China, India's foreign exchange reserves were badly depleted, and gold became an important concern of the government.

No authoritative figures were available, but estimates of the gold reserves of the people of India in 1962 ranged from Rs 1,800 crores to 4,500 crores ($3.78 billion to $9.45 billion). Economists pointed out that public hoarding of gold was unproductive investment and not in the national interest. The government offered gold bonds, to be given in exchange for gold in any form, at the prevailing international price, plus interest. Government leaders appealed to the public to purchase these bonds in order to mobilize private gold stocks and to refrain from buying gold oranments so that the price of gold would drop and smuggling be discouraged. Patriotic sentiment led many Indians to contribute gold to the national cause, but compliance was much less than had been hoped for (*Economic Weekly*, 1962: 1753-4; "Croesus", 1962: 869-70; *Eastern Economist*, 1962: 851-52; Stern, 1970: 24).

In 1963 the government enacted Gold Control Rules forbidding the manufacture and sale of jewelry of gold purer than fourteen carats and placing other important restrictions on rights to own and sell gold. It was hoped that the new rules would encourage public investment in industrial development rather than gold and would ultimately result in government ownership of all the gold in India. These rules were met by a public outcry and widespread noncompliance. Goldsmiths and jewelers mobilized against the rules, with significant political consequences (see Stern, 1970). In 1966, the government finally abandoned controls on the purity of gold, although other restrictions on the possession of gold have remained in effect. In 1974, the Government Planning Commission proposed that no couple should be permitted to possess gold or gold ornaments in excess of ten *tolas*, upon pain of imprisonment of up to five years. Public response to this proposal was, predictably, largely negative (e.g., Sahasranaman, 1974: 30). Today the demand for gold in India remains high, and gold smuggling is a continuing problem.

Clearly, then jewelry remains important in the lives of millions of Indians and will almost certainly remain so for some time. Why is jewelry so important? What does it do for those who own and wear it? I cannot answer these questions in full or for all of India, but I wish to examine the place of jewelry in the lives of villagers in one area of Central India as a step toward understanding the importance of jewelry in the Indian context.

THE CULTURAL SETTING

Jewelry and the Area

From 1965 to 1967, and in 1973, I carried out a study of the roles of women in the Bhopal area of Madhya Pradesh. I focused on the women of Nimkhera, a village in Raisen District, about 45 miles east of Bhopal, the capital of the state. Even before my research in the village began, I became aware of importance of women's jewelry in the area. The bazaars in Bhopal and other towns in the region had large numbers of shops devoted exclusively to jewelry. Long chains of linked silver bracelets hung beside loops of silver belts outside each shop, and would-be purchasers clustered beside heaps of toe rings and ankle ornaments. Glittering cylinders of stacked glass bangles of every conceivable hue filled several bazaar stalls in Bhopal, and nearby, artisans could be seen studding bright lac bangles with bits of mirror. Women in the crowds at local country fairs wore large quantities of jewelry.

After I moved to Nimkhera, the importance of jewelry in the lives of the villagers made itself even more evident. The ornaments of the village women clanked and jingled as they walked, and jewelry was always a topic of conversation at women's gatherings. The village women criticized me for going about with "naked" (i.e., unornamented) feet and ankles, and my purchase of a set of toe rings and ankle chains drew outspoken approval from both men and women. At weddings and on certain festivals, some women were so heavily laden with sparkling jewelry they gave the appearance of mobile jeweler's stalls. It·would have been impossible to ignore jewelry during my study.

The Region and the Village[4]

Nimkhera is similar in many respects to hundreds of settlements in Central India. The village houses of whitewashed earth and stone cluster on the side of a hill of the Vindhya range overlooking fertile fields on the flat land of the Malwa plateau below. Most of the 621 villagers are farmers, laborers, and craftsmen supported by the abundant wheat crop grown on the village fields. Rice, gram (*chanā*), pulses, maize, millet, linseed, and several varieties of vegetables and fruits are also grown by the villagers. A small number of men work at urban jobs, and a few men have recently begun quarrying, trucking, and road contracting to supplement their agricultural income. The village population is approximately 80 per cent Hindu and 20 per cent Muslim. The Muslims include a group of well-to-do Pathans, originally from Afghanistan, and poorer groups of Fakirs, "Sheikhs", and recent converts. The Hindus include representatives of 21 castes, ranging from prosperous landowning Brahmans and Thakurs to landless weavers and sweepers. A Beragi temple priest, Raoji farmers, carpenters, barbers, tailors, vegetable growers, potters, goat butchers, washermen, and leather workers all reside in village. The composition of the village population is not unusual for villages in this region.

The village is about 15 miles east of Raisen, the district headquarters and site of a weekly bazaar. The district is almost completely rural and includes much uncultivated forest land, reflected in the low district population density of 170 per square mile (compared with 471 for all of India). As in many other parts of the the country, there are fewer females than males (900 to 1000). The district is relatively undeveloped agriculturally and educationally, but consistently produces a wheat surplus, even in years of subnormal rainfall (Tiwari, 1964: xliii-iv, lvi, lxxx; Pandya, 1974: 114).

The character of Nimkhera and its population today reflect diverse cultural influences of many centuries' duration. The village is situated hardly 25 miles from Vidisha, an important provincial capital of the Magadhan empire four centuries before Christ, now a busy market town of primarily Hindu population. Nearby is Sanchi, a world-famous Buddhist site. Raisen Fort, an impressive hilltop complex, was the scene of many battles between Hindu Rajputs, Gujarati Muslims, and Afghans, and was controlled by the Moghuls for over a century. A powerful Gond kingdom extended to within a few miles of Nimkhera and may have included the site of the village for some time. In the seventeenth and eighteenth centuries the area was plundered by the

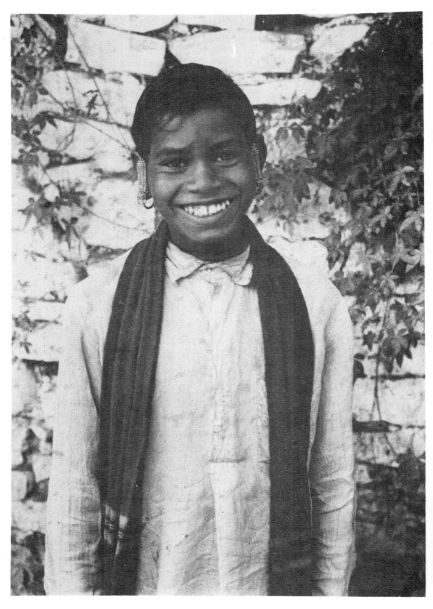

A Brahman youth attending a wedding wears gold earrings for the occasion;
he normally does not wear these ornaments.

At a Koli (weaver) wedding, women of the bride's village critically examine the silver jewelry presented to the bride by the groom's family.

Dressed to celebrate a festival, a young high-caste Hindu woman is
ornamented with much of her silver jewelry.

A well-to-do Pathan Muslim woman dressed up for a holiday wears gold earrings and pendant, rings set with precious stones, and glass bangles.

Marathas, Hindu armies from Bundelkhand, and Afghans. In 1722, Dost Muhammad Khan, an Afghan adventurer, established himself as the ruler of Bhopal state, which included Nimkhera, Raisen, Sanchi, and Bhopal, with Bhopal as its capital city. Vidisha became part of Hindu Maratha-ruled Gwalior state. In succeeding years Bhopal state became a British protectorate, ruled from 1819 to 1926 by a succession of four female rulers (Begams). In 1949 the state became part of independent India, and in 1956 Bhopal was made the capital of Madhya Pradesh. Previously a quiet town of arched gateways and narrow bazaars peopled by bearded men wearing turbans and fezzes and women veiled in black, Bhopal became an active center of modern government. An influx of well-educated civil servants and technicians from all over India has swelled the population of the city to about 400,000.

There are no written records indicating when Nimkhera was founded, but numerous broken stone carvings dating from the eleventh or twelfth century have been found in the village. The Bagheli Thakurs, the most numerous caste in the village, came into the area with their Brahmans and other service castes from Bundelkhand about 250 years ago. In 1916 a family of Afghan Pathans moved into the village and became quite prosperous.

The Hindu village women's dress of this area reflects strong influences from western India, particularly Rajasthan. Traditional Hindu women's garb includes a bright bordered sari worn over a printed or patchwork blouse and full ankle-length skirt (*ghāghrā*). Many of the traditional heavy pieces of jewelry resemble those worn in Rajasthan today and in the past.[5] Today young village women of the region are increasingly adopting the printed sari, blouse, and petticoat worn throughout much of North India. Muslim village women, like their urban relatives, wear a tunic and gathered ankle-length pants (*salwār-kamīz* with head scarf, while some sophisticated young Muslims in the area wear the currently fashionable bell-bottom pants and tops.

Kinship and Marriage

Patterns of kinship and marriage among Hindus in the region differ from those of the Muslims. Every Hindu belongs to an endogamous caste (*jāt*), and exogamous patrilineal clan (*got*), and an exogamous shallow patrilineage (*khāndān, kuṭum*). Marriage to any person known to be a consanguineal relative is prohibited. Marriage within the village is not forbidden, but the vast majority of Hindu marriages are contracted outside the village, in settlements from one to 40 miles distant from Nimkhera.

Most Hindu girls are married before puberty, and virtually all are married before the age of 16. Boys almost all marry before about age 22. The young couple do not normally begin living together until after the *gaunā* ceremony, which takes place about three years after the wedding and consummates the union.

Divorce and the remarriage of widows and divorcees are strongly disapproved of only within the high-ranking Jijotiya Brahman and Brahmbhat Raoji castes, although in most groups in this region divorce carries at least a slight social stigma. Divorce is seldom formally decreed but is considered to have occurred when a woman marries another man or is clearly rejected by her husband. In Nimkhera, 14.7 per cent of women have been divorced.

Residence is ideally patrilocal, but other forms of residence are not uncommon. The joint family is the ideal although only 45 per cent of the villagers live in joint households.

A married Hindu woman is formally regarded as a member of her husband's patrilineage. In most cases, however, village women of this region for many years after marriage act as important members of both their natal and conjugal households (called *m āīkā* and *s u s r āl* respectively), periodically travelling back and forth between the two. A striking feature of village life is the constant procession of women coming and going on such visits. The flexibility of the married woman's position as a member of two households seems to fulfil important functions for her, her kin groups, and her caste (see Jacobson, 1976). The amount of time a woman spends in her natal home usually diminishes as she grows older. Generally, young women spend long months in their parental homes, while middle-aged women may visit for a week or a month once or twice a year.

Members of affinally linked kin groups may assist each other in a number of ways, but the groups remain structurally distinct. Hindu affines often stand in opposition to each other, and tensions between them may be great. The most common point of contention between affines is the woman linking them, particularly her husband's relatives' treatment of her, and the issue of the length of time she may stay in her parental home for visiting and helping with household and agricultural work.

Muslim groups in this area are not strictly endogamous, although the high-ranking Pathans feel strongly about maintaining the "purity" of their blood lines.[6] The Muslim kindred (*azīzdār*) is bilateral, and marriage within it is common and approved. Cross and parallel cousin marriage and brother-sister exchanges are encouraged, although marriage between nonkinsmen (*gair*) is occurring with increasing frequency. Residence is usually patrilocal or virilocal, although a significant proportion of couples deviate from this ideal. Muslim girls are married after puberty—some immediately, and others several years after, and boys usually marry before age 25. The bride and groom normally commence marital life immediately after the wedding.

Divorce and the remarriage of both men and women are permissible, although not frequent, in all groups. Divorce (*talāk*) is obtained formally in accordance with Muslim religious law.

Property Ownership and Inheritance

Among Hindu villagers in this region, wealth, including land and houses, is normally inherited patrilineally only by males, ideally sons, but in their absence, by brothers or other patrilineally related male kinsmen of a deceased person. At the division of a Hindu joint family, the family houses and lands are divided among the males of the household; females get no share.

Hindu widows have rights to the fruits of their husband's lands, but traditionally they have no right to alienate the property. If a widow remarries, she loses all rights, even of maintenance, in her husband's land. Upon the death of a Hindu widow without living sons, her lands and property revert to her husband's kinsmen rather than to her own natal kinsmen or daughters.

A Hindu woman normally owns absolutely only that property which is presented to her by her natal kin as gifts during the lifetime of the donors (typically, cash, clothing, and jewelry). Her dowry, presented at the time of her marriage by her natal kinsmen to her husband's family, is not part of her personal property. In recent years, a few men with daughters but no sons have willed land to their daughters.

The Hindu Succession Act of 1956 passed by the Government of India gives equal inheritance rights to a Hindu man's widow, his sons and daughters, and his mother, to the exclusion of other heirs, and grants Hindu women absolute ownership and control of their inherited property. Despite the existence of this legislation, traditional inheritance rules are observed by villagers in the Nimkhera region, as they are by many villagers in other areas (see Luschinsky, 1963).

The Muslims of Nimkhera, particularly the Pathans, attempt to follow Islamic rules of inheritance. Both daughters and widows inherit shares of wealth, including land and houses, from their parents and husbands. Some women receive their property shares from their parents at the time of marriage. Muslim women, even if childless, remarried, or divorced, have complete rights to their inherited property, and may sell or give it to whomever they wish. In addition, every married Muslim woman is the potential owner of a sum of money known as *mehr*, which her husband and his family pledged to pay her at any time she demands it. The amount of *mehr*, which varies from a token sum to many thousands of rupees, is written into the marriage contract and is considered legally binding. Most women never demand the *mehr* payment, but a woman scorned, mistreated, or divorced without just cause may insist on receiving the money, which is hers to do with as she wishes. Nevertheless, the power of Muslim women in economic matters is generally less than that of men. Women inherit smaller shares of wealth than men do (a son's share is twice that of a daughter's), and purdah (the traditional seclusion and segregation of women from men) imposes limits on women's participation in money-earning activities. As among Hindus, Muslim women cannot normally claim dowry goods as personal property.

The Status of Women

In this region of India, women enjoy a status relative to men apparently somewhat higher than that of rural women in the Gangetic plain area. Young Hindu girls, like goddesses, are worshipped by males in annual rituals, and parents touch their daughters' feet as a gesture of respect. Son's feet are not touched. In most groups women perform economically significant tasks, and this as well as the shortage of women in the region, enhance women's power within their residential and kin groups. That most women are not completely isolated from their natal kinsmen after marriage and *gauna* adds to their strength and sense of well-being. Meekness is seldom to be found among village women of the Raisen region.

Nevertheless, all women of the area acknowledge the cultural ideal that women should be subservient to men. No matter how domineering she may be, no woman will openly admit that she does not obey her husband. In fact, most women refrain from confronting or quarreling with male cognates or affines, and independence is usually displayed subtly rather than boldly. Women play no obvious part in village politics, are expected to act modestly in public contexts, and usually observe some form of purdah. Hindu women veil their faces in the presence of elder relatives of their husbands and before other categories of affines, and, at least while young, should remain virtually housebound in their husband's villages. They do, however, have some freedom of movement and need not veil within their natal households or villages. Traditional Muslim women of the area, on the other hand, wear all-covering veils (*burkās*) on their rare outings beyond the confines of their courtyards, both in their conjugal and parental homes, and should not communicate with men who are not close kinsmen.[7]

Few rural women of this region visit town and city bazaars; marketing is normally done by men. However, village women sometimes make purchases from local shops and itinerant vendors, and in Nimkhera, two middle-aged women run small shops.

Ideally, husband and wife make joint decisions pertaining to family finances. A passage in the Hindu marriage ceremony explicitly admonishes the husband to consult his wife on all matters involving money and jewelry.

In 85 per cent of Nimkhera households, a woman keeps some or all of the family money, guarding the cache in a locked or secret spot, and she may exercise considerable influence over its disposal. A few women secretly lend money and keep the interest. Virtually all women have access to the household grain stores, and some secretly sell grain to build up private nest eggs for themselves.

The power of a woman to make decisions governing significant aspects of her own life and the lives of her family members depends upon several factors. The amount of wealth she and her family control is obviously a limiting factor. The woman's age and position in the residence unit are crucial: generally, the least influential adult woman is the youngest daughter-in-law in a joint family, and the most influential is the older wife in a nuclear family. A woman's health, knowledge, cleverness, and confidence in herself are also very important determinants of her ability to influence and make decisions. The personalities of a woman's male affines are also significant; it is difficult for a woman to openly challenge a husband or father-in-law determined to be autocratic.

JEWELRY IN NIMKHERA

Pounds of Silver and Gold

All female villagers wear at least a few ornaments, and some women always wear substantial quantities of jewelry. On festivals and at weddings a high percentage of the jewelry owned by village women is taken from its storage places and worn. Most of the pieces owned by village women of this area are of silver—often pounds and pounds of it—but a few items are of gold. The monetary value of each piece derives not from the beauty of the workmanship involved in its manufacture but from its weight and the purity of the metal. Pieces are weighed by the jewelry seller and the price is computed according to the current local price per *tola* (11.67 grams) of the metal, plus a small "making charge". In 1973, a pair of moderately heavy silver bracelets could be purchased in Vidisha for about 100 rupees,[8] and a small pair of silver earrings for Rs 5. A set of three amulets made of very thin hammered gold was purchased in 1972 for 232 rupees.

The number and value of a woman's pieces of jewelry are clearly related to the wealth of her family, since silver and gold jewelry is definitely expensive by village standards. The poorest women may own only a pair of silver ankle ornaments, a pair of thin silver bracelets, and some glass bangles, worth in all barely a hundred rupees, while a well-to-do woman of the village may decorate herself with a large number of pieces together weighing as much as 20 pounds and valued at several thousand rupees. Women occasionally discuss their jewelry in terms of its actual retail value or even of its exact weight, but they tend to refer to specific pieces, qualified by such descriptions as "very heavy" or "thin and light", as well as "silver", "gold", "pure", "impure", or "mixed". However, when discussing jewelry purchases, men usually refer to the weight and price of jewelry. No one readily indicates to non-family members the total value of his or her ornaments or of jewelry owned by other members of the family.

The array of different pieces of jewelry is large, with each differently designed ornament designated by a specific name. With few exceptions, men and women, and Hindus and Muslims wear differently designed and named pieces. Some ornaments are worn by members of some groups more than others; for example, the head peak (*rikrī*) is worn primarily by Thakurs and almost never by Brahmans, barbers, sweepers, or members of most other castes. Thus, here as elsewhere in India, ornaments of different design indicate or suggest caste and religious affiliation.

The designs of most jewelry worn in the village seem to be traditional, or at least not very new. Novelty or originality *per se* are not valued;. a woman who wears an item never before seen in the village is usually not regarded as a style-setter, but is rudely asked where she got that "foreign" thing. Old women still wear pieces they received as brides, and in one case, the joints on an old woman's ankle ornaments had completely solidified and melted together from years of continuous wearing.

Nevertheless, fashions in jewelry do change, and some of the older styles are seldom worn by young women in the village. The current trend is away from heavy toward lightweight jewelry. Ornaments for the head and upper ear are rapidly falling into disfavor, and jewelry for the upper arm is now seldom seen. Men now wear very little traditional jewelry. As pieces wear out and styles change, old ornaments are melted down to make new ones.

In general, heavier pieces are worn in higher proportion by women with few urban contacts. In Nimkhera, women of the almost exclusively rural Bagheli Thakur caste wear the heaviest jewelry, while wealthy Muslim women with many urban kinswomen wear relatively little jewelry. For all young villagers, lightweight jewelry, and among wealthy Muslims, ornaments of nontraditional western-influenced design, are gradually becoming valued marks of sophistication. For men, a watch is now an essential indicator of urbanity.

Appendix I (pp. 212-17) lists local names for specific pieces of jewelry tradionally worn in Nimkhera and other villages in the region. The list is probably not complete, but the extent and variety of the terminology provide an indication of the significance of jewelry in the culture of the region.

It should be noted that ornaments of gold are worn only above the waist, particularly on the head and neck. Wearing gold on the upper— and purer—portions of the body reflects the traditional Indian respect for gold as the most precious metal.[9]

The numbers of different ornaments suggest that jewelry is less important among Muslim women than Hindu women and much less significant among men than women. (Hindu women, 61 pieces; Muslim women, 36 pieces; Hindu men, 22 pieces; and Muslim men, 6 pieces). The lesser emphasis on jewelry among Muslims can be attributed not only to urban influence and the wealthy Pathans' view of heavy traditional ornaments as being rustic and old-fashioned, but also to the fact that unlike Hindu women, Muslim women can hope to claim *mehr* if necessary and to inherit shares of any property left by parents and husbands. For them, jewelry is but one form of valuable property they may own. For both Hindu and Muslim men, ornaments are relatively insignificant in value in comparison with the houses, lands, animals, and machines they own or control.

The Aesthetics and Symbolism of Jewelry

The wearing of jewelry is imbued with a variety of aesthetic and symbolic meanings in this region, as it probably is in most parts of India.

Firstly, jewelry is considered beautiful. The glistening of precious metals on the human form is pleasant to look upon, and for most villagers, jewelry is considered an essential adjunct to beauty. Jewelry cannot be worn haphazardly:on women, the pieces must be arranged in bilateral symmetry, with each half of the body exactly balancing the other, except for the single nose ornament in the left nostril. Pieces must be worn in correct sequence and on the appropriate places: for example, on the ankle, *kaṛe* must be worn above *tore*, which in turn are worn above *chhagale*. On the toes, *joṛue* are worn with *bichhiye*, never with *bichhuriye*, and so on.

The unornamented female ankle or wrist is deemed ugly and inauspicious and is rarely seen. Even the young Hindu women and wealthy Muslims who scorn the more traditional heavy jewelry load their wrists with glass bangles and wear ankle chains.

Traditionally, the woman decked out in all her jewelry has been considered the essence of femininity. The tinkling and jangling of the ornament-laden bride or young wife remains a happy symbol of prosperity and well-being. When going to her new home, the bride always wears as much of her jewelry as possible, and she may wear much of it for months at a time, not removing it even to sleep or bathe. Upon the departure of her daughter-in-law for a long visit to her parental home, one old woman said sadly, with tears in her eyes, "I'll miss the jingling of her jewelry; the house will be empty without it."

The glitter and tinkling of glass bangles are also considered sexually alluring. A Pathan woman once scornfully described modern urban Muslim girls who wear the ostensibly modest *burka* with sleeves cut short enough to reveal wrists laden with bangles.[10]

A Hindu woman with a living husband (*suhāgan*) must always wear the essential emblems of the married state: bangles and toe rings. The forehead spangle or a colored dot, and red powder in the parting of the hair are also worn by the *suhāgan*. Conversely, the sorrowing widow breaks off her bangles,[11] strips her feet of ornaments, and leaves her forehead bare as signs of her misfortune. Among Muslims, the bride is frequently presented with a nose ring and chain which she wears for two months to signify her new condition.[12] She should also wear bangles and toe rings.

It is considered bad luch for a married woman to remove any of her ornaments at the well or tank while she is bathing, since after the death of her husband, a widow ceremonially removes her jewelry at the well or tank and bathes there. Otherwise, no misfortune is thought to attach to the removal of ornaments, except perhaps for protective amulets worn by many villagers.

Among Hindus the fracturing of bangles is associated not only with widowhood but motherhood as well. The bangles worn by a parturient woman are ritually polluted by the birth process, and the midwife breaks them off the new mother's wrists. But unlike the widow's, the new mother's wrists do not remain bare. Ten days later, in preparation for the *Chauk*, a blessing ceremony welcoming the infant to the family, the new mother is bathed, has new lac bangles put on her wrists, and dons all her jewelry. The association of jewelry and fertility is strong when the new mother, with wet bejeweled hands, blesses the household water pots and, in another ceremony, the village well.

In one situation, an earring symbolizes a bride. Among Hindu castes which allow women to remarry, a previously unmarried man cannot wed a previously married woman. For high-ranking castes, this rule is a strict one and prevents some men from ever marrying. But in middle-and lower-ranking castes a particular ceremony called *Ḍūri Byāo* marries a bachelor to an earring which, for ritual purposes, is considered to be his bride. The man's previously-married human fiancee attends the wedding and is presented with jewelry by the groom's kinsmen, but otherwise acts as a guest. She afterward resides with the groom as his second wife. The earring may be worn by the man or his wife or kept safely put away. If the ring is lost or breaks, a death feast should be given, as if the "wife" had died.[13]

In another situation involving remarriage, a piece of jewelry is symbolically equated with a woman. The second wife of a Hindu widower wears on a string around her neck a silver amulet representing her husband's first wife. If she failed to accord her dead predecessor this respect, the second wife would be "twisted and killed" by the dead woman.

At the *gauna* (consummation ceremony) jewelry is the object of a ritual struggle for power. When the Hindu bride is first brought to her new home, she and the groom fish with their hands seven times in a platter of turmeric water for a bead necklace, a silver ring, and a silver rupee. The partner who grasps these items first most frequently during the contest (*kankan jītnā*) is said to be the partner who will dominate in the marriage. The bride is usually more reticent than the groom and seldom wins.

Jewelry clearly represents status and wealth in more general ways. Obviously, only the well-to-do can afford large quantities of heavy jewelry, and a woman laden with ornaments bespeaks prosperity. Women attending weddings typically don as many ornaments as possible to maintain or enhance family prestige, and young marriageable girls are likely to be especially well ornamented with jewelry borrowed from married kinswomen. During the annual Divali festival, Lakshmi, the goddess of wealth, is worshipped. In Hindu village households, cattle ornaments of tinsel and twine (representing their bovine wearers, important items of a farmer's wealth), coins, and the gleaming jewelry of the household's womenfolk are placed beside the image of goddess. These items are worshipped in the hope that they, and the general prosperity of the household, will increase.

Poorer people cannot afford large numbers of ornaments, and they actually may be enjoined against wearing them. Ideally, members of very low-ranking castes should not wear large quantities of gaudy ornaments or toe rings, as a sign of their lower status.

Many villagers, particularly children, wear amulets, which are intended to provide supernatural protection for their wearers. According to Russell and Hiralal, who wrote of castes and customs in Central India in 1916, almost all pieces of jewelry were originally invested with symbolic and protective functions. These authors say, for example, that the *bichhiya* toe rings represent a scorpion and protect from the sting of that creature; that the *haslī* necklace is shaped like, and protects, the collar bone; that a silver pendant shaped like a betel leaf (*pān*) is "very efficacious in magic", and so on (Russell and Hiralal, 1916 (IV): 517-25). They indicate, however, that the protective and magical functions of ornaments are now largely forgotten which, if such functions ever existed, is certainly true. No villager with whom I spoke could suggest any such associations with pieces of jewelry other than amulets. They denied that ornaments protected, or that the lack of them invited bad luck or danger of any kind. Even the removal of bangles or toe rings (at sites other than the well or tank) was said to be acceptable. In fact, they found the whole notion rather amusing and laughed at my questions. "We wear jewelry because we like it", they explained. Even so, a married woman who deliberately went without bangles would meet with criticism, since bare wrists on an adult woman imply widowhood.

Ultimately, jewelry symbolizes happiness, prosperity, and life, and the lack of it sorrow, poverty, and death. The new mother dons pristine bracelets and all her jewelry to celebrate the introduction of her child to the community. The infant is given small pieces of jewelry and is fed its first solid food from a silver rupee or silver dropper. The bride must be adorned with ornaments. But the widow has her bangles broken off and keeps her wrists bare for many months or years, and a generation ago, she was expected to abjure the wearing of ornaments of any kind for a year and a half. The poor with but little jewelry serve the well-ornamented wealthy. The body of a dead Muslim should be completely unornamanted for burial. A Hindu corpse wears jewelry for its final journey, but all ornaments are stripped from the body at the cremation ground. The jewelry of the dead is purified with fire and water and returned to the living, to whom it rightfully belongs.

The Acquisition of Jewelry

Jewelry may be acquired at different times during the life of the individual. From the point of view of individual jewelry owners and their kinsmen, jewelry is divided into three categories: gifts from natal kin, gifts from the spouse's kin, and items purchased jointly by a couple after their marriage.

Hindu girls receive small gifts of jewelry from their parents and other natal kinsmen: bangles, *ṭikkīs* (forehead spangles), thin silver bracelets and anklets, nose studs, necklaces, and earrings. But a young woman's jewelry collection is expanded primarily at the time of her wedding and *gauna* ceremonies. Her groom and his party present her with expensive gifts of clothing and jewelry in formal ceremony (*Chārhāunā*) at the wedding. The bride's parents and other relatives present gifts of money, jewelry, clothing, and sometimes cows to the bride and groom during another wedding ritual (*pāū pūjā*). Ideally, the bride's family should present her with a forehead ornament (*dāurī*), ear chains (*jhelā*), four sets of bracelets (*bangrī, chhalā, batānā, chūṛā*), and a silver head peak (*rikri*). Some parents adhere to this ideal, but many parents present fewer items. In certain groups, the bride should receive a silver pendant from her family, or she will be chided by her in-laws. In most castes, the groom's family is expected to present the bride with a silver amulet representing the special deity of the groom's patrilineage, indicating the bride's formal admission into the group. In addition, the groom's party may bring any other pieces of jewelry; their contribution should always be larger than that of the bride's parents to their daughter. Among Thakurs, a typical array of jewelry given by the groom's party to the bride might include a heavy silver belt, two or three sets of heavy ankle and foot ornaments, one or two gold necklaces, some bracelets, and a gold head peak.

At the wedding of a well-to-do Nimkhera Thakur youth, the bride's parents presented the bridal couple with jewelry of gold and silver worth Rs. 2,800. The groom's party gave the bride gold and silver pieces worth Rs. 5,800 (5 kilograms of silver, 14 *tolas* of gold). The less prosperous family of a Brahman groom gave jewelry worth about Rs. 2,000 to the bride. A landless Soriya laborer gave his bride only a pair of anklets worth less than Rs. 100.

At her *gauna*, a Hindu girl should receive additional pieces of jewelry from both affines and cognates. Toe rings (*bichhiya*), the symbol of the married state, are presented by natal kin among Thakurs and conjugal kin among Brahmans. One Thakur bride was escorted to her new home wearing, in addition to a massively full skirt (about 25 yards), sari, and cover-all veil, rings on her ears, fingers, and toes, several necklaces, a chain belt, and on each arm seven heavy silver bracelets reaching almost to the elbow.

Upon her arrival at her husband's home at her *gauna*, the young bride is completely veiled. For the privilege of lifting her veil to look at her face, the bride's mother-in-law and other female affiness pay her money known as *mūh dikhāī* (face-viewing). Her father-in-law and other male affiness do not see her face but also present her with *mūh dikhāī*. The bride may use this money to buy clothing or other things for herself. Typically, however, her father-in-law takes the money to buy ornaments for her, regarded as jewelry received from the affines.

In the Hindu wedding, both bride and groom have ritual assistants (*Sawāsan* and *Sawās*), ideally the father's sister and her husband. They receive gifts, often of jewelry, from the sponsor of the bride or groom. Such jewelry is considered a gift from natal kin.

Like Hindu girls, Muslim girls receive most of their jewelry at the time of marriage. There are no rules prescribing the presentation of particular pieces by particular kinsmen, except that the nose ring and chain representing the married state cannot be presented by the bride's natal kinsmen, and the bride's mother should given her a gold head ornament (*tīkā*) decorated with the Islamic star and crescent.

As among Hindus, the amount of jewelry received by Muslim brides varies greatly. One poor Muslim woman said she received no jewelry at all from her husband's family. "I'm married into a poor household", she wistfully explained. Her sister, married at the same time, received a necklace, bracelets, and anklets worth about Rs 200 from her groom. The sister's parents gave each of them three sets of bracelets, a locket, and a pair of earrings, worth about Rs 250. A younger sister received jewelry valued at Rs 400 from her husband's family, but it was counted as half of her *mehr*. Among wealthy Pathans, a bride may receive several sets of jewelry of gold and precious stones, consisting of errings, necklace, and bracelets, from both natal and conjugal kin.

After marriage, when a woman visits her parental home, her natal kinsmen may present her with pieces of jewelry from time to time. A woman's parents often celebrate the birth of her first child with gifts of jewelry and clothing for the child and its mother.

A woman in a nuclear family may acquire jewelry by purchasing it or having her husband purchase it for her. The funds for the purchase may derive from her own earnings or the household savings.

Young boys may receive a few items of jewelry from their parents—a pair of thin anklets, a few amulets, gold earrings. At his wedding, the groom marrying a bride from a prosperous family may receive substantial sums of money as well as gold amulets, earrings, a necklace, and even a watch (the earrings and necklace are usually not worn after the wedding). Adult men also purchase watches for themselves.

Jewelry is presented to brides, grooms, and young women for various reasons. Perhaps most important among these is the fact that jewelry is given and worn publicly, and the donor of an ornament becomes known for his generosity. Gifts of jewelry are always displayed and examined by guests at wedding and *gaunas*, and new jewelry worn at any time attracts attention. A gift of money or clothing, while also showing generosity, may be less conspicuous and is less enduring. Parents who give their daughter jewelry add to the regard in which she and her natal kinsmen are held by her husband and his family. A daughter-in-law seen laden with metallic wealth enhances the reputation of her affines both in the village and in the marriage circle. Conversely, parents and parents-in-law who can afford it, yet fail to present jewelry when it would be appropriate to do so may lose the esteem of their affines and neighbors. As one Hindu woman explained, "Everyone wants to see their daughter-in-law laden with ornaments; no one wants to see their daughter-in-law naked of jewelry."

Among Hindus, giving jewelry is also an acceptable way for prosperous parents or a widowed mother without sons to contribute to the private wealth of a daughter without antagonizing patrilineal heirs to the family's real estate (see Bailey, 1958:78). A gift of jewelry is also preferable to a gift of a large amount of cash, since that could be discovered and "borrowed" by a daughter's affines.[14] In Nimkhera, an elderly childless woman often gave expensive gifts of clothing and jewelry to members of her brother's family, since she did not want all her wealth to be inherited by her husband's brothers.

A married woman who purchases jewelry for herself out of her own and her husband's earnings shows that she is clever both in accruing funds and putting them to good use.

Ownership and Control of Jewelry

The rights an individual has over his or her jewelry differ according to whether the jewelry was presented by natal or conjugal kin or purchased by a couple after their marriage. The differing rights of the ostensible owner in jewelry reflect the ideal and actual relationships between the individual and different categories of kinsmen.

HINDUS

Jewelry from Natal Kin (for a woman, *maika* jewelry)

Jewelry presented to a man by his natal kin may be his to keep or dispose of as he chooses, or it may be reclaimed by his agnates in time of need. Since men possess little jewelry, disputes over men's ornaments are rare.

Ideally, the jewelry a woman receives from her natal kinsmen belongs exclusively to her, and she is free to keep it, sell it, or give it away. None of her affines have a claim on it during her lifetime, but they may inherit it after her death. If she dies childless her husband or his kinsmen will take possession of it. If she has children, she may give some to a daughter during her lifetime, and the rest will be inherited by her son. A woman's natal kin do not expect to get back any of the jewelry they have given her or her children.

Thus, a woman's control over her *maika* jewelry parallels her bonds of kinship with its donors: virtually indissoluble, indisputable, and generally free of tension. However, like herself, her jewelry has been formally given away, and at her death is claimed by those to whom she was given.

Jewelry from Conjugal Kin (*Susral* Jewelry) and Joint Purchases

Jewelry a man receives from his wife's relatives is usually considered to be his personal jewelry, but if he lives in a joint family, he may be asked to pawn it to add to the family funds in times of need. It is usually difficult for him to refuse, as his agnates may remind him of the expenses they bore in sponsoring his wedding.

A man's *susral* jewelry belongs to him and his patrilineal group no matter what happens to his marriage. In this area, as in much of North India, the givers of a bride expect to give presents to their son-in-law and his family but never to receive unreciprocated gifts from them. Ideally, a gift presented to a son-in-law is regarded as given forever, without thought of return—for example, the dowry of a bride (*dahej*), which usually includes valuable brass vessels and frequently cows. However, where a marriage breaks up due to the questionable behavior of the groom or his kinsmen, the bride's kin group may attempt to reclaim their goods. Such disputes are adjudicated by *panchāyats* (council meetings of senior male members of the caste) and are usually decided in favor of the groom's side. However, a locally famous case of about 15 years ago involved a Thakur woman who refused to care for her own young son and was then rejected by her husband, who took another wife. The *panchāyat* awarded the woman and her family all the dowry they had given and even some items belonging to her husband. The woman's mother-in-law noted that it was a sin for people to take back the things they have given to the groom's family in a wedding.

It is recognized that gifts presented to a bride by her husband's family are hers only conditionally. Like her ties to her conjugal lineage, her rights in her *susral* jewelry are ideally permanent and clear, but in fact are very possibly impermanent, equivocal, and subject to a great deal of negotiation and manipulation.

Under ideal conditions, a woman's *susral* jewerly belongs exclusively to her, and she may keep or sell it as she sees fit. She might give some of hr ornaments to her daughters: such jewelry then becomes *maika* jewelry for them. She may not, however, give her jewelry to her own natal kin, nor should they accept it from her. If the marriage ends in divorce, and the husband is adjudged the guilty party or willingly lets his wife go, the woman should be allowed to keep her jewelry as long as she remains unmarried. If, however, the marriage ends through the error or desire of the woman, the *susral* jewelry should be returned to the husband's family.

Ornaments purchased jointly by a husband and wife, or even ornaments bought by a married woman for herself out of her own earnings are generally considered to be the woman's *susral* jewelry. As one woman explained, " Even if you work and buy jewelry with your savings, your husband will say, 'Didn't I feed you and put a roof over your head so you could spend your money on jewelry?'" Thus, a woman leaving her husband for another man might have to give such jointly purchased jewelry to her husband. A clever woman anticipating such a situation could, of course, secretly give her savings to her natal kinsmen and ask them to buy jewelry to present to her as a "gift". In contrast, jewelry purchased for himself by a married man in a nuclear family is considered the man's personal property no matter what happens to the marriage.

A Hindu widow should keep her *susral* jewelry, unless she marries again, at which time she should return her first husband's jewelry to his kinsmen and accept another set of ornaments from her second husband.

A woman's *susral* jewelry should be inherited by her husband, who is free to distribute it to his relatives (usually his sons) as he wishes. If the husband is dead, it should be inherited by her son, who gives it to his wife, or if she has no son, by other males of her husband's kin group.

As long as she is married to her husband, a woman ideally has full control over both her *maika* and *susral* jewelry. However, the ideal rules are not always followed. If the need for cash is great, a woman's affines may pressure her into allowing her jewelry to be pawned. When a woman's husband's younger brother is getting married, she may be asked to give her *susral* jewelry to the new bride "temporarily"; jewelry is sometimes thus passed from bride to bride within a joint family. A young bride who has received an expensive gold necklace from her husband's family may be told that it would be too dangerous for her to wear such a valuable object; the necklace will be "kept safe" for her by her mother-in-law—in fact, perhaps pawned or sold. Only fear of shame can prevent a woman's affines from taking back the jewelry they have given to her. A woman so deprived will tell her natal kinsmen and neighbors, and the reputation of her husband's kin group will be lowered. Further, the fact that women's jewelry is so conspicuously displayed daily and on special occasions increases a woman's control over it, since the absence of a piece is immediately noticed by friends or natal relatives. A woman whose affines have taken her jewelry does not hesitate to explain to the curious the loss of her ornaments.

Some women must resist pressure from their affines to allow their *maika* jewelry to be pawned in addition to their *susral* jewelry. One young Brahman mother allowed her father-in-law to pawn all the jewelry his family had given her. She explained, "A woman has no choice; she must do what her husband and others tell her to do." But on further questioning, she admitted that she had refused to allow her affines to pawn her *maika* jewelry as they had wanted to do. She also refused to hand over a small gold forehead ornament (*bendi*) which she planned to present to her husband's younger brother's bride.

The Brahman woman was asked before her jewelry was pawned, because, like other village women, she kept it in a trunk to which only she had the key. Some women bury their jewelry in pots in the floor, or secrete it in walls, ostensibly to protect it from thieves. Some women deny keeping jewelry in the house and say publicly that most of it has been pawned. In truth, a woman fears the loss of her jewelry as much to her affines as she does to burglars, and she never leaves it unprotected for any long period of time. When she goes to visit her natal village, she takes all of her jewelry with her in her suitcase. When, later in life, she departs from her marital home for a pilgrimage to the Ganges or other holy places, she invites her daughter to guard the house—and her valuables. A woman's brother or sister are also considered trustworthy guards. As one woman said, " You can't trust anyone in your husband's house, not even neighbors or friends. But you can leave things in your parents' home; there you can trust people more."

It is at the time of divorce that serious disputes may arise over the rightful ownership of jewelry. A woman who goes to her parent's home leaving some of her *maika* jewelry behind and fails to return to her husband can expect that her affines will confiscate her *maika* jewelry and then deny having done so. A woman who goes to her parent's home wearing all of her *susral* jewelry and then fails to return to her husband may be able to retain possession of the *susral* jewelry if she claims she does not have it. One such case involved a Thakur woman married to a relative of a Nimkhera family. A young Thakur girl spoke of the incident.

> My father's sister who lives in Thikri had a daughter-in-law who was very beautiful. There's no one in Nimkhera who's half as good-looking as she was. My cousin's wife was very fair and was always laden with jewelry. She wore a wide silver waist band, and she wanted one even broader. She never took off her head peak. She was just perfect in appearance and the way she wore her jewelry. Then, after only the second or third visit to her husband's house after her *gauna*, she went to her parent's house and didn't

come back. Her parents made her marry another man. They took lots of money from that man; that sold her for about 2,000 rupees.[15] She didn't want to go, but her parents forced her to go. My Thikri aunt and her son got only a few of the ornaments back from that daughter-in-law; she took the rest with her. My aunt called a *panchayat* meeting, and the daughter-in-law came and swore on a jug of the sacred water of the Ganges that she had left all her jewelry at their house and that she had nothing of theirs on her body now. The *panchayat* people couldn't do anything.

Clearly, possession may be nine points of the law in such disputes, and villagers are very much aware of it. In 1966, after the divorce and remarriage of her daughter (and prior to the marriage of her son), a barber woman explained:

If a woman and her husband get divorced, the husband and his family take the jewelry, clothes, and all the pots and pans given to them in the Pau Puja at the wedding. But if the girl is clever, she brings lots of things back to her parents' house, for example, the ornaments given to the groom by the bride's people. She may ask to wear them and come back wearing them. My daughter didn't do that, and we didn't get any of our things back, even though the divorce took place because of the misbehavior of her husband's kinsmen.

A few years later, the same woman acted forcefully to retain physical possession of the jewelry given to her son's errant wife. In 1973 she described the scene:

My son Gulab came home one day and saw his wife with her face unveiled talking and laughing with my daughter Halki's husband. Gulab was suspicious, but he kept quiet and said he was going to take a bath. He gathered his clothes and a bucket as if he were going to the well, and then he circled around the village, came up behind the house and sat on the roof. From there he overheard their conversation and saw them begin to make love inside the house. He came down and accosted them and began to beat Halki's husband. He told him he would kill him, but he didn't want to make Halki a widow. We kicked out the girl. We stripped off all her jewelry and the clothes we had given her. We gave her an old torn sari to wear and told her to go home. She had no *maika* jewelry—she came to us naked and we sent her away naked....We have given the first wife's jewelry to Gulab's new bride.

In another case, a carpenter widow contracting a second marriage was allowed to keep the jewelry given to her by her first husband's kinsmen, with the agreement that when her son by her first husband marries, the jewelry will be given to his bride. *Panchayat* members carefully recorded in writing a list of the ornaments involved. If the carpenter woman were to leave her new husband for any reason, she could properly come away with all the listed pieces.

Some woman secretly convert wealth derived from their conjugal households into *maika* jewelry. These women take advantàge of their access to cash and grain in their marital households and convert such wealth into jewelry belonging exclusively to themselves. For example, it was rumored that the daughter-in-law of a wealthy high-caste family secretly lent out part of the family hoard with which her husband had entrusted her. She saved the interest for herself, took it home with her to her parents' house, bought silver jewelry with it, and returned to her husband's home wearing the jewelry which her parents had supposedly given her. Other women were said to secretly sell quantities of grain and stash away the proceeds for similar conversion to jewelry. Some women make purchases and tell their husbands they have spent more than they actually have; the surplus money resurfaces later as the "gift" of clothing or jewelry from the woman's natal home. Thus, wealth over which a woman has but limited control is converted into property over which she has complete control. Clearly, such a transfer would be of most benefit to a woman residing with her husband in a joint family, where property rights are shared by several adults, with the rights of males being absolute and the rights of women contingent upon their relationships to the males. Normally, the wife in a nuclear family would have sufficient control over wealth in her conjugal home that she would not feel the need to convert it to *maika* jewelry. Several village women indicated that such secret dealings were much more common among women of joint families than women of nuclear families.

The transfer of jointly owned property to a woman's private property is often done with the knowledge of the husband.   Thus, through his wife, a man has access to funds he may use without securing permission from his elders. The private hoard is often collected in anticipation of the division of the joint family property, which should ideally be divided equally among males.[16]

The woman making such property transfers may gain in several ways. Firstly, she improves her personal economic position by adding to her store of *maika* jewelry. Secondly, by representing her natal kin as wealthy and generous enough to give her expensive presents, she may increase the prestige of her natal kin, and by extension, herself, in the eyes of her affines. She may be subjected to fewer derogatory comments about her origins and receive better treatment than might otherwise be her lot. Thirdly, she may be allowed more frequent visits to her natal home than would otherwise be the case. A daughter-in-law bedecked with increasing amounts of jewelry reflects well on her kinsmen. A woman's affines may be eager to have her visit her generous parents as often as possible so that they can have a well-ornamented daughter-in-law without having to pay for the privilege. The affines may also hope to prevail upon the woman to allow them to pawn the pieces and thus profit from them.

A woman's parents may be well aware of the secret transfers and happy to be considered more wealthy and generous than they actually are. Some parents also keep safe secret caches of money collected by their daughters and occasionally benefit by borrowing from the supply.

Women earnestly strive to keep such financial manipulations secret from all persons in their conjugal homes and even from non-family residents of their natal villages. No woman ever admits to engaging in such activity. Nevertheless, since so many women do it, each may suspect if of the other. For example, one old woman said of a young neighbor, "Her parents are poor, so how could they give her as much as she says they do? Ha, I know where she got those new ankle ornaments."

MUSLIMS

The rights of a Muslim woman in her jewelry are similar to those of a Hindu woman. Jewelry received as gifts from her natal kin is absolutely her own, and ornaments received from her husband's family as part of her *mehr* are also hers to keep or sell as she wishes. Other jewelry received from her affines or purchased after her marriage is hers conditionally. If she leaves her husband without just cause or is rejected by her affines because of her disgraceful behavior, her husband's family will claim the jewelry they gave her. If her marriage remains intact, she should be able to control all of her jewelry. A few older women, however, refuse to allow a daughter-in-law to keep her own clothing and jewelry and lock it in their own trunks, rationing out the items to be worn each day. A man may also cajole his wife into letting him dispose of her jewelry.

A Muslim woman's jewelry is inherited by her children, with both sons and daughters ideally dividing the ornaments amicably. A childless woman's jewelry usually goes to her affines, but a claim advanced by natal kin may be honored. In any case, a Muslim woman's affines are frequently also related to her consanguineally,and distinct lines between natal and conjugal kin are often hard to draw.

Uses of Jewelry

As an expensive, valuable, portable, non-perishable commodity, jewelry is frequently pawned by its owners. Its intrinsic value is not open to significant debate: its weight is readily discernible, and the current price of gold and silver per *tola* is common knowledge among ordinary villagers as well as jewelry merchants and moneylenders. Most owners of jewelry would share the view of a Vidisha jewelry vendor who declared to a hesitating customer, "Jewelry is the same as money".

Jewelry is, of course, not the same as money: it is not currency as such, but it is readily acceptable as security against a loan of money, or it may easily be sold, usually for a reasonably fair price (see Bailey, 1958 : 80). However, a moneylender usually gives only about half the full value of the security, since he must allow for interest and possible default on the loan.

There are a number of advantages to owning jewelry. First, jewelry is a form of savings against hard times, and the desire to own jewelry encourages saving. In an extreme example, one Thakur wife refused to return to her husband until he had given her more jewelry, and she remained in her parental home for over two years. Her desperate husband prevailed upon his parents to forego a long-planned pilgrimage so he could use the family savings to buy Rs 1,100 worth of jewelry for his wife. A poor young Soriya man bought only one pair of silver ankle ornaments for his bride, but he spent Rs 100 to have a brass band play at his wedding. Village women were critical of his deployment of scarce funds. One woman remarked, "What good did that band do? If he had bought jewelry with that money his wife would have worn it all her life".

As a form of savings, jewelry is preferable to cash, because cash is too easily frittered away on a day-to-day basis, while jewelry is less liquid. This is so partly because of the resistance of the women who keep it, and also because it often can be realized only at a loss. Further, hoarded money depreciates in value, while the market value of silver and gold is always increasing (Bailey, 1958: 76-79), probably at a rate at least equal to the general rate of inflation. For example, the price of 10 grams of gold on the Bombay bullion market in 1962 was about Rs 120, in 1973 was Rs 360, and in 1975 was Rs 568. Similarly, the price of a kilogram of silver rose from Rs 210 in 1962 to Rs 680 in 1973 and Rs. 1,061 in 1975 (*Economic Weekly*, 1962; *The Economic Times*, 1973: *The Times of India*, 1975).

Through constant wearing, jewelry does become thinner and wears through in places, but the amount of metal thus lost is not enough to equalize the increase in the value of the piece through time. Worn-out jewelry is not worth significantly less than new pieces of the same weight, since old pieces can be melted down and fashioned into new ornaments for very small sums. In the case of gold there is sometimes a premium attached to older pieces, since these are made of gold of greater purity than is currently available.

As liquid capital, jewelry is also preferable to land. The many different pieces of jewelry are available in different weights, and consequently the prices paid for jewelry cover a wide range, from a rupee or two for a ring, to hundreds of rupees for a silver chain belt or a gold necklace. Thus the seller can easily adjust the amount of jewelry he liquidates to coincide with his specific needs. This would not be the case with land, except in special circumstances.[17] More importantly, since jewelry is not productive, its sale does not diminish annual income, as would the sale of land (Bailey, 1958: 79-80). The loss of land to a moneylender affects the total economic well-being of a family very significantly, whereas the loss of jewelry does not. Jewelry can always be replaced by gradual purchases of new pieces, but recovering or replacing land is much more difficult. Land is not readily available, and in any case its purchase requires a large initial payment. For those without land or bullocks, jewelry may be the only collateral they own for obtaining loans.

Thus, from the point of view of a man and his household, jewelry provides a good source of cash when needed. When a man, or a man in conjunction with his wife and other members of the family, decide that money is required, the man asks his wife for her jewelry and takes it to a known moneylender, either within the village (for small sums) or in Raisen (for larger sums). A Nimkhera Brahman recently pawned almost all of his wife's jewelry to obtain funds to hire a lawyer to defend him in a legal action threatening his lands. His wife grumbled that she was without ornaments, but she recognized the need to pawn them. The village barber family suffered the loss of a bullock and needed to purchase another one immediately. They found one at a bargain price—Rs 300—but they had only Rs 150 in cash. They obtained the rest of the money by pawning head ornaments (*jhela*) they had given their married daughters. The daughters agreed to this readily, since they trusted their parents to redeem their ornaments. Several years earlier, the same family needed money for medicine for their sick son and daughter. Bracelets were pawned for Rs 100 and were ultimately redeemed after a long period of time for Rs 200. The same family also pawned ornaments to help pay for a big wedding for their son.

From a woman's point of view, ownership of jewelry is particularly important, since it is usually the only form of wealth she actually controls or can manipulate without encountering opposition from others. *Maika* jewelry and, if she remains married to her husband, *susral* jewelry, provide a woman with security and the ability to take certain actions, without permission or assistance from others, if necessary.

Ideally, a woman does not pawn her jewelry without her husband's permission. When asked, women repeatedly indicated that they would always consult their husbands before pawning ornaments. Women in nuclear families often replied, "Wouldn't you ask your husband before doing such a thing ? Don't you think that would be the right thing to do?" In any case, they said, it is usually men who do the actual pawning. One clever old woman, Tulsibai, has pawned her heavy *hasli* necklace several times herself, but always with the knowledge of her husband, she said. Tulsibai originally purchased the necklace about 20 years ago with her earnings from harvesting wheat in the fields of others. Although she is the wife of the village temple priest and high caste, she is poor and has had to use her intelligence to better her position. Over the years the necklace, beautifully made of a hand-worked solid silver bar, has alternately ornamented her neck and languished in pawn shops. Whenever she pawns it, she ties a thread around it and weighs it carefully to ensure that she gets the same one back when she redeems it. One year her husband was very ill, and Tulsibai pawned her necklace to buy medicines for him. The next year she pawned it to buy goods to sell at a local nine-day village fair, "I pawned my necklace for Rs 100." she said, "and I used the money to buy things to sell at the Havan celebration. I made enough profit to feed myself and about seven house guests during the fair. And after the fair, I redeemed my necklace, paid 2 rupees interest, and still had 25 rupees cash profit."

Another poor high-caste woman, a widow, pawned much of her jewelry to buy stock for a little shop. The shop proved profitable, and she was able to quickly claim her ornaments as well as continue running the shop.

In at least one case, a young Thakur woman, Priya, used her jewelry to help her natal kinsmen. At the time of her younger brother's marriage, her parents were forced to borrow money to help pay for the wedding expenses. Purchasing ornaments for the new bride would have added to their debt. Priya lives in a nuclear family with her husband, and with his knowledge and consent gave many of her ornaments to her brother's bride. This transaction, which in fact amounted to the transfer of wealth from Priya's conjugal kin to her natal kin, could not have been properly effected with cash. It would have been highly inappropriate for Priya's parents, as bride-givers, to accept cash from Priya's affines or even from Priya herself. However, after their marriage, Priya and her husband had begun living separately from the husband's parents, and Priya retained control of her *susral* jewelry. This jewelry provided a potential source of capital for the new household, and in this case, for Priya's brother bride, to whom it was not inappropriate for Priya to give jewelry as a wedding gift.

In the absence of trust and mutual understanding between a woman and her affines, she may dispose of her ornaments secretly or without their consent. This is much more likely to occur in joint than nuclear families. One woman explained, "Yes, some women do pawn their jewelry secretly. They give it to a friend and say don't tell anyone. The men don't ask about their jewelry; otherwise, they wouldn't be able to do it." A young Thakur woman, stricken with tuberculosis, was denied medical care by her husband and his relatives. The husband was dissatisfied with her and hoped she would die so he could marry someone else. She sold most of her jewelry, including that given her by her affines, to pay for vital medical care. After she had sold all the jewelry given her by her first husband's family, she married again and accepted new ornaments from her second husband. She was within her rights to sell her first set of ornaments as long as she remained formally attached to her first husband; it would not have been acceptable for her to go to her second husband wearing ornaments from the first. This bright woman ultimately died, but her jewelry helped prolong her life by several years.[18]

Jewelry and Power

The conditions under which women obtain and retain control of jewelry relate very much to power and the lack of it.

In general, members of prosperous groups with significant economic resources are able to purchase more jewelry than those who have little economic power. Women who need jewelry the most are those of poor families: landless laborers and servants. Lacking land, valuable animals, rich relatives, or other resources, jewelry may be their most valuable material possession and potential source of funds in an emergency. Nevertheless, women of wealthier families who need it less tend to own much more jewelry than do the poor.

However, *within each kin group*, the possession of jewelry is associated with the lack of other overt economic power. Jewelry is owned primarily by women, who tend to have less control of other forms of wealth than men do, and by young daughters-in-law in particular, who usually occupy the weakest position among adults within the household. The most heavily ornamented women, young Thakur brides, usually belong to prosperous joint families in which land is owned and controlled by men, and the family purse is kept by the oldest woman and controlled primarily by her and the family males. The young daughter-in-law in such a family may not be asked for advice or preferences on even the smallest purchases, even clothing for herself. Thus, within each household, jewelry is usually worn by those who need it and can benefit from it the most.

In her relatively weak position, a daughter-in-law may be prevailed upon by her affines to allow them to pawn her ornaments; she may find it impossible to resist. But, it is improper for a woman's affines to ask for the jewelry given her by her natal kin, and she is perfectly within her rights to refuse to acquiesce to such a request.

Conversely, the achievement of a position of strength and security within her household may encourage a woman to give up her jewelry. Clearly Priya, the young Thakur woman who gave her jewelry to her brother's bride, trusted her husband and natal kinsmen to assist her if she should require aid. A wealthy Pathan woman in the village was given several sets of gold jewelry at her marriage, but she has allowed her husband to give away almost all of her jewelry to friends and relatives. She and her husband, who live in a nuclear family, have a relationship of deep affection and trust, and she is in charge of the family savings, which are many times the value of her jewelry. She also inherited from her father a house and urban property worth much more than a few necklaces and earrings. In addition, this woman has voluntarily relinquished her right to *mehr* as an act of trust in her husband and acknowledgement of her secure position.

In most joint families, the older females loan or give their jewelry to the younger women. One old grandmother, who has retained only a small set of bracelets and ankle ornaments for herself and has given the rest of her ornaments to her daughters-in-law and grand-daughters-in-law, said, "Lots of jewelry doesn't look nice on an old woman". Her relative lack of adornment reflects the cultural ideal that old people should turn away from worldly pleasures toward more ascetic living but also reflects the fact that she has absolutely no need to control jewelry. She is responsible for all family funds and is the much revered senior woman member of a large and prosperous family.

CONCLUSION

The shiny and jingling jewelry of Central India is set in a context of elaborate aesthetic and ritual symbolism and firmly linked to a strong social fabric. The investiture of jewelry with symbolic meanings and its association with specific social forms is an ancient and widespread tradition in India. All of the ideological and social associations of jewelry are positive: beauty, prosperity, youth, marriage, fecundity, auspiciousness, and life itself, while the lack of jewelry connotes the negative opposites of these. Ornaments are essential gifts at marriage and consummation rites and highly favoured offerings on other occasions. Except among the most wealthy and urban sophisticates, every cultural norm encourages the acquisition and ownership of jewelry.

In modern Madhya Pradesh, and much of the rest of India, significant amounts of money are spent on silver and gold molded and hammered into ornaments for the human form. This expenditure on precious metals has added to India's national economic problems by increasing the internal demand for gold and putting much-needed capital into a form not available for investment in business and industry. Despite government attempts to curb such investement, much of the primarily rural public continues to spend a high percentage of their savings on ornaments.

Where there is so much ideological commitment and support for the ownership of a particular commodity, we would expect to find that commodity to fulfil significant positive functions for its owners. Such is in fact the case with jewelry.

For the villager, jewelry is a relatively prudent form of savings. It can be purchased at any price, regularly increases in value, and can be quickly converted into cash as needed. In emergencies, it is a dependable source of funds for individuals, couples, and families and may make the difference between an opportunity grasped or missed, a problem solved or left unresolved, or even life and death. Clearly, the positive reinforcement for collecting jewelry provided by the culture helps to ensure that each family owns such an insurance policy, be it large or small.

Jewelry, when displayed, enhances family and individual prestige. Prestige, of course, is a currency that may be used to "buy" advantageous affinal and political alliances and can contribute to the ability of individuals and kin groups to consolidate wealth and power.

In the joint family, all property other than personal clothing—and women's jewelry—is ideally held in common and disposed of only with the approval of the senior members of the family. Within this structure, jewelry provides an element of flexibility. Women can use money derived from the sale of their ornaments for their own purposes, whether sanctioned or not by other members of the joint family. Some men also avail themselves of the proceeds of their wives' jewelry in order to circumvent the elder's power of authority. Thus, in some cases, needs of individuals and couples can be met without direct confrontation and quarreling which might endanger a marriage or a joint family.

A woman's ability to secretly transfer wealth received or taken from her affines into *maika* jewelry controlled only by herself is an important means of adding to the economic power of an economically disadvantaged group—women. Jewelry is needed to fulfil many aesthetic, ritual, and prestige requirements, thus tending to ensure that every woman owns as much jewelry as is possible within the limits of the financial resources of her natal and conjugal kin groups. From one point of view, then, given the present Hindu and even Muslim systems of inheritance and property control, the high esteem in which jewelry is held could be said to contribute to women's economic well-being. From another point of view, however, the positive associations of jewelry can be seen as a sugar coating on the bitter pill of economic inequality between the sexes. Jewelry is beautiful, auspicious, connotative of prosperity, etc.—but it is also much less valuable than the real estate, animals, and other goods owned by men. Much of women's acquisition and control of jewelry derives from their associations with men (fathers, husbands, and male affines), and the rupturing of a woman's relationships with these men, particularly her husband, threatens her control of her most valuable material property. It is small wonder then that the emblems of marriage are pieces of jewelry worn by women, since for women, marriage and jewelry are so intimately related. In contrast, men's acquisition and control of their most significant wealth has nothing to do with their relationships with women. Even jewelry given to a man by his wife's kinsmen remains his in case of divorce.

Some women attempt to circumvent this situation by stealing from their affines or by running away to their natal homes, carrying with them as much jewelry as they can, but these are subterfuges which not every woman is audacious enough to try. These measures, if discovered, may also be severely condemned by affines and neighbors, and a woman thus risks losing the esteem of others in such attempts to gain economic power.[19]

It is surely revealing to note that among women, those with the fewest rights in immovable property and with the least secure economic positions treasure their jewelry the most (young Hindu wives), and those with the most property rights and economically secure positions are virtually bare of ornamentation (older Muslim women). And among all villagers, it is the owners and inheritors of most land, houses, and animals who take the least interest in jewelry— men. A cavalier lack of concern for ornaments is found only among those to whom they are economically insignificant trinkets.

The present trend away from wearing heavy jewelry toward wearing lighter and fewer pieces may lead to a diminution of some women's financial resources, but it is at the same time probably indicative of a potential increase in women's overall economic power.

The diminishing regard in which village women hold traditional ornaments is due partly to influences from urban centers, where heavy ornaments are considered rustic and old-fashioned. City women today often have their old pieces melted down or broken up to be fashioned into smaller pieces. For educated women who hold jobs or are potentially employable in clerical or professional capacities, jewelry has become relatively unimportant economically, and is worn to a much lesser extent than a generation ago.

Also emanating from the cities is the knowledge that under modern Indian law, all women have the right to inherit and absolutely own land and other valuable family property. As one old village woman said, "The government is giving power to women." Few village women with brothers avail themselves of this legal right, since the social penalties for doing so would be high (see Luschinsky, 1963). But in relatively recent years, two Nimkhera Hindu women without brothers were willed land by their fathers, and their male kinsmen did not contest their absolute ownership of the land. One childless Hindu widow recently sold the land she inherited from her husband for a substantial sum. Her husband's agnates attempted to prevent the sale, but district officials upheld her right under modern law to dispose of the land. She now resides with her natal kin.

Muslim women, too, are coming out of purdah and taking more active roles in supervising their own lands. One wealthy married Pathan daughter of the village owns a farm near Indore and rides there daily (unveiled) from her city house on a motorscooter. Her mother, once completely sequestered, now personally oversees workmen in her fields. The jewelry worn by these women is relatively low in value.

Even with these changes, women's control over property remains significantly less than that of their male kinsmen: equalizing economic power between the sexes will doubtless take some time. Until such equality is achieved, women may be expected to keep their ornaments secure in their houses, even if they do not wear them as frequently as they did in the past. Most Nimkhera women who wore traditional jewelry five years ago but now prefer less ornamentation say they have kept or pawned their jewelry and have not sold it outright or otherwise divested themselves of it. Village women of this region may come to favor lightweight pieces of gold in preference to heavy silver pieces of equal or lesser value.

With increasing contact between the village and the city, cash is being spent on an increasing number of different items, some of which have resale value and function as repositories of savings: watches, radios, bicycles, and impressive houses. Some villagers are also investing in tractors, bulldozers, jeeps and stone quarries. As the easy availability and profitability to villagers of diverse forms of investment increase, it may be expected that the emphasis on jewelry as a form of savings for family units will decrease. However, as long as there is a need for a form of capital which can be manipulated and utilized by individuals, couples, and joint families, and by men and by women, in a variety of ways to help satisfy diverse needs, it is probable that jewelry will continue to be highly valued in India.

APPENDIX I
THE JEWELRY OF NIMKHERA AND ITS REGION
Hindu Women's Jewelry (Jewelry=*rakam, jewar*, or *gehne*)

Head Ornaments

rikrī	:	gold or silver peak worn atop the head
sīsphūl	:	small head ornament, half gold, half silver
daurī	:	forehead ornament, a cluster of silver beads
chhaugā	:	small silver forehead pendant
bendī	:	small gold forehead ornament
ṭikkī	:	gilt glass or plastic spangle, glued to center of forehead
kilap	:	silver hair clip

Nose

katā, long	:	nostril stud of gold or gold alloy
nath	:	gold nose ring, no longer worn
nakphūlī	:	large gold nostril stud, with flower design

Ear

karanphūl, kanphūl	:	flower-shaped large gold or silver earrings
jhelā	:	chains from earrings to top of head, with dangles (*ghunghru*), of silver
ongne	:	silver rings worn in upper ear
barīye	:	gold rings worn in upper ear
ḍiraniye	:	flower-shaped silver or gold earrings, with central red stone
ṭāpas, eran	:	earrings of relatively modern design, of gold or brass
jhumkā	:	pendant earrings, gold or silver

Neck

haslī, khangwārī	:	solid silver collar, rarely of gold
bajaṭṭī	:	flat necklace of three rows of gold beads, with central ornament
timnī, pachmaniyā	:	necklace of large beads of thin gold (three and five beads, respectively)
thussī	:	gold bead necklace
janjīr	:	silver chain
sīk sākar	:	silver toothpick and ear cleaner, hung on silver chain

mālā	:	glass bead necklace
chhaṭā	:	glass beadwork choker
katlā	:	necklace of silver rupees, with center amulet (*tawij*)
takār	:	necklace of silver rupees, with betel-shaped pendant (*pan*)
tāwīj, hāī putrī	:	amulet, amulet with sun and moon figures

Upper Arms

bājū	:	flat silver clasps for upper arm
botā	:	rounded silver clasps for upper arm
bānkrā	:	zig-zag upper arm clasp of thick silver wire

Wrists

chūṛī	:	colored bangles of lac or glass
chūṛā	:	silver bracelet; includes a few different designs
tīn tār kā chūṛā	:	bracelet of three twisted silver wires
gajrā	:	thick silver bracelet, with five clusters of dangles
batānā	:	thinner silver bracelet with four clusters of dangles
dorī	:	silver bracelet embossed with two rows of circular bumps
kaknā	:	silver bracelet with segmented design
bangrī	:	silver bracelet, with flower designs
chhalā, kakaniyā	:	circle bracelet with large silver balls
chail chūṛī	:	silver bracelet, with rings attached
hāthphūl	:	ornament for back of hand, attached to finger rings and wrist, of silver

Fingers

| *angūṭhī* | : | ring; includes several different designs |

Waist

| *kardhonā, chhūtā* | : | belt of silver chains and buckle |
| *guchchhā, kilīm* | : | ornamental key ring worn at the waist |

Ankles

| *kaṛā* | : | plain silver anklet, round in cross section |
| *neoriyā* | : | circular anklet, with floral design |

torā	:	heavy silver anklet, of segmented design
torī	:	circular anklet, close-fitting, often worn by children
awlā	:	circular anklet, with segmented design
lachchhe	:	large thin silver circlets, usually worn in groups of six or more
āīl	:	circlets, with dangles, worn with *lachchhe*
chhāgal	:	silver ankle chain, with dangles
pāujeb	:	heavy silver chain, with dangles
kalar	:	thin ankle chain

Feet

anotā chhingarī	:	toe rings, silver, linked by a chain with dangles
joruā	:	thick bronze ring for big toe
bichhiyā	:	toe rings with two large lumps on each, worn in groups of three, on the middle toes, of silver or bronze
bichhūrī	:	small toe rings, worn on second joint of second toe

Muslim Women's Jewelry (Jewelry=*zewar* or *rakam*)

Head

ṭīkā, bindī	:	gold or silver forehead pendant
jhūmar	:	triangular spangled piece worn on the side of the head

Nose

long	:	nostril stud of gold or brass
nath and jhālar	:	nose ring, with supporting chain to ear
pejbān, pesar	:	gold ring in septum; rare

Ear

tāps, tāpis, eran	:	earrings of modern style
jhumke	:	rounded pendant earrings of gold or silver
bunde	:	long dangly earrings
janjīr	:	chain, attaches to *bunde*
bāliye	:	upper ear rings
kuṇḍal	:	dangly costume jewelry earrings

Neck

guluband	:	silver chain necklace
hār	:	silver or glass bead necklace
champakalī	:	solid silver necklace with flat dangles
tauk	:	solid silver necklace with dangles
thussi	:	gold bead necklace
lāket, rāket	:	pendant necklace of silver or gold
tāwīz	:	amulet

Wrists

dastband	:	silver bracelet with flower design
karā	:	twisted silver bracelet
batānā	:	thin silver bracelet with four clusters of dangles
gajrā	:	thin silver bracelet with clusters of dangles
paunchiyā	:	tight silver bracelet with dangles
parīband	:	flat silver bracelet with flat dangles
chūṛī	:	glass bangles

Fingers

angūṭhī	:	thick ring
chhale	:	thin rings worn together

Anklets

pāujeb	:	ankle chain with dangles
jhānjhā	:	thin silver anklet
āīl lachchhe	:	thin silver circlets with dangles
neorī	:	thick round silver anklet
chharā	:	thick chain anklet with round and flat dangles
lachchhe	:	thin silver rings, worn in groups
kalar, patiyā	:	thin silver ankle chain

Feet

bichhūrī	:	small toe rings, worn on second joint of second toe

Hindu Men's Jewelry (Traditional)

Ear

bhīkbārī	:	single gold ring in upper ear

murkhī	:	gold ring worn in ear lobe
chokŗe	:	gold rings worn in pairs in each lobe
kuṇḍal, bālā	:	large gold ring worn in lobe
jhelā	:	chain over ear, usually gold

Neck

gop	:	solid gold necklace
selī	:	gold chain necklace
kānṭhā	:	gold wire necklace
gunj	:	gold bead necklace
baṭan	:	silver buttons linked with chains and dangles, worn in shirt front
kaṭlā	:	necklace of silver rupees and amulets (*tawij*)
tāwīj	:	amulet

Waist

chhūtā	:	chain belt, usually silver

Wrists

chūŗā	:	silver bracelet, thin
paūchī	:	emossed silver bracelet
karā	:	plain silver bracelet, thick
gharī	:	modern wristwatch

Fingers

angūṭhī	:	ring
gorakh dhandho	:	silver wire puzzle ring, with stones

Upper arms

bhujbal	:	silver clasp

Anklets

torā	:	thin silver anklet for baby or child
berī	:	silver anklet, for left ankle

Muslim Men's Jewelry

Ear

murkhī	:	gold ring worn in ear lobe
kuṇḍal	:	larger gold ring worn in ear lobe

Neck

baṭan : silver shirt buttons linked with chains and dangels

tāwīz : amulet

Fingers

angūṭhī : ring·

Wrist

ghaṛi : wristwatch

NOTES

* A comprehensive study of the jewelry of India, copiously illustrated with hundreds of photographs, is currently (1994) being prepared by Oppi Untracht, an authority on the symbolism and technologies involved in the design, creation, and uses of jewelry (Harry N. Abrams, Inc., New York, forthcoming).

1. This paper is concerned with jewelry and its relationships with those who purchase and wear it. No attempt has been made here to deal with jewelry manufacture and commerce.

2. For detailed discussion of the history of laws of property ownership as they relate to Indian women, see Altekar, 1962: 212-78.

3. For a rather thorough and richly illustrated compendium of data pertaining to Indian jewelry, see Hendley, 1909. For other references, see Chandna, 1961.

4. The data on which this paper is based were collected by the author during approximately two years of anthropological fieldwork in "Nimkhera" from 1965 to 1967, and a month in 1973, with the assistance of Kumari Sunalini Nayudu. I am very grateful to the residents of Nimkhera for their hospitality and cooperation and to Miss Nayudu for her valuable insights and aid at all stages of the fieldwork. I am indebted to numerous state and district government officers in Bhopal and Raisen for the many courtesies they extended. My husband, Jerome Jacobson, provided essential assistance, advice, and moral support.

The field research was supported by a pre-doctoral fellowship and grant from the National Institute of Mental Health, United States Public Health Service. Preparation of this paper was made possible by an Ogden Mills Fellowship, awarded by the American Museum of Natural History, New York, for which I am most appreciative. I wish to thank Suzanne Hanchett, Miriam Sharma, Sylvia Vatuk, and Jerome Jacobson for their helpful comments on an earlier draft of the paper.

The pseudonym "Nimkhera" refers to a large *nīm* tree in the center of the village, whose leaves are used by all the villagers for soothing medications. All personal names used in this paper are pseudonyms.

The language spoken in Nimkhera is a variety of Hindi. In this paper, Hindi words are written with diacritics only at the first appearance of each word.

5. Sharma's book on social life in medieval Rajasthan includes a labelled drawing of a woman wearing traditional Rajasthani jewelry. Many of the pieces closely resemble ornaments worn in the Bhopal area today, and several of their names are the same (Sharma, 1968: [26]).

6. Muslim groups are similar to Hindu castes in some respects but differ significantly from castes in other respects (see Mines, 1972).

7. For full discussion of women's status and purdah in this region, see Jacobson, 1970, and 1974. For comparative material from North India, see especially Luschinsky, 1962, and Minturn and Hitchcock, 1966.

8. A rupee is worth about 13c at the current rate of exchange, but in practical terms is treated very much like a dollar in the United States.

9. The only gold toe rings I saw in Central India were on the feet of the former Rani of Kanker (a small princely state in eastern Madhya Pardesh), indicating, perhaps, a privilege of the high-born. Hendley also observed gold toe rings on women "of the highest rank" (1909:26).

10. On rare chaperoned outings, strictly secluded Muslim women in Hyderabad ride fully concealed in curtained rickshaws and also tie their bangles with string to prevent them from jingling (Schmidt, 1969:56).

In the Ramayan, Rama's attention is first drawn to Sita by the sounds of her jewelry:

> Hearing the tinkle of her bracelets and anklets and the bells on her girdle, Rama pondered in his heart and said to Laksman. 'It sounds as though Love were beating his drum, ambitious to vanquish the world!' So saying, he turned and looked in that direction. ....When he saw Sita's beauty, he was glad; he praised her in his heart but spoke no word (Hill, 1952:104).

11. In this region, lac bangles should not be worn by a widow, although bracelets of other materials are not forbidden and are often donned after a period of mourning. Widows who remarry may wear all items normally worn by a married woman.

At the remarriage of a widow, any glass bangles on her wrists are broken off and replaced with a new set. A divorcee remarrying does not have bangles broken.

Among a few urban-influenced women in the village, a necklace of black beads (*mangal sūtra*) is worn as a mark of the married state.

12. A sophisticated Muslim woman said the nose ring and chain symbolized the bride's enforced servitude to her husband. "She is chained," she said.

Some Hindus present a solid silver necklace (*hasli*) to the bride at the engagement ceremony. One woman explained, "It means the bride and groom are chained together from now on."

13. In a variant of this ceremony, an earthenware pot represents the bride. The equation of a woman with a clay pot (vs. the equation of a man with a brass vessel) is verbally expressed in other parts of India (e.g., among the Gonds, see L. Dube, 1957; and in North India, see Luschinsky, 1962:254).

14. Women do retain secret stores of cash for themselves, which they use for a number of purposes. For an account of a system of private savings and the uses to which such savings are put in a village of Western Uttar Pradesh, see Vatuk and Vatuk, 1971.

15. Taking money for a bride is considered sinful and reprehensible.

16. Interestingly, both publicity and secrecy may be used to enhance a woman's control over her private property. In the Bhopal region, the obviousness of a woman's jewelry and the publicity attendant upon its disappearance help her retain control of it in the face of attempts by her affines to pawn or sell it. Among the Hakka of Taiwan and some other Chinese, secrecy is the prime means by which a woman guards her private property (mostly cash) from her husband and his family. Among both Central Indians and Hakka Chinese, maintenance of secrecy about the full extent and manner of acquisition of women's holdings provides a measure of autonomy for individuals and couples within a joint family. As among Hindus, Hakka women acquire most of their personal property at the time of marriage which, as Cohen has suggested, is hardly coincidental (see Cohen, 1968:167-69, 172-74).

17. Land must normally be sold in cultivable units, valued in thousands of rupees. In recent years some Nimkhera farmers have begun renting out their fields or portions of them for cash advances of considerable size in order to obtain funds to invest in stone quarries. This may jeopardize the income of the landowner for a year or two but does not itself involve the risk of losing the land.

18. At least two important Muslim leaders of the late nineteenth and early twentieth centuries owed their educations to funds their

mothers obtained by pawning jewelry. One of these mothers, a widow, secretly pawned her jewelry to provide western education for her son over the objections of a domineering and conservative uncle (Andrews, 1929:52; and Muhammad Ali, 1966:4-5, quoted in Minault, 1973;6-8).

19. In an article on women in Rajasthani folklore, Bhatnagar has written, "Rajasthani folklore is mostly the music of bracelets and anklets, armlets, bangles, and costumes of folk women. But the sweet voice of her ornaments does not shield the bitterness of her life" (1969:59).

References

Altekar, A.S. 1962 *The Position of Women in Hindu Civilization*. Delhi : Motilal Banarsidass.

Andrews, C.F. 1929 *Zaka Ullah of Delhi*. Cambridge : W. Heffer and Sons.

Apte, V.M. 1951a "Social and Economic Conditions." In R. C. Majumdar, A.D. Pusalker, A.K. Mujamdar (eds.), *The Vedic Age. The History and Culture of the Indian People*, pp. 387-406. Bombay: Bharatiya Vidya Bhawan.

————1951b "Political and Legal Institutions." In R. C. Majumdar, A.D. Pusalker, A.K. Mujamdar (eds.), *The Vedic Age. The History and Culture of the Indian People*, pp. 429-41. Bombay : Bhartiya Vidya Bhavan.

Bailey, F.G. 1958 *Caste and the Economic Frontier*. Bombay : Oxford University Press.

Basham, A.L. 1959 *The Wonder That Was India*. New York : Grove Press.

Bhatnagar, Manju 1969 "Women in Rajasthani Folklore." In Sankar Sen Gupta (ed). *Women in Indian Folklore; Linguistic and Religious Study, a Short Survey of their Social Status and Position*, pp. 59-78, Calcutta : Indian Publications.

Bhushan, Jamila Brij 1964 *Indian Jewellery, Ornaments and Decorative Designs*. Bombay : D.B. Taraporevala.

Chandna, Suman (Compiler) 1961 *Bibliography of Indian Arts and Crafts*. Census of India, 1961, Vol. I, Part XI (ii). New Delhi : Office of the Registrar General of India : Ministry of Home Affairs.

Cohen, Myron L. 1968 "A Case Study of Chinese Family Economy and Development." *Journal of Asian and African Studies* 3 : 161-80.

Coomaraswamy, Ananda K. 1964 *The Arts and Crafts of India and Ceylon*. New York : Noonday Press. (First Edition, 1931.)

"Croesus" 1962 "Golden Opportunity to Give Away Gold." *Eastern Economist* 39 : 869-70.

Dube, Leela 1957 The Gond Woman. Ph.D. dissertation. Nagpur : University of Nagpur.

Eastern Economist 1962 "Gold Bonds." *Eastern Economist* 39 : 851-52.

Economic Times, The 1973 "Market Trends." *The Economic Times* 13 (26 September) : 2.

Economic Weekly, The 1962 "Trading in Gold." *The Economic Weekly* 14 : 1753-54.

Fuchs, Stephen 1966 *The Children of Hari* : *A Study of the Nimar Balahis in Madhya Pradesh, India*. Bombay : Thacker and Co.

Hendley, Thomas Holbein 1909 "Indian Jewelry." *The Journal of Indian Art and Industry* 12 : 95-107.

Hill, W. Douglas P. 1952 *The Holy Lake of the Acts of Rama.* (An English translation of Tulasi Das's Ramacaritamanasa.) London : Oxford University Press.

Hutton, J.H. 1963 *Caste in India* : *Its Nature, Function and Origins* (4th edition). London : Oxford University Press.

Jacobson, Doranne 1970 Hidden Faces : Hindu and Muslim Purdah in a Central Indian Village. Ph.D. dissertation, New York : Columbia University.

——————. 1974 " The Women of North and Central India : Goddesses and Wives." In Carolyn Matthiasson (ed). *Many Sisters* : *Women in Cross-cultural Perspective*, pp. 99-175. New York : the Free Press.

——————. 1976 "You Have Given Us a Goddess : Flexibility in Central Indian Kinship." In S. Devadas Pillai (ed.), *Aspects of Changing India* : *Studies in Honour of Ghurye*. Bombay : Popular Prakshan.

Luschinsky, Mildred Stroop 1962 The Life of Women in a Village of North India. Ph.D. dissertation. Ithaca, New York : Cornell University.

——————. 1963 "The Impact of Some Recent Indian Government Legislation on the Women of an Indian Village." *Asian Survey* 3 : 573-83.

Minault, Gail 1973 "Muslim Women in Conflict with Parda : Their Role in the Indian Nationalist Movement." Paper presented at the Berkshire Conference of Women Historians, New Brunswick, New Jersey. [In Sylvia A. Chipp and Justin J. Green (eds.), *Asian Women in Transition*. University Park, PA: Pennsylvania State University Press, 1980, pp. 194-203.]

Mines, Mattison 1972 "Muslim Social Stratification in India : The Basis for Variation." *Southwestern Journal of Anthropology* 28 : 333-49.

Minturn, Leigh and John T. Hitchcock 1966 "The Rajputs of Khalapur, India." *Six Cultures Series*, Volume 3. New York : John Wiley and Sons.

Muhammad Ali 1966 *My Life, a Fragment*. Lahore : S. M. Ashraf.

Pandya, A. K. 1974 *Raisen District, District Census Handbook, Census of India 1971*. Bhopal : Government of Madhya Pradesh.

Russell, R. V. and Rai Bahadur Hiralal 1916 *Castes and Tribes of the Central Provinces* (4 volumes). London : Macmillan and Co.

Sahasranaman, M. 1974 "How Much Gold Do You Possess?" *Femina* 15

(July 19) : 30.

Schmidt, Ruth 1969 Structural Analysis of Hyderbadi Dakhini Urdu. Ph. D. dissertation, Philadelphia : University of Pennsylvania.

Sharma, G. N. 1968 *Social Life in Medieval Rajasthan*, 1500-1800 A.D. Agra : Lakshmi Narain Agarwal.

Stern, Robert W. 1970 *The Process of Opposition in India* : *Two Case Studies of How Policy Shapes Politics*. Chicago : University of Chicago Press.

Times of India, The 1975 "Bullion Firm." *The Times of India* 137 (April 7) : 5.

Tiwari, G.N. 1964 "Introducing the District." In G. Jagathpathi, *Raisen District, District Census Handbook, Census of India 1961*, pp. xxxvii-lxxx. Madhya Pradesh, Government of Madhya Pradesh.

Vatuk, Ved Prakash and Sylvia Vatuk 1971 "On a System of Private Savings among North Indian Village Women." *Journal of Asian and African Studies* 6 : 179-90.

The "Village Indira": A Brahman Widow and Political Action in Rural North India

Susan S. Wadley

In 1984 while doing research in Karimpur[1], a village in north India, I had a provocative encounter one day in a village lane.

> You should do something for women so that they have work to fill their own stomachs.

Startled, I could only look at the speaker in amazement. Facing me was a scrawny old Brahman woman, dressed in a not-so-white sari, wearing only a silver bangle for jewelry. The voice was sharp, the eyes full of fun and vitality. She had followed me from her house where I had been seeking permission for my research assistant to conduct a time study. Now I was being lectured in the village lane. "Women work to fill their stomachs?" This was a radical idea in a village where most felt women's only proper role was housewife, inside a closed courtyard. I muttered a response and left. But I was intrigued by this encounter and sought further information. I learned that my acquaintance was called "the village Indira": that she headed the women's section of the village *carca mandal* (government initiated educational cum development organization); that she was active in district politics; and that she was a firm supporter of that other Indira.

This chapter is about my protagonist, here called Saroj[2] (known to me as Caci, literally, father's younger brother's wife), and hence about the obstacles that women face as they seek a greater voice in economic and political life in rural north India. Very few economic opportunities are open to and acceptable for the wives of high status landowners. The demand from the central and state governments for female political leadership, however muted that demand, conflicts with village norms of women's proper roles, particularly as defined by the local system of honor, a gendered system in which women's good reputations are attained in ways markedly different than those of men. For a women to enter politics marks her as 'acting like a man', rendering her vulnerable to public ridicule and criticism, in contrast to the successful male politician. Understanding Saroj's demand for economic opportunities for women and her choice to be critically judged for behavior in conflict with traditional norms demands that we look at the sources of honor that she values and ultimately at her own marginal position in Karimpur society. As I shall show, Saroj is a fervent believer in the values of her rural Brahman heritage. Yet she often acted in opposition to them as she sought new roles for herself and her daughters. Hers was truly a "balancing act," pushing against the barriers facing women, but careful not to push excessively.

Saroj and Her Community

Let me begin with Saroj's story. It was told to me over many months, and I have reordered it and condensed portions here to provide a coherent outline. When appropriate, I will quote her exact words. At the time that she told me of her life, she was 59 or 60 years old.

When I was one and a half years old, my father died. We were one brother and three sisters. We faced a lot of hardship and misery. One sister was married before the death of my father, but he had not yet done her *gauna* (consummation ceremony).[3] When I was ten years old, my mother sent me to this house as a bride. Here I also faced a lot of difficulties. As soon as I came here, the problem of bread and butter became a bit tolerable. I had the strength of my youth. My first children did not live long. They all died. Later on seven more were born. And they are alive up to now. So again I became happy. Then again I began to march toward sorrow. After some time, Panditji (her husband) died, eight years ago. Right from that time, I have been passing through hardship and difficulties. So I am leading a miserable life. My older son began to live out of the joint family two years ago. And these two children (unmarried son and daughter) are a burden on my head. I barely feed them. This son does not do well in school. This daughter reads willingly, and she is wise in her studying. So I am giving her education.

This brief statement introduces the outlines of Saroj's life. Her father died; her mother struggled to raise and marry her off. She married at nine, moving to Krimpur only one year later. She had fourteen pregnancies, with seven living children, five daughters an two sons. The two older daughters and oldest son were married before her husband died. After his death in 1976, she arranged marriages for two more daughters. In 1982, her older son separated his small family, leaving her with an unmarried son and one unmarried daughter. Her son separated both because his mother and wife quarreled constantly and because by doing so he avoided bearing the expenses of the remaining two marriages.

When Saroj came to Karimpur as a young bride, there were three persons in the house: her mother-in-law, husband and herself. Her father-in-law had died when her husband was two years old. The house and land were in fact in her husband's *nansar*, that is, the village of his mother's father. Her husband's mother had no brothers and hence had inherited the land. At that time, the house was one room of crumbling clay bricks. Although the family owned considerable land, there was no one to work it. After laborers and sharecroppers took their share, Saroj's mother-in-law had to pay the rent to the *zamindar* (landlord) and lived off the remainder. With no adult men to supervise, her share was minimal. Saroj says that her dowry was one rupee, as both her mother and mother-in-law were widows and equally poor. That Saroj moved to Karimpur before puberty indicates her mother-in-law's need for an extra pair of hands.

Between 1930 and 1970, the family grew prosperous. The land was there and Panditji was soon able to farm it himself. They initially bought a buffalo calf, raised it, sold it and bought two calves. Selling these, they obtained adult animals, and eventually bullocks. Saroj attributes the family's prosperity to their hard work. She loves to tell of building their brick house. Working stealthily at night, she and her husband dug trenches, leveled foundations and carried bricks. It was highly improper for a Brahman wife to labor at such tasks, hence the nighttime activities. While not the largest house in the village today, her several rooms of brick are more than adequate for her family of three.

The one teenage son living with Saroj owns five acres of land. Since he doesn't farm himself, the land is let on one-half shares to men of a neighboring village. Saroj does have two water buffalo and one calf (fed with fodder grown on their land) and sells milk to cover daily costs that allow a higher than usual standard of living, with vegetables and fruit from the market, tea, oil and spices.

The family also benefited by not having to marry children while the parents were still young and struggling to gain an adequate livelihood. Since Saroj had no surviving children until she was almost thirty, she and her husband had more than 25 years of working life before their family faced exorbitant marriage costs. Starting in 1970, the weddings of four daughters began to drain family finaces. By the early 1980s, each wedding cost a mininum of 15,000 rupees, (up to a year's cash income) but usually much more. A minimum 15,000 rupees for weddings every three years would impoverish any farm family owning only ten acres of land. The family bought a tractor in 1973 with a government loan and sold it after Panditji's death in the late 1970s to pay for a daughter's wedding.

Saroj's family was the first Brahman household in Karimpur to educate all daughters to grade 8 or more. The oldest finished 8th grade, the middle three all finished high school, and in 1984 the fifth was in her first year of intercollege (11th class), only the third village girl to continue past tenth class. Both sons finished high school. Rajani, the unmarried intercollege student, rides a bike daily to town seven miles away for schooling, where she also does the family shopping. Saroj says that education is necessary for girls to make good marriages. Educating girls is not without problems, however; Rajani's reputation is endangered because of her behavior on the roads. Saroj hopes that her youngest can obtain a service job: perhaps, given her political connections, this is realistic dream.

Saroj's attitudes are a curious mix of modern and Brahman conservative. As a Brahman woman married into Karimpur, Saroj is a member of the dominant *jati*[4] of the village. Karimpur is an agricultural community located 150 miles southeast of New Delhi; in 1984, it contained 327 families (2048 individuals) divided among twenty-three *jati*. The Brahman *jati* owns nearly 60 percent of the village lands, but had controlled almost 80 percent of the land when Saroj married into the community at the age of nine in 1934. Since only 21.6 percent of the population is Brahman, their control of community resources marks their political and economic dominance.[5] A second large *jati* of farmers (*Kachhi*), comprising 20.4 percent of the population, owns another 17 percent of the land. The other *jati* groups are small farmers, sharecroppers, laborers and members of the service *jati* who are tied to patron families through the *jajmani* system of hereditary ties between patron landowning families and client serving families such as the washerman, watercarrier, flowergrower, midwife, carpenter, and priest.[6]

One's birth into a given *jati* is a result of actions in a previous life: birth is a matter of fate (*karma*). The Brahmans of Karimpur are sure about their superiority. Saroj herself said,

These Brahmans, they are Brahma (one of the three major Hindu gods). It is the top *jati*. If Brahmans act properly according to their fate even a little, if they do good work, they are *devata* (gods). We say Brahman *devata*.

A Brahman male also called the Brahmans "god" and added,

It has been told in the scriptures that Garuda? asked Kagbhasur, "Tell me this: what is the best *joanj* (shape, life form)?" And he said, "I have feeling for all, but I have more love for humans. And among humans. I have more love for Brahmans. I have much love for Brahmans, who are knowledgeable."

Having knowledge gives one the right to rule others, whether the higher *jati* rule the lower, men rule women, or parents rule children. Male dominance of women is based on male control of knowledge. In a discussion one day with a Brahman male, he claimed that women have power. The conversation continued: 'If the woman is more powerful, how does the man control her?'

Control. They don't have much knowledge. How is the lion locked in a cage? It lacks reason. Man protects her from everything.

"If a woman progresses, then she would be knowledgeable. Then how can you shut her in a cage?"

I say that if the sun begins to rise in the west, then what? It is a law of nature.

Saroj's viewpoint is similar.[7] She discussed women when talking about her own situation:

The woman is inferior. A woman can only do the work of discipline. She can never leave the customs. If my daughters wander outside of the house, I may be the target of defamation, as well as my dead husband. So it is against my dignity. For this reason, she is inferior to man. Women have given birth to such great persons—Prahlad, Dhurt, and others. In this she becomes major: because she has given birth to all the great saints, she becomes major. Man cannot give birth to such great persons. Actually speaking, men could never

produce women. But what can I do? I am a woman. A woman can
do only what she possesses as right. My girls can never go out of
control. Had I not guided them in connection with the social
conditions of *purdah*, how could they live inside the curtain? As a
girl sees her mother's activities, the girl imitates them unconsciously.

Later that day, I asked Saroj what she would think if she were a man.

I would feel good if I were a man. I could go whenever I wanted. Now
I am a woman. We live under control and behind the curtain
(*purdah*) and live in discipline and we work according the wishes of
our husband.

In these comments, Saroj articulates many of the values that ultimately
underlie her ideas about work and politics. She adheres to the ideas of the
superiority of Brahmans and males that form the traditional value system
of Karimpur. Many of these ideas revolve around the dual concerns of
honor (*ijjat*) and *purdah*.

Honor and Purdah

Reputation in Karimpur is a gendered concept: what makes a good
man differs from what makes a good woman.[8] Reputation in north India is
defined by the term *ijjat*, honor. Honor belongs not just to a person, but
extends to that person's family, lineage, *jati*, and community. Thus if a
woman has honor, she contributes to the honor of her family, lineage, *jati*
and village. And if the village has honor, that in turn reflects upon the
individual person.

A man from a middle ranking *jati* put it this way:

Sometimes there is a very honorable man who is rich and everyone
knows him. But others live in his house who destroy honor. That
Brahman has four sons, but when I was a child, he purchased a wife...
So they didn't keep any honor.

For men, wealth is the main criterion of honor. When asked about
honorable men in the village, no one ever spontaneously listed a non-
Brahman, suggesting that wealth is the main criterion of honor. Raghunath,
quoted above, added:

Honor comes in every way: honor comes from wealth; honor comes from land; honor comes from your daughters-in-law living inside the house and not speaking to others. A person who never steals is also honorable.

Male honor, then, depends upon wealth, one's own righteous behavior, giving aid to others, and on the behavior of the women of one's house. "If the woman runs away, the nose of the whole family is cut," said one poor man. Raghunath elaborated on the behavior necessary for a woman, and hence her family, to have honor;

The woman who has honor lives inside the house. Suppose, if I go to someone's house and from outside I call, "Anyone here?" The one who has honor comes quietly, face hidden by a veil and answers softly. We say she keeps much honor (*ijjat rakhti hai*). On the contrary, if I come from outside and call out and the woman comes quickly to the door and asks unshamefully and unhesitantly, "Who is it?", and says, "He is not here, he is coming. Come in and sit down"...she speaks unnecessarily and too much. She is not a woman of honor.

A woman who has honor, then, speaks softly and seldom, remains veiled, and most critically, keeps *purdah*, literally "curtain," as is commonly required of women in north India rural communities such as Karimpur. Saroj is clear about the role of *purdah* in her own life for as a Brahman wife, she faced the greatest *purdah* strictures.

When I was a daughter-in-law (*bahu*), the order was given to me not to call my mother-in-law when she was out of the house. I used to knock the chain of the window against the wood. The men and women sitting with her used to tell her that perhaps your *bahu* is calling you. Then she used to come inside the house and I asked her whatever was neccessary. But nowadays it isn't like this. In this era, everything is wrong. Today I don't understand the fashions. The family is not doing proper work when it should be done. If you follow the traditions of the village and society, there lies your prestige. If you ignore traditions and customs, it means the total annihilation of your honor and respect.

On another day we discussed her mobility again. I asked, "Previously your husband did everything, things like shopping in Mainpuri?"

Yes, he did everything outside. He went to market. He worked in the fields. He brought the bundles of grain to the house, then I would store it. He threshed. If he went in some marriage procession, I asked him to bring all the *sili* (threshed grain) to the courtyard and I would winnow it. (Marriages typically take place near the end of the spring harvest, often before the crop is stored. Only men go to bride's house and are often gone three days.) Until the marriage procession came back, I would winnow all the threshed wheat and make a pile of grain. I packed that in the bags, I finished all the work. But I never went out. The girls could go out to see the cattle, if they were grazing in the fields. I never went to the threshing floor, never. I also never went beyond the door to give him food. When I used to go into the village lanes to get to a women's ceremony (*balava*), I used to cover my face with this much *ghungat* (the end of her shawl. She demonstrated enveloping herself in it). My husband's younger brother (fictive kinship) used to tease me and say, "See this is the *bahu* of *gauna*" (i.e. she is newly married). When I used to go out of the house, they used to say, "She is the newly married *bahu*". Nowadays *bahus* move about the village with uncovered heads. Even the newly married ones. They don't follow the customs. I never went in the lane or out of the gate without a shawl. I also cover myself with a shawl. I cannot go without a shawl even now. But earlier I never went anywhere. He had to come home for food. When these children were older, they used to take food to him. I never went. Since he died, I have seen everything of ours.

Here Saroj articulates the village rules for women to maintain family honor through the maintenance of rules of *purdah*. Women, whether Hindu or Muslim, should be not seen by strange men nor should they talk to them. Younger Brahman wives are rarely allowed out of their houses, except for a morning or evening trip to the fields which serve as the village latrine. Unmarried teenage girls are also restricted in their mobility, perhaps visiting the village shop for some spices or supplies for a festival, but always accompanied by other children. Only older Brahman women like Saroj's mother-in-law, sitting on the verandah, are allowed out of the houses on a regular basis. Hence older women make and store cow dung cakes in an empty lot or milk cattle in the cattle yard or lane. *Purdah* restrictions are clearly age-based and eased as a woman ages. But as Saroj noted, even at sixty years and widowed, she must wear a shawl and restrain her mobility.

Women of poorer families, but never Brahman women, may help their husbands in the fields or labor beside their husbands in other jobs. Four kinds of work are recognized in Karimpur. Wage labor (*mazduri*) is unacceptable for women, and only a widow or the very poorest woman engages in it. Agricultural work (*kheti ka kam*) is acceptable for most non-Brahman women only when they accompany male kin. Housework (*ghar ka kam*) is women's work, and, in addition to the chores of cooking, cleaning and child care, includes making cow dung cakes, milking and feeding animals, and grain processing as Saroj noted above. More recently, "service" (teacher, bank clerk, policewoman) has become acceptable prestigious work for women.

In north India, agriculture is primarily a male activity. While women of some groups help their male kin plant certain crops, weed, harvest, or irrigate, women do not plough or prepare fields. In contrast to women in other parts of India, Karimpur women do not do agricultural work unless accompanied by male kin (father, brother, husband or son). Unless widowed, a woman would not work for wages unless male kin were also employed by that farmer. Hence even the lower class women who are seen working in the fields are unlike those in other parts of India who obtain jobs independent of their male kin. In addition, the *purdah*-bound "housewives" like Saroj, belonging to richer farming families, do a significant amount of processing of harvests, including threshing and winnowing, often on their verandahs or in courtyards.

Some income-producing activities traditionally part of the *jajmani* system of hereditary patron-client relationships are solely or mainly female as well as tied to particular *jati*. The *purdah* system of north India demands that non-family men be denied regular access to women's quarters, so in those quarters, the duties of the watercarrier, the sweeper, the washerwoman, the flowergrower, and the barber were all performed by women. The act of keeping one's women in *purdah* is a marker of the "power of money," because women's potential labour value in the fields or income producing jobs is overtly denied and must be replaced by hired labor. Even "household" activities sometimes require additional hired help because of women's confinement: the water carriers who brought water from public wells were providing a service that was necessary only because secluded women were forbidden to move about outside their homes.

Nowadays *jajmani* plays only a minor role in Karimpur life. Pump sets in family courtyards render the watercarrier superfluous. In a curious twist, more women use the fields as a latrine than previously so that the daily services of the sweeper are rarely demanded. Given better supplies of water, richer families are choosing to wash their own clothes using commercial soap powders or to send them to Manipuri where they can be pressed and starched, rather than using the village washerwoman, who uses no soap powder, starch or iron. As *jajmani* has declined generally, the flowergrower and barber find themselves less needed and their ties to patron families cut. Hence many women's work opportunities as defined by hereditary *jajmani* ties have been displaced since the early 1970s rendering many of these women "jobless".

Women have few other opportunities to earn. Women can earn some money by making and selling cow dung cakes (50 paise, about 5 cents, per 100 cakes), raising cattle and selling milk (which for the poor involves obtaining grass daily for fodder), or less often by raising chickens. But these occupations all require mobility beyond the household and hence are closed to those who seek to maintain their social status through *purdah*. The only acceptable jobs for high status women are "service" jobs, bank clerk, schoolteacher, office worker, or policewoman. Only one woman in Karimpur has a service job: a Brahman widow now in her 50s, she has been a schoolteacher for thirty years.

A key factor for women's lives is that north Indian marriages are both village exogamous and hypergamous within their local *jati* group.[9] Hence married women live in a community where they are strangers, often some distance from their natal home, generally with no close relatives nearby. Further, as the lowest ranking persons in their new households, they are required to display regular respect to those senior to them, especially to their husband's female kin. Saroj put in this way:

> She (a new bride) is inferior to her husband, father-in-law, mother-in-law, sister-in-law and husband's sister. If she becomes servant (*dashi*) for these persons, she might be called the queen (*rani*) of the family.

Women show respect in a variety of ways. A *bahu* asks her *sas* (mother-in-law) what to cook, how much spice to add, whether she can go to the fields, and so on, even when she is forty and the mother-in-law sixty or more. Showing this respect within the household is crucial to maintaining the joint families so desired by Brahmans, who believe that jointness demonstrates the power of the united household, where one voice can speak for all.

Actions, whether leading to honor or dishonor (*veijjati*), are motivated by modesty (*sharam*). Modesty is a matter of conscience and leads to right and wrong behavior. It is learned from parents and peers and also upon experiencing insult. The person without modesty (*vesharam*) acts crazily and dishonorably. One man said, "The woman who is immodest says whatever comes to her mind, she acts in an upside-down way." So, if a woman should show respect or act in ways which gain honor, but doesn't, she is acting immodestly.

Saroj ties these aspects of women's proper behavior to *dharma*, righteous behavior, and to household prosperity. To explain *dharma* to me, she told the story of Lakshmi, the goddess of prosperity, and her sister, Kulakshni, the "misbegotten one". The two sisters are married to the god Vishnu, who asks them what kind of house they will keep. Lakshmi desires a house where the women rise early, bathe, worship and work hard. Kulakshni wants a house where the women are slovenly, rise late, gamble and drink. Vishnu says that he will live with Lakshmi, for he desires a house that is prosperous. Saroj added, "Tell this story to women in America."

Saroj continually articulates patriarchal values, although certainly not in the same manner as men do. Nevertheless, her position within the hierarchies (male-female, '*jati*', class) of Karimpur demand adherence to patriarchal norms if her own position is to be enhanced. She emphasizes the need for women to control the labor and sexuality of yet younger women, all aimed toward reproducing patriarchal domination (see Sen 1984). It is from within this ideological framework that Saroj negotiates her life in the 1980s, as she seeks new roles for herself and for women in Karimpur.

Karimpur in the 1980s

Beginning in the 1950s, government agencies and programs penetrated many aspects of village life. In 1952, a government tube well, funded by the German government, was installed. In the 1950s, *zamindars* (landlords) were abolished and farmers became landowners (though significant sharecropping continues). A Cooperative Bank and Seed Store opened in the mid-1960s. In the late 1960s, there was land consolidation, new seeds and fertilizers were introduced, and a Village Level Worker, an agent for development programs, was present. Each state divided its districts into smaller units called Blocks. The Blocks are the primary units for development programs. Government loans aided the acquisition of pump sets and paid for the drilling of tube wells in the 1970s, so that by 1984 irrigation was available to anyone with money to pay for it. The result is a significant change in Karimpur's agricultural economy. With increasingly widespread education and growth of the District town, a market town servicing a rural population of over 1 million located only seven miles away, labor relationships in Karimpur changed markedly beginning in the mid-1960s.

Several factors have affected women's work, all of them producing a marked decline in income-producing opportunities for women. First, with a relative decline of male employment in agriculture and the shift of landless men to urban-based jobs, women who had worked in agriculture alongside their male kin are displaced. Second, women who were traditionally employed in *jati*-based occupations as servants through *jajmani* no longer are. Third, mechanization has replaced female labor in a variety of agriculturally related arenas (including grinding grain, oil pressing, threshing, irrigation). Finally, changes in cropping patterns have made female help in the fields less necessary. (see Wadley 1993 for more details on these issues.)

Other factors that have changed women's status in recent times include a greater disparity in education, with more males becoming literate and receiving considerably higher levels of education; an increase in dowry payments for women of all *jatis*, in contrast to some brideprice marriages among the poor and other more reciprocal marriage payments in the past; and greater female-specific child mortality, especially among the poor (Wadley 1989). At the same time, a very few women are becoming relatively well-educated, and daughters and daughters-in-law are sometimes (though rarely) given training to allow them to pursue outside employment.

Brahman economic dominance has given Karimpur Brahmans political dominance as well. During British colonial rule, the appointed headman was a Brahman. Since Independence in 1947, the elected headmen have all been Brahman. This Brahman control of the village *panchayat* (governing body) gives them control of many development endeavors, such as the *carca mandal* that Saroj heads.

The community and especially the Brahmans have prospered over the past several decades. Measures of material prosperity include longer life spans, better health care, and more consumer goods (radios, bicycles, watches, synthetic clothing, pumps in courtyards, sewing machines, etc).

The "green revolution" (fertilizers, new seeds and irrigation) has quadrupled some yields, while cash crops for the urban market permit some farmers to make substantial profits. Nevertheless, the Brahman community decries their situation. To them, their life situation has deteriorated. There are two factors contributing to this vision. First, their political and economic dominance has decreased substantially. Men who work in the urban center are no longer dependent on the Brahmans. Banks have replaced money-lenders. Democracy propounds a rhetoric of equality, and untouchables seek entrance to the village school, participation in some rituals, etc. Second, their aspirations have changed. They now have relatives in small towns with gas stoves and televisions. This consumer-oriented middle class provides a new reference group, and farm incomes do not necessarily permit achieving it. Hence, Karimpur Brahman feel poorer, though by gross material measures they are not (Wadley and Derr 1989). This then marks the social context in which Saroj has sought a role as a female leader.

Saroj as Politician

After her husnand's death, Saroj first became involved in the village *carca mandal*, an organization of the Block Development Office designed to educate rural men and women. She explains her involvement and the organization this way:

It [*carca mandal*] was started six years ago (1978). It was started by the government because the government thought that women lead a miserable life. So do their children. So orders were given to the Village Level Worker (VLW) to make a report about the women in your community and present it to the government. A VLW was renting my room. He was asked, "Who is the most intelligent and wisest woman is your community?" So he gave my name saying that my aunt is the most intelligent woman in the village. No other village woman is her equal in wisdom. The Block sent someone to interview me. They appointed me an important woman of the village. All because my interview went well.

Then they said, "Improve conditions in your village. We have appointed you. You must choose the other women." So, as I was ordered, I chose twenty women who were poor and in distress. I taught them what I had been taught. I took them to the Block Training Center. The teacher of the Block Center taught us, "Keep the children healthy. Feed them nourishing food. Feed them this thing and don't feed them that...This training was given for five days. At the end of the fifith day, 25 rupees was paid to every woman. The program continues till now.

Twelve years later, Saroj still headed the women's division of the *carca mandal*. No one seems ready to replace her and only one or two other women are active in its infrequent activities. One active member is a middle-aged Muslim widow who is a daughter of the village. It is unlikely that the Block would appoint a Muslim leader in this Brahman-dominated village. Saroj's position remains secure.

The *carca mandal* has twenty members per year. Its main function is to provide a week's training in childcare and nutrition at the Block headquarters some seven miles away. All *jati* groups should be represented and members should be married women under 40 years of age. These requirements are seldom met. The first year, Saroj invited many unmarried village girls to attend. Almost all were Brahman (and educated from landowning families). When this list was condemned, Saroj invited only married women, but they continue to be overwhelming Brahman. In 1984, her membership numbered eighteen: thirteen were Brahman, two accountants (*kayastha*), one Muslim, one shepherd (*gadariya*) and one Farmer (*kacchi*). There were no untouchables. Eleven were over forty, four in their thirties, and three in their twenties. Twelve of the families owned engines for pumping irrigation water from tube wells, marking them as well-off. Saroj mainly invites friends to participate. It is her own private patronage system.

The problems attracting younger wives and girls are serious. The Block's goal is to train young mothers. Instead, they are training grandmothers. The younger women are in *purdah*, and bear the burden of household tasks. Getting them free for a week's training is difficult. But the problems are greater; sending a young woman for a week's training is perceived as dangerous . In a discussion of why young women do not join, Saroj's neighbor told this story she had heard being told by a wandering beggar.

The were three boys and one girl. At the district fair there is a market called Mina Bazar. They bought her toe rings [a symbol of marriage, comparable to our wedding band]. She was unmarried, but they had her put them on. A Home Guard [paramilitary force] saw them and followed. They went to the cinema. Then they came out and sat under a tree. The man called the police. The police called them one

by one. They asked each one, "What is your relationship to the girl?"
The first said, "she is my wife. "The second and third also said,"she
is my wife." Then they called the girl and asked her what relationship
she had to each. She said that the eldest was the husband's younger
brother...The younger was her husband. Then the police beat her. So
she admitted that one was her paternal cousin, one was her maternal
cousin, and one was the brother of her sister's husband. The police
beat them and sent them to the police station.

The discussion following this story focused on the potential for mischief;
since the two cousins were her "brothers" by north Indian kin reckoning,
only her sister's husband's brother could have caused her harm. As one
woman put it, "What harm could he cause before two brothers?" Yet the
potential of a girl being inappropriately chaperoned excludes women's
participation in the *carca mandal*.

In the spring of 1984, Saroj had an opportunity for even greater
patronage. The Block sent smokeless hearths (*chula*) to be installed in
thirty homes. The traditional hearth is a horseshoe- shaped mud stove. It
is fired with cow dung and kindling and allows one pot to cook at a time.
Women generally prepare vegetables, then set them aside and cook the
family breads. Since the hearth is most often in a purified space, bounded
by high mud walls, the smoke of the fire causes eye irritation and infection
and possible lung problems. The smokeless hearths contained two cooking
spaces and had a metal pipe off the back to take smoke up and out of the
cooking area: they were to be a remedy to eye infections and one-pot
cooking, thus saving women time and energy and protecting their health.
Saroj and her male counterpart chose thirty families. Here wider
networks were cast: fourteen families were Brahman; three were of the
Midwife *jati* (*dhanuk*); two were Leather workers (*chamar*)[10]; five were
Farmer (*kacchi*); two were Muslim; one was Accountant (*kayastha*); one
was a Shepherd (*gadariya*); and two were Carpenters (*barhai*). By late
May, the new hearths were installed: six months later, they had all
disappeared. Women did't know how to use the two burners efficiently.
The smokeless hearths used more fuel than the old hearths, making them
more expensive to run. The metal piping could be put to use elswhere.[11]
Despite their ultimate failure in village eyes, the initial grants gave Saroj
significant opportunities for patronage. The 100 rupees ($ 10) that she and
four friends each received for installing the new hearths was also welcome.
Further, as Saroj noted.

I work for the Block because I get things from the Block. And if you need a subsidy or loan, I can get it for you. And I choose twenty members every year.

Not surprisingly, most Karimpur women had never heard of the *carca mandal*. Its infrequent activities affecting only a few women a year, and then mostly Saroj's Brahman neighbors and relatives, makes it a rather invisible activity to most. The smokeless hearths gave it a temporary visibility in a few sections of the village, but since all the stoves were abandoned within six months, even this visibility was of short duration.

Two years after she became head of the *carca mandal*, Saroj joined the Congress Party as an active member. The *carca mandal* was actually instituted under the Janata government in the late 1970s.[12] By 1979, Saroj realized that the Janata government was likely to fall in the next election and switched allegiance, since Janata programs and appointees would be banished. She also ties her switch to aid given her by a prominent Congress politician. She says that she had gone to the District Magistrate to seek a permit for diesel fuel to irrigate her fields, as none was available. The local MLA (member of the Legislative Assembly) was there, read her petition, asked her situation and had the District Magistrate give her a permit 20 liters of diesel fuel. Saroj claims that he then said, "Mother, I belong to Congress." So she responded, "Okay, I shall join the Congress. Write down my name."

Active involvement with the Congress party has taken Saroj to Lucknow, the state capital, and other cities. She had organized Karimpur villagers for rallies in Delhi; in March, 1984 she organized a group of more than 30 villagers to attend a farmers' rally there. Ironically that trip was cancelled at the last minute due to lack of diesel fuel for the bus. But in 1981 she took thirty villagers to Delhi for a large farmers' rally. The free trips, the accommodations, and meeting or seeing national leaders have been major events in her life. In 1985, she described for me a rally for women leaders held in conjunction with the 1984 election after Indira Gandhi's assassination.

I went and lived there (Lucknow) for one week for training.... Both the Chief Minister and Rajiv (Gandhi) were there. Women from all over the state were there... The helicopter landed at the airport. He stayed there for a long time. He met us one by one. Then we returned to the office and ate food there. There we were told that we should be together, that Congress should not be defeated. We all promised that Congress should not be defeated: we would all help... Indira died, but the Congress [party] is still alive.

In describing another rally, Saroj dwelled on the arrangements— the tent, bolsters, crowd, main speakers, foods. They received lot of sweets, thick fried cakes (*puri*) that Saroj found wonderful because she could eat them ("They were good for me because I have no teeth."), and tea. At this rally, she herself spoke. She discussed, she reports, the prices received by farmers.

> When I was called before the mike. I spoke of my desires. My potatoes are rotting. I said that if you intend to eliminate poverty, and make the poor happy, you must do it carefully. No one is listening to the farmers... When a farmer goes to a cloth merchant to buy a *dhoti* (a wrap for men), the cloth merchant asks twenty rupees for it. When he receives twenty, he gives you the cloth... But farmers cannot fix the rates of their goods. The government fixes the rates. Farmers are not valued. Everyone eats the grain grown by farmers, whether he is poor or rich. If farmers don't grow grain, what will Indira and others eat?...Others get good rates, but not farmers. Potatoes are two rupees per maund [approximately 20 cents for 80 pounds]. If I pay these two rupees to a cloth merchant, I won't get anything!

"What did they reply?"

> Don't worry, a strike is taking place right now. The government will buy potatoes. Sister, don't worry. The potato rates will go up." And now the rates are about 22 rupees per *maund*.

In publicly speaking before thousands, Saroj is breaking the norms that she herself articulates for Karimpur women. Other ideas that she reports from these rallies also challenge her values, yet she reports them positively. She tells of Mrs. Gandhi asking them to go to their village sisters and explain why they should vote for Congress. Saroj also notes that the new hearths are an election ploy to bring women to the Congress side. A friend asked her, "Do you think men will vote according the women's desires?" Saroj responded.

> You are a fool, Listen, Indian people have lost their religion. Earlier,

women used to serve their husbands. Nowadays, women are more likely to break their husband's head. Indian brothers have lost their religion. Perhaps only one or two in a hundred are controlled by their husbands.... It is the aim of Indira to bring women forward and push men back. To make them self dependent. To give ladies more comforts. And to give them rights.

Here again Saroj contradicts her more frequently stated views on the necessity of women being controlled by men. But the contexts are very different, and Indians often hold contradictory beliefs, using the answer appropriate to a given context.[13] Saroj as politican holds different beliefs than Saroj as Brahman housewife, widow and mother.

She herself sees no discrepancy between being a Brahman widow and going from house to house or city to city in search of votes and political gain. She is, after all, close to sixty years old. Her appearance—white hair and white sari, a single silver bangle, seldom even sandals—immediately marks her as an older woman cum widow. Middle aged women are noted for their increased power, authority and autonomy (Vatuk 1992). Her age gives her a certain amount of mobility within the village. Older women are family representatives at social functions and are allowed to freely visit neighbors. Older women can visit the town to shop or take younger women to see doctors or relatives. *Purdah* is minimalized, though Brahman women of any age should not freely roam the village. Yet Saroj does just that. She visits her fields, visits other women in far corners of the village, and goes to the nearby town almost daily.

Her mobility is in direct contradiction to the *purdah* norms that she herself advocates in other contexts. *Purdah* acts to curtail women's mobility, preventing free interaction with other women and preventing exactly the kind of organizing that Saroj does. When women have no knowledge of the potential of group action, and no ability to gather as a group, they have no opportunity to develop strong women's associations. Saroj is beginning to break some of those barriers in Karimpur, though with difficulty and at the risk of personal censure.

The ideal widow is one who lives a simple life, who is chaste and ascetic. Although dressing as a widow, Saroj does not adhere to the other norms for widows. This is one focus of criticism against her. Her husband is dead and she runs about here and there. Has she no shame? Her sexuality is also questioned and rumors of a liaison with a lower status male were rampant. Saroj herself criticizes those women who she sees as breaking the rules of honor and *purdah*.

Women who used to live inside the house, in *purdah*, nowadays those very women are wandering outside on the road and in the fields to collect fuel or cut grass or get dung for cooking.... Does honor lie in these activities? Dung should be gathered by the boys, and men should do the field work.

Her attitudes toward women and work are revealing. She would allow her daughter to work in an acceptable service occupation, listing teacher, bank clerk, and police as alternative possibilities. But women should also work at home. She once said,

Brahman women can do any work inside the house, whether the work of the spinning wheel, weaving cloth, so that all the family members can wear it, make quilts, carpets.

Asked if women could sell what they made, she responded, "Of course, it's all right. Go and sell it in the market."

This view is shared by few other Karimpur women, rich or poor, who generally feel that women should not earn an income, should not sell handicrafts. In fact, only since 1985 have women sought paid work that can be done in their courtyards. By 1990, women from three of the poorest families were rolling *bidis* (cigarettes); rolling 1000 per day brings in between 5 and 10 rupees, enough for flour for breads. Saroj further thinks that village women are useless.

My suggestion is, do the work by your hands, and so eat the food you earn, and wear clothes of cotton. If you do not labour in this way to earn your livelihood, what will you eat? Nothing at all. If you work hard, you will never stay hungry.

Saroj herself works hard. She buys raw cotton which she spins herself. She winnows grain brought by her sharecroppers. She feeds cattle, cuts fodder, makes cow dung cakes, cooks. With only one son and daughter at home, she has little help. Her son seldom works and Rajani is often at school and unable to help. And as we have seen, she attributes her family's prosperity to hard work. But she feels that the younger women, especially, are spreading poverty. She is especially vehement about the synthetic clothes.

They ask for terycot and terylene [synthetic fabrics] clothes to wear. These ladies want cream and powder for make up and chairs to sit on. These terylene clothes have led to austerity in every family. Previously people used to wear cotton clothes and use cotton sheets. So there was no pinching poverty. But these terylene clothes have led to debts and loans. The fact is that terylene clothes are so thin and light that if women put them on, all the organs can be seen, even from far away. Women are so immodest in putting on terylene saris; they don't care that their organs are visible.

The contradictions in Saroj's own world view are best seen when she confronts the criticisms aimed at her from other villagers. She is indeed known as the "village Indira" (*ganv ki Indira*). One old Brahman woman claimed that Saroj has no honor left: her mobility and activities demonstrated that she had no modesty. A younger male thought that she acted too much like a man, especially poking her nose in other people's business. However one middle-aged housewife spontaneously named her as the village woman with the most honor. She then added that it was because Saroj knew people at the Block and in the District town. Saroj has connections that no other women and few men have. These connections are valued, for only through connections do things get done in rural India.

Saroj twice discussed her nickname with me. The first time I asked her why she was called "Indira".

I myself arranged the marriages and functions according to my own ideas. I never ask others for help and advice. So they call me "Indira". Generally people make a comparison between the intelligence of Indira Gandhi and me. She serves her purposes well. Other women are incapable of even working on their own. Hence they named me "Indira". I got my daughter married into a wealthy family. I also arranged my son's marriage. I never asked them for help.... Why should I seek the advice of others? Can they help me? No, they can't assist me so why should I make them directors of my personal affairs?

Understanding Saroj's position within the Brahman community of Karimpur makes her independence more comprehensible. Karimpur is her husband's *nansar*, her mother's father's village. Given hypergamous marriage rules, her family is actually higher than the other Brahmans of Karimpur, who are mostly descended from a common ancestor some ten to twelve generations back. This higher status has several ramifications. Saroj's family has no close kin in Karimpur and hence few possibilities for feuds and for the petty fights over honor that are frequent among the Brahman community. (People in Karimpur say that some men think about honor so much that they can't even take a piss without considering whether it will cause an enemy dishonor.) Saroj's family accepts its superiority and hence can ignore the Brahman community to some extent.

Their role vis-a-vis the rest of the Brahmans was manifested when Saroj's son was married in March, 1984. Only one Brahman male (the village headman) from Karimpur was invited to be part of marriage party. Normally twenty or more Brahman men would participate in a Brahman wedding party. Instead, her son's *barat* (wedding party) was made up of affinal kin—her daughters' husbands and relatives of her sisters' families. Not only did Saroj not need to rely on Karimpur's Brahmans; she purposefully ignored them. Women were called for some women's ceremonies, but their labor, usually needed to roll breads to be fried by the men, was not called on. Rather, her daughters and sisters and their families provided the labor. Since women's networks in northern India are primarily defensive, i.e. women join together in times of crisis for mutual aid,[14] Saroj's denial of these female links also marks her separateness in Karimpur.

Saroj might be concerned about her reputation with other women. Married women deny that they have "friendships," which are felt to be found only in one's parents' village. But Saroj does have women with whom she regularly gossips. Yet her closest companions are themselves aberrant. Two are daughters of the village who inherited land from their fathers. A third is an older woman who has been widowed for fifty years; her daughter, now also widowed, is Karimpur's one educated employed woman. A final frequent visitor is the second wife of her next door neighbor. Physical proximity plus troubles with her husband's family have led the woman to Saroj. But Saroj is bound to no women in Karimpur through affinal links. She has no sisters-in-law with whom to battle or to surpass. Her female friends are themselves outside of Karimpur Brahmans' normal status games.

It has been suggested that few women seek leadership roles in northern India because they are unwilling to assert authority over other women (Sharma 1980:192). Asserting authority risks disturbing the traditional defensive associations of women (March and Taqqu 1987). Yet as we have seen, Saroj has little need for these intra-village defensive associations. Hence she risks less than most women when she seeks to influence thier votes or pushes to have them join the *carca mandal.*

Two other possible connections with the Brahman community are also obviated. Saroj lets her land to men from another village. These sharecroppers use their own electric pump to irrigate her fields. Hence two potential dependencies—labor and water—are absent. As Saroj herself states, why should she seek advice from those who cannot in fact offer help? Her advice instead comes from her sisters' and daughters' families; Saroj's own source of status recognition does not come from the village, as is usual, but rather from progressive outsiders. Her daughters have all married well, are themselves highly educated for their time and place, and appreciate their mother's achievements. Saroj's structural marginality to the dominant clan organization of the Brahman community allows her the personal freedom to chose alternative sources of reputation and honor.

Nevertheless, her behavior is in marked contrast to the ideology that she proclaims. One day she told me that "If a widow keeps her tongue quiet, she gets fed. If she moves her lips, she is told 'get out'." She herself talks frequently, sometimes in public places and to many people. To gain some insight into this behavior, we must look again at her family responsibilities. When her husband died, her oldest son was 18, not yet ready to take on family. When he finally separated his family,she was left once again with a son incapable of heading the household. So she either took charge or saw their prosperity decrease. In the absence of older family member or fully adult sons, her widowhood made her a dominant figure at home.

I think that it is also important to remember that she was raised first by a widowed mother and then by a widowed mother-in-law. There were few male authority figures in her homes. She and her husband, fourteen at the time of their marriage, seem to have formed a working partnership. As they reached adulthood and his mother grew old and blind, they jointly ran the house. Growing up with women who were forced to manage their own affairs, Saroj had role models for females in authority. Moreover, living in a small family unit, the normal power struggles between women (and men) were lacking. Certainly her ability to run her own family is not surprising.

Saroj returned to the "Indira" nickname another day. She claimed that at a Lucknow rally in 1984 attended by Mrs. Gandhi

> The Chief Minister of the state said, "When all our sisters do great work, people might call them 'Indira.' But let them say it. What you are doing, continue it." Then I thought that people call me "Indira." But what these people (Chief Minister) said pleased me. If I pass through the lane and people call me Indira, it doesn't affect me.

Should I say. "Don't call me by the name of Indira?" Should I not go out because of worry? They can say what they want. It doesn't affect me. No defect comes to me if they call me Indira. That man can think that this old woman is adulterous, wicked or a thief. But am I bad just because you say it? I know that I am good. If I am very bad and you say that the old woman is good, doesn't she still get the result of her bad actions?

Like those anywhere, Saroj opens herself to criticism by becoming a public figure. She has her own defenses. She also clearly understands the implications of "Indira."[15]

Saroj is undoubtedly rare in northern India. Few female rural leaders are found. The lack of leadership can be attributed to a variety of reasons, ranging from the restrictions of *purdah* to an unwillingness to assert authority over neighbors. But as I have shown, Saroj is in many ways a marginal person in Karimpur. Pellow (1983) shows the role of marginality for female leaders in Africa. While the cultural components of marginality differ from society to society, Saroj is without doubt a marginal person in Karimpur, whether as female head of household, as superior by kinship to other Karimpur Brahmans, as independent economically, as the daughter of a widow herself, as having her reference group clearly outside of the village. Some of this marginality she carefully constructed, using bits and pieces of Karimpur culture to create a particular niche for herself and her family. And she is aware of the ambiguity of her situation, of being the "village Indira" and yet advocating roles for women that perpetuate the patriarchal society in which she lives.[16] I am also certain that Saroj has personality attributes that faciliate her taking on new roles. Other women, in the same social nexus, might not become leaders. Saroj is articulate and aggressive; she dominates her sons although her daughters seem to have her wit and vigor. After all, when I first asked her to tell me her life story, she responded, "Of course, I am the cleverest woman in the village".

Notes

1.   Karimpur is a pseudonym given by William and Charlotte Wiser in their initial writing on this community in the 1930s. I have continued to use it. All personal names are also pseudonyms; again I have kept those names given by the Wisers and added others as neccessary. See Wiser, W.1933, 1958: Wiser, C.1978; Wiser, Wiser and Wadley 1989. The research on which this paper in based was funded in 1967-69 by the National Science

Foundation, in 1975 and again in 1990 by the American Institute of Indian Studies, and in 1983-84 by the Smithsonian Institution and the U.S. Dept. of Education program for Faculty Reacarch Abroad. My thanks to those who participated in the latter research: Bruce W. Derr. Monisha Behal, Umesh Pandey, and Ant Ram Batham. Above all my gratitude to Saroj and her family for providing many cups of tea and enduring hours of questions. Their friendship is invaluable.

2. Saroj also appears in Wiser and Wiser and Wadley 1989 and Wadley 1994.

3. The process of marrying is composed of three steps. First is the actual marriage ceremony (*shadi*), with all its attendant rituals, often before the girl reaches puberty. At this time, the girl does not spend more than a week in her in-laws' household and has essentially no contact with her husband, aside from some mandatory rituals supervised by the women. Some years later, usually after the girl reaches puberty, the marriage is consummated in another ritual (*gauna*). At this time the girl spends a month or two in her in-laws' household. Finally, she goes to live with her in-laws permanently, called *rona* (literally, 'to cry'). Brahman families who are marrying their daughters at older ages (as late as 24 years) now collapse the *shadi* and *gauna* into one event.

4. *Jati*, cognate with the Latin *genus*, more clearly captures the essence of social groups in Karimpur than does the English cum Portuguese "caste". *Jati* marks different kinds of human beings, each with its own moral codes, rights and duties. You are born into the *jati* of your parents and cannot change that status. These groups should not intermarry ("caste endogamy") and have a traditionally defined occupation. Brahmans have the right to be priests (*pandit*), serving Hindu families at life cycle and other ceremonies and in some temples. They can also pursue other occupations and in Karimpur are landlords and farmers. Unlike some north Indian Brahmans, Karimpur Brahmans plough their own fields.

5. See Srinivas 1959 for a discussion of dominant castes in rural India.

6. The classic description of this system is Wiser 1933. See also Wadley 1994.

7. There are subtle differences in the male and female views that require a separate analysis.

8. There are also class differences in what makes a good reputation that I do not deal with here.

9. Hypergamy within the *jati* is often confusing to outsiders. In addition to ranking among *jati*, the various *gotras* (clans) forming each local *jati* are also ranked within the *jati*. Marriages should be made with a male from a *gotra* of higher rank than one's own. Further, marriage is directional. Karimpur Brahmans believe that their homeland is Kanauj, site of a medieval Hindu kingdom, to the southeast of Karimpur. The Brahman marriages move towards Kanauj, with brides coming from the northwest and daughters moving towards the southeast. Most other *jatis* in Karimpur believe prestigious marriages are made in the reverse direction, from the

southeast to northwest.

10. A *dhanuk* man was the assistant headman and his wife also helped with the installation, thereby receiving 100 rupees ($5). The Midwives and Leatherworkers are untouchable.

11. Charlotte Wiser discusses a similar installation of smokeless hearths in the 1960s (Wiser and Wiser1989). They too disappeared.

12. In 1975, Indira Gandhi as Prime Minister and head of the Congress party declared an "emergency" which gave her extraordinary powers. Especially hated was her birth control policy. Her government fell in elections in 1977 to Janata Party coalition government. The Janata government lost its mandate in 1979 and Congress regained control. It is this later shift from Janata to Congress which propelled Saroj into politics.

13. See especially O'Flaherty 1989.

14. See March and Taqqu 1987 for a discussion of female defensive and offensive organizations and their role in development in India and elsewhere.

15. In 1992, a student, Bhuvana Rao, reported to me that a woman in the community where she is working in Tehri Garhwal in the Himalayan foothills was nicknamed "Indira." This Indira was a younger educated woman who had returned to the village for political activities aimed at organizing the women.

16. See Ryan 1990 for a discussion of a similar process in the United States.

References

March, Kathryn and Rochelle Taqqu. 1987. *Women's Informal Organizations and The Organization Capacity for Development.* Ithaca: Rural Development Committee, Cornell University.

O'Flaherty, Wendy Doniger. 1989. "Impermanence and Eternity in Indian Art and Myth," in Clara M. Borden, ed, *Contemporary Indian Tradition.* pp 77-91. Washington D.C.:Smithsonian Institution Press.

Pellow, Deborah. 1983 *Marginality and Individual Consciousness: Women in Modernizing Africa.* Women in International Development Working Paper 28, East Lansing: Michigan State University.

Ryan, Mary. 1990. *Women in Public: From Banners to Ballots, 1825-1880.* Baltimore: John Hopkins University Press.

Sen, Gita. 1984. "Subordination and Sexual Control: A Comparative View of the Control of Women." *Review of Radical Political Economics* 16: 133-142.

Srinivas, M.N. 1959. "The Dominant Caste in Rampura." *American Anthropologist* 61: 1-16.

Vatuk, Sylvia. 1992. "Sexuality and the Middle-Aged Woman in South Asia," in J. Brown and V.Kerns, eds., *Anthropological Perspectives on Middle-Aged Women.* pp. 155-170. Urbana: University of Illinois Press.

Wadley, Susan S. 1989. "Female Life Changes in Rural India." *Cultural Survival*

Quarterly 13: 35-38.

————. 1993 "Family composition Strategies in Rural North India." *Social Science and Medicine,* 37: 1367-1376.

————. 1994 *Struggling with Destiny: Karimpur Lives 1925-1984.* Berkeley: University of California Press.

Wadley, Susan S. and B.W. Derr. 1988. "Karimpur Families over Sixty Years." *South Asian Anthropologist,* M.S.A. Rao Memorial Issue. 9: 119-132.

————.1989. "Eating Sins In Karimpur," *Contributions to Indian Sociology* 23: 131-148.

————.1989. "Karimpur 1925-1984: Understanding Rural India Through Restudies," in P. Bardhan, ed., *Toward a Dialogue Between Anthropologists and Economists: Understanding Socioeconamic Changes in Rural India.* Pp. 76-126. New Delhi: Oxford University Press.

Wiser, Charlotte V. 1978, *Four Families of Karimpur.* Foreign and Comparative Studies Program, South Asian Series, No. 3, Syracuse University, Syracuse, NY.

Wiser, William H. 1933. *Social Institutions of a Hindu Village in North India.* Doctoral Dissertation. Cornell University.

————.1958. *The Hindu Jajmani System.* Lucknow: Lucknow Publishing House.

Wiser, C.V. and William, Wiser. 1989. *Behind Mud Walls, 1930-1960.* With a sequel, "The Village in 1970," and a new chapter by Susan S. Wadley, "The Village in 1984," Berkeley: University of California Press.

Index

Abortion, 129
Agricultural work, 233
All-India Handicraft Board, 91
Anglo-Indians,101
Azīzdār, 185

Bangrī, 194
Basham, A.L., 173
Batānā, 194
Berreman, Gerald, 102
Bombay Khoja Muslim Family, 39
Brahmanical practices, 129
Bichhiya, 195
Bichchuriye, 191
Brahmbhat Raoji, 185
Brother's Second (relationship with brothers), 161-164, 169, 170
Burka, 188, 191

Chārhāunā 194
Chauk see Childbirth
Chagale 191
Chhālā 194
Child marriage, 89
Childbirth: ceremonies following delivery, 146-148; *chauk* ceremony, 148-153, 192; continuing cycle of ceremonies for child, 153-154; delivery, 144-146; Hindu childbirth rituals, 137-155
Childless couples, 73
Children, 70, 72, 73, 74, 75, 76
Christians, 89, 90, 92
Chūra, 194
City women (*see also* Urban), 89, 100; poor women, 83

Code of Manu, 174
Cultural setting and Nimkhera village, 138-142

Dahej, 198
Dāurī, 194
Devadasis, 125
Dharma, 235
Discrimination against women, 91
Divorce, 51, 56, 129
Dowry, 46
Dress and Appearance, 20-23
Dūrī Byāo, 192

Economy: Economic equality, 129: family economy, 89
Education, 87: Educational parity, 56
Emotional release, 95
Equality: Economic equality, 129
Family and Household Rites of Hindu women, 157-170
Family living, 66-76
Family planning, 73
Femaleness: Hindu perspective, 112-116
Festival of Lights, 168-170
Freed, Ruth, 96

Gandhi, Indira, 6, 62-63, 127-128
Gandhi, Mahatma, 88
Gair, 186
Gaunā, 185, 187, 192, 194, 195, 196
Gold Control Rules, 177
Green revolution, 237
Gypsy women, 101

Haslī, 193
Hindu arranged marriages, 140
Hindu beliefs, 5
Hindu childbirth rituals,, 137-155
Hindu classical laws, 117
Hindu cosmology, 112, 116
Hindu girls, 35-44
Hindu ideology and practice relating to women, 111-130
Hindu joint family, 186
Hindu orthopraxy, 111
Hindu practices and rituals surrounding pregnancy, 137-155
Hindu religious practices, women in, 122-127
Hindu rituals, 92-93
Hindu social organisation, 122
Hindu Succession Act (1956), 186
Hindu traditional customs, 57
Hindu traditional teachings, 164-166
Hindu wedding ceremony, 58
Hindu women, 35, 38, 59, 61, 78, 84, 92, 95, 102, 111-130, 165, 169: Family and Household rites of, 157-170: Hindu widow, 85: Ideal Hindu woman, 116-122: village Hindu woman, 67
Hinduism, 95, 111: religious specialization in, 123-125: wifely role in, 120: women in, 112-130
Hiralal, 193
Housework, 233
Husband, duties of, 118: importance of, for women (marriage worship), 164-166, 169,170, relations of woman (husband-wife relations), 63-66

Ijjat, 230
Inheritance, 186
Ishvani, 39, 101

Jains, 92
Jajmani system (system of intercaste exchanges of goods and services), 83, 228, 233, 234, 236
Jat, 184
Jati, 230, 233
Jewelry, acquisition of, 194-97; area, 178; control of, 197; design, 176; from conjugal kin, 197; Hindus, 197-203; in modern India 175-78; in Nimkhera, 188; in rural India 171-212; Muslims, 203-09; ownership of, 197; power and, 208; symbolism of, 191-94; tradition, 173-75; uses of, 204-07
Jhelā, 194, 206
Jijotiya Brahman, 185
Joint family, 63,66, 67, 158

Kankan jītna, 192
Kaṟe, 191
Karimpur, women's rituals in, 159-160
Khāndān, 184
Kinship, 184
Kutum, 184

Lambadi, 176
Lampblack Mother (Siyao Mata) (Women's desire for sons), 167-168,170
Life-cycle rites, participation of women in, 126
Life styles, 18
Lucknow rally in (1984), 246

Mahabharata, 57
Māikā, 185
Māikā jewelry, 197, 198, 199, 200, 202, 203, 210
Manu, Laws of, 56: *Laws of Manu*, 113, 117
Marriage, 40-56, 184: affectionate marriages, 65: *gauna* ceremony, 54-55, 185, 187, 192, 194, 196: Hindu arranged marriages, 140: Hindu wedding ceremony, 58:

love marriages, 43-44: matrimonial advertisements, 46: Muslim wedding, 50: negotiations, 46: prepuberty marriages, 129: Rajput marriages, 72: widow remarriage, 45, 51, 56, 128-129: worship, marriage (Husband's importance), 164-166,169,170, *Mehr,* 187, 196, 209
Monogamy, 51
Mother-in-law, 68
Mūh dikhāi, 195
Mukerji, D.P., 100
Murphy, Robert, 155
Muslim women, 6, 21, 37, 50, 61, 78, 85, 92: girls, 38: religious Muslim women, 96: village women, 21

National Community Development Programme, 90
Nayudu, Sunalini, 102
Nehru, Jawaharlal, 63
Nimkhera village and cultural setting, 138-142: childbirth rituals and practices in, 139-140
North and Central India, growing up in, 24-40
Nuclear family living, 66

ornamentation, 171

Parsis, 89, 92
Pau puja, 194
Pregnancy, 142-144: Hindu practices and rituals surroundings, 137-155
Property ownership, 186
Prostitutes, 100
Purdah, 37, 38, 61, 68, 71, 89, 126, 129, 162, 230-35, 238, 242, 247: rules of, 38
Pure gold, 174

Ramabai, Pandita, 90
Ramayana, 118-119, 164
Ray, Satyajit, *Mahanagar* film by, 91
Religion, 66, 92-97: Religious-activities, 96, Muslim women, 96, parity 56, roles, 5, specialization in Hinduism, 123-125, tradtionál religious-based rules for women, 128, women in Hindu religious practice, 122-127
Rig Veda, 173
Rikrī, 180, 194
Rituals, 6, 92-93: activities, 94: ceremonies following delivery, 146-148: *Chauk* ceremony, 148-153, 192: continuing cycle of ceremonies for child, 153-154: Hindu, 92-93, 157-170: Hindu childbirth, 137-155: matters, 60: practices, 129: vedic, 122-123: in Karimpur, 159- 160
Russell, 193

Saroj as politician, 237-47
Saroj's story, 226
Sati, 128
Sawās, 195
Sawāsan, 195
Secular roles of women in South Asia, 111-130
Sexual desires, 102
Sexual segregation, 126
Sharam, 235
Sikhs, 92
Smuggling, 177
Snake's Fifth, (*nag panchmi*) 168, 170
Social practices, 129
Stridhana, 175
Subbalakshmi, Sister, 90
Suhāgan, 191
Susrāl, 185
Susral jewelry, 197, 199, 207

Talāk, 186
Thakurs, 50
Tīkā, 195
Tikkīs, 194
Traditional religion-based rules for
    women, 128
Traditional tasks, 76-87
Tribal peoples, 65, 101

Urban women, 18, 21, 72: traditional,
    84

Vedas, 122-123
Vedic rituals, 122-123
Veijjati, 235
Veiling of women, 57, 67
Village siblings, 70
Village women (Rural) 18-105: Hindu
    woman, 67: traditional, 98

Wage labor, 233
Widows: better treatment for, 89:

Hindu widows, 85: remarriage
    of, 45, 51, 56, 128-129
Wife, duties of, 118;; wifely role, 120
Women: Amusements, 97-103, Ap-
    pearance and dress 20-23, Grow-
    ing up, 24-40, Home activities,
    60, In-laws, relationship with,
    67, Male dominance, 64,
    Occupations, new 87-92, Older,
    103-105, Poor, 83, Recreation,
    97-103: Recreation release 95,
    Rights of,88-89, Role of, 56,
    Rural 18-105, Seclusion of, 57,
    67, Sequestered, 61, Secular
    status, 129, Status of, 2, 56-66,
    187-88, Urban, 18, 21, 72 Value
    of, 57, Movement, 7
Work: new occupations, 87-92; tradi-
    tional tasks, 76-87; Work centres,
    76

Yolanda, 155